HOT Springs
& Hot Pools
of the Southwest

HOT Springs & Hot Pools of the Southwest

Jayson Loam's Original Guide

Marjorie Gersh-Young

AQUA THERMAL ACCESS

Hot Springs and Hot Pools of the Southwest: Jayson Loam's Original Guide

Copyright 2001 by Marjorie Gersh-Young

Design, layout, and production
by Marjorie Gersh-Young

Front Cover - Stagecoach (Manby) Hot Springs, New Mexico, Debbie Johnson

ISBN 1-890880-03-5

Manufactured in the United States

Published by: **Aqua Thermal Access**
55 Azalea Lane
Santa Cruz, CA 95060
831 426-2956
email: hsprings@ix.netcom.com
web page: www.hotpools.com

Please Note: It is not possible to include all of the dangers encountered in getting to and making use of the hot springs described in this book. It is up to you, the reader, to use common sense and learn as much as you can about the risks involved and the safety measures needed.

Grateful acknowledgements

All of the regional contributors who always went above and beyond their assignment to make this book interesting and accurate. All of you who have written in with updates and information. Staff members at state parks, national forests, national parks, and hot springs resorts for their cooperation and encouragement. Athena Reschke for her detailed editing and suggestions. Debbie Johnson who was a superior traveling partner and is now a "hot-springer" in her own right. Henry Young for his "eagle eye" and computer help. Wally Bran and Steve Nickovich up at CDS who were so helpful and are always great to work with. A special thanks to Jane Leche, Public Affairs Specialist for the US Forest Service for her help with the Caring For the Outdoors section.

TABLE OF CONTENTS

INTRODUCTION

By Marjorie Gersh-Young

This book was written with the premise that there is nothing more enjoyable than to soak in a hot spring in ideal conditions. To me this means a beautiful pool with water at 104° cascading in over the rocks out in the middle of the forest at the end of a moderate hike. While definitions of the perfect pool may differ, there does seem to be some standard information that everyone wants to know in order to make an informed choice.

Our hot springs research program started with an analysis of the 1,600 springs listed in the NOAA springs list published by the National Oceanic and Atmospheric Administration. Only seven percent of the listed springs were on public land, accessible without charge, and another fifteen percent were private, commercial enterprises open to the public. Nearly one-third of the locations had temperatures below 90°, so we eliminated them as simply not hot enough. The remaining two-thirds required individual investigation, usually involving personal inspection, which reduced the NOAA list to a usable twenty-two percent. The unusable seventy-eight percent were often old resorts that had burned down, seeps too small to get into, functioning as cattle troughs, or on posted, private land, making them not usable by the public (NUBP).

As many of you may know, Jayson Loam was the original creator of these hot spring books almost twenty years ago. At that time, he did the initial field work and made many decisions as to what information should be included or excluded. Over the years we have refined the format, but without going into an analysis of the chemicals in the water, have maintained the basic premise that soaking in geothermal water does feel good. We have continued to designate hot water as anything above 90° and to include hot wells, treating them the same as hot springs. (Occasionally, I will include a spring at a lower temperature due to its natural beauty or location.) Rental tub locations, which have now become an integral part of many people's lives, are also included. And, as a special service and option for many of our readers, there is now a listing of nudist/naturist resorts and parks in those states where there are springs listed that welcome visitors with advance reservations. One thing we do not do is send people onto private property where they can get arrested or shot.

This edition retains these basic criteria while expanding the descriptions, providing more detailed directions with GPS sightings, and adding a bit of history whenever possible. I feel sure that the blending of our styles and interests will ensure you, the user, continued enjoyment from the book.

Jayson Loam
1918-1994

There is no way I can publish a new edition without including a special mention of Jayson. Without his passion for doing what he truly loved to do most, searching out hot springs and writing about them, this book would not exist and many of us would never have been introduced to the pleasures of hot water. He was truly "King of the Hot Springs."

REGIONAL CONTRIBUTORS

PHIL WILCOX, also known as "the Solar Man," is mostly retired and lives comfortably in his solar home in N o r t h e r n California. He loves to travel, usually in his solar equipped camper van, most often in the Northwest. He also designs, sells, and installs remote home solar power systems. Send $4.00 for a complete catalog to THE SOLAR MAN, 20560 Morgan Valley Rd., Lower Lake, CA 95457. Email to: thesolarman@hotmail.com. GPS: N 38.5354 W 122.3136.

CAMILLA VAN SICKLE AND BILL PENNINGTON have fulfilled their dream. After many years of traveling to track down hundreds of remote locations, with an emphasis on hot springs where hiking and camping are permitted, they now own El Dorado Hot Spring near Phoenix, Arizona with natural, hot mineral water which they are developing for your pleasure. They have provided details on springs across the United States. All of this information is published in hard copy or on a series of disks that can be ordered from PO Box 10, Tonopah, AZ 85354. 623 393-0750. HotSpring@El-Dorado.com.

CHRIS ANDREWS, who lives and works in Idaho seems to like nothing better than to hop in his truck and travel to hot springs all over the west. He takes wonderful photographs and doesn't mind how far he has to hike to find a spring he hasn't visited. He's also a whiz with a map and a GPS recorder and many of the accurate detailed directions are due to his dilligence.

DEBBIE JOHNSON discovered hot springs through her interest in travel and collecting wild mushrooms. Fungi and hot springs are found in beautiful, remote areas, so it's a perfect pairing. A soak after a day's hiking, bending and picking is certainly a welcome pleasure, and another soak in the morning is even better. When she can arrange time away from her work in women's health, Debbie and her partner enjoy trips to investigate new hot springs and revisit old favorites.

SKIP HILL, intrepid hot spring adventurer and writer and publisher of the *Hot Springs Gazette*, has been more than kind in offering advice, directions, and bits of information to make the information in this book more accurate and allowing me to add some of his "finds."

To subscribe to this offbeat and delightful journal see the ad in the back of this book or proceed to his website: www.hotspringsgazette.com.

ROB WILLIAMS has devoted his life to locating, soaking in, and now developing hot springs in remote areas of Baja California. Four-wheel drive vehicles are used to reach hidden canyons filled with palm forests and natural hot springs. The best time of year to explore these remote, dry wilderness areas is during the winter and spring. To reserve a place on one of Rob's tours, or to acquire maps and up-to-date information, contact Rob's Baja Tours, PO Box 4003, Balboa, CA 92261. 949 673-2670.

HUNTING FOR HOT WATER:
Where it Comes From

The cataclysmic folding and faulting of the earth's crust over millions of years, combined with just the right amount of underground water and earth core magma, has produced a hot surface geothermal flow that often goes on for centuries.

As volcanic activity dies down, igneous rocks which have solidified from hot liquids such as magma are formed in pockets deep in the earth below the remains of the volcano. The magma produces heat which is conducted through a layer of solid rock into the porous level where new water, or water which has never before been on the surface, is believed to be formed from available molecules. Fissures are formed in the solid rock layer above the porous layer and steam and hot water escape producing hot springs, geysers, and fumaroles. A hot spring is considered to be a natural flow of water from the ground at a single point. It is called a seep if it does not have enough flow to create a current. Springs may come up on dry land or in the beds of streams, ponds, and lakes.

Natural geothermal areas lie in the earthquake and volcano belts along the earth's crustal plates. In many areas, due to the earth shifting and moving, the hot magma has worked its way closer to the earth's surface. Surface water (water from rain, for instance) soaks into the earth through cracks and crevices down to the area where the hot magma again provides the heat source for the water. If there are no fissures or cracks for the water to use to come to the surface, wells can be drilled, for example. Each of the resorts in Desert Hot Springs, California has its own well.

Water temperatures vary greatly. When the water is at least fourteen degrees hotter than the average temperature of the air it is considered to be thermal water (or a hot springs). This definition means that there is a very wide range of what is considered thermal water as the air temperature in Iceland is certainly different from that of a California desert. The overall temperature of the water can range up to the boiling point. Geothermal resources in Italy, New Zealand, California, and Iceland have been used for a number of years to heat municipal and private buildings, and even whole towns. In Iceland, the early Norse carried hot water to their homes through wooden pipes.

As the water travels up through varying layers of the earth, it accumulates different properties. These are classified as alkaline, saline, chalybeate or iron, sulfurous, acidulous, and arsenical. At least as far back as the time of the Greeks and the Romans, medicinal cures were attributed to the different chemicals and certain springs were alleged to cure certain ailments from venereal diseases to stomach and urinary tract weaknesses. The waters were administered in a combination of drinking and soaking.

Of the thousands of hot springs found in the United States, most are found in the Western mountains.

A Bit of History

Long before the "white man" arrived to "discover" hot springs, the Native Americans believed that the Great Spirit resided in the center of the earth and that "Big Medicine" fountains were a special gift from The Creator. Even during tribal battles over territory or stolen horses, it was customary for the sacred "smoking waters" to be a neutral zone where all could freely be healed. Back then, hot springs belonged to everyone, and understandably, we would like to believe that nothing has changed.

The Native American tradition of free access to hot springs was initially imitated by the pioneers. However, as soon as mineral water was perceived to have some commercial value, the new settlers' private property laws were invoked at most of the hot spring locations. Histories often include bloody battles with "white men" over hot spring ownership, and there are colorful legends about Indian curses that had dire effects for decades on a whole series of ill-fated owners. After many fierce legal battles, and a few gun battles, some ambitious settlers were able to establish clear legal titles to the properties. Then it was up to the new owners to figure out how to turn their geothermal flow into cash flow.

Pioneering settlers dismissed as superstition the Native Americans' spiritual explanation of the healing power of a hot spring. However, those settlers did know from experience that it was beneficial to soak their bodies in mineral water, even if they didn't know why or how it worked. Commercial exploitation began when the owner of a private hot spring started charging admission, ending centuries of free access.

The shift from outdoor soaks to indoor soaks began when proper Victorian customers demanded privacy. Then, affluent city dwellers, as they became accustomed to indoor plumbing and modern sanitation, were no longer willing to risk immersion in a muddy-edged, squishy-bottomed mineral spring, even if they believed that such bathing would be good for their health. Furthermore, they learned to like their urban comforts too much to trek to an outdoor spring in all kinds of weather. Instead, they wanted a civilized method of "taking the waters," and the great spas of Europe provided just the right model for American railroad tycoons and land barons to follow and to surpass.

In 1882 Captain Isaac Cooper purchased the land in Colorado which would turn his dream into reality. In 1888, the first stone bathhouse at Glenwood Hot Springs was contructed. Land where the pool now stands was an island before the diversion of the Colorado River. The combined length of the modern pools is two city blocks.

Photo courtesy of Glenwood Hot Springs

Around the turn of the century, American hot spring resorts fully satisfied the combined demands of Victorian prudery, modern sanitation, and indoor comfort by offering separate men's and women's bathhouses with private individual porcelain tubs, marble shower rooms, and central heating. Scientific mineral analysis of the geothermal water was part of every resort's merchandising program, which included flamboyant claims of miraculous cures and glowing testimonials from medical doctors. Their promotional material also featured social amenities, such as luxurious suites, sumptuous restaurants, and grand ballrooms.

In recent decades, patronage of these resorts has declined, and many have closed down because the traditional medical claims were outlawed and modern medical plans refuse to reimburse anyone for a mineral water "treatment." A few of the larger resorts have managed to survive by adding new facilities such as golf courses, conference and exhibition spaces, fitness centers, and beauty salons. The smaller hot spring establishments have responded to modern demand by installing larger (six people or more) communal soaking tubs and family-size soaking pools in private spaces for rent by the hour. Most locations continue to offer men's and women's bathhouse facilities in addition to the new communal pools, but most have discontinued the use of cast iron, one-person bath tubs.

In addition to the privately owned hot spring facilities, there are several dozen locations that are owned and operated by federal, state, county, or city agencies. States, counties, and cities usually staff and operate their own geothermal installations. Locations in US National Forests and National Parks are usually operated under contract by privately owned companies. The nature and quality of the mineral water facilities offered at these locations varies widely.

Although natural mineral water (from a spring or well) is required for a truly authentic traditional "therapeutic soak," there is a new generation of dedicated soakers who will not patronize a motel unless it has a hot pool. They know full well that the pool is filled with gas-heated tap water and treated with chlorine, but it is almost as good as the real thing and a lot more convenient. We chose to include in our hunt for hot water those locations that offer private-space hot tubs for rent by the hour.

According to California legend, the historic redwood tub was invented by a Santa Barbara group who often visited Big Caliente Hot Springs. One evening, a member of the group wished out loud that they could have their delicious outdoor communal soaks without having to endure the long dusty trips to and from the springs. Another member of the group suggested that a large redwood wine cask might be used as an alternate soaking pool in the city. It was worth a try, and it was a success. Over time, other refugees from the long Big Caliente drive began to build their own group soaking pools from wine casks, and the communal hot tub era was born.

USING THIS GUIDE

The primary tool in this guide is the KEY MAP, which is provided for each state or geographical subdivision. The KEY MAP INDEX on the outside back cover tells the page number where each of the KEY MAPS can be found. Each KEY MAP includes significant cities and highways, but please note that it is designed to be used with a standard highway map.

Within every KEY MAP, each location has been assigned a number that is printed next to the identifying circle or square. On the pages following the KEY MAP you will find descriptions of each location listed in numerical order.

The Master Alphabetical Index of Mineral Water Locations is printed at the end of the book and gives the page number on which each location description will be found. If you know the specific hot spring name, this alphabetical index is the place to start.

The following section describes the quick-read symbols that are used on the KEY MAPS and in the location descriptions.

● Natural Locations with Minor Improvements

On the key maps and in each hot spring listing, a solid round dot is used to indicate a natural hot spring, or hot well, where no fee (or minimal fee) is required and pools are generally created by the rearranging of rocks or by using other materials, such as cement, to create a place to soak (bathtubs and stock tanks qualify). At a few remote locations, you may be asked for a donation to help maintain the spring, or to pay a parking fee.

■ Commercial Mineral Water Establishments

On the key maps in this book and in the hot springs listings, a solid square is used to indicate a mineral water commercial location. A phone number and address are provided for the purpose of obtaining rates, additional information, and reservations.

❑ Tubs Using Gas-heated Tap Water or Well Water

Listings of rent-a-tub locations, indicated by a white square, begin with an overall impression of the premises and with the general location, usually within a city area. Premises are described. Nearly all locations require reservations, especially during the busy evening and weekend hours.

HOT SPRINGS ETIQUETTE

A Word about Nudity

You had best start with the hard fact that any private property owner, county administration, park superintendent, or forest supervisor has the authority to prohibit "public nudity" in a specific area or in a whole park or forest. Whenever the authorities have to deal with repeated complaints about nude bathers at a specific hot spring, it is likely that the area will be posted with NO NUDITY ALLOWED signs, and you could get a citation without further warning.

The vast majority of natural hot springs on public property are not individually posted, but most jurisdictions have some form of general regulation prohibiting public nudity. However, there have been some recent court cases establishing that a person could not be found guilty of indecent exposure if he removed his clothes only after traveling to a remote area where there was no one to be offended.

In light of these court cases, one of the largest national forests has retained its general "nude bathing prohibited" regulation but modified its enforcement procedure to give a nude person an opportunity to put on a bathing suit before a complaint can be filed or a violation notice issued.

In practical terms, this means that a group at an unposted hot spring can mutually agree to be nude. As soon as anyone else arrives and requests that all present put on bathing suits, those who refuse that request risk a citation. If you are in the nude group, all you need from the newcomers is some tolerance. You may be pleasantly surprised at the number of people who are willing to agree to a policy of clothing optional if, in a friendly manner, you offer them an opportunity to say "Yes."

In a separate section titled "For the Naturist" we have included a special listing of landed clubs in those states where there are hot springs to give skinny-dippers alternatives to conventional motels/hotels/resorts. Most of the nudist/naturist resorts specifically prohibit bathing suits in their pools and have a policy of clothing optional elsewhere on the grounds. Most nudist/naturist resorts are not open to the public for drop-in visits, but the resorts listed in this book are often willing to offer a visitor's pass if you phone ahead and make arrangements.

Those resorts listed in the Palm Springs section are definitely open to the public. Just call for reservations.

Common Sense and Safety Tips

Respect is the key word when considering using a wilderness hot spring–respect for both the water and the area surrounding it, and for the people using it. Safety is also a key issue. The following guidelines will help make your soak safe and enjoyable.

It's Hot: Always, always check the temperature of the water before entering. Even if you have been to a spring several times, conditions affecting water flow and temperature change constantly.

It's Smelly or Not: Structures built over hot springs often prevent natural gasses from escaping. These can often build up and cause you to become dizzy and pass out. Be extremely cautious about staying within structures for any length of time.

Heads Up: Because many forms of bacteria and other organisms live in hot water, it is recommended by many that you do not put your head in the water.

Check it Out: If there is a ranger station in the area it is a good idea to talk to someone in the office to check for back country weather conditions, to see if any permits are needed, get maps, and make sure you have appropriate and sufficient supplies for your hike.

Over the River: The roads to many of the hot springs are often very primitive, cross deep washes, and are heavily rutted; stay on the roadway. Make sure your vehicle can make the trip. It is also often necessary for you to walk across running rivers to get to a springs. Cross at a wide, shallow spot that isn't above rapids or falls in case you get pulled downstream. Test rocks and logs before putting your weight on them. Face upstream while crossing and unbuckle the waiststraps of your backpack. Use a stick to increase stability.

The Gang's All Here: This is where consideration for other soakers comes in. If you arrive at a full pool, ask how long they plan on staying; or ask if you may join them. If you're the first person there, invite others to join you. You'd be amazed at the interesting people you meet. If people are waiting for you to get out before they get in, determine a reasonable length of time, and leave when agreed upon. Take a walk, watch the sky, read a book, and return later.

Cry of the Wild: Dogs go with their owners, and kids go along with their parents. It is up to the adults in this situation to take care of their children and their pets. Dogs do not belong in the pools, and loud barking is intrusive on an otherwise quiet time. As most of us know, when going to the bathroom in the wilderness, it is necessary to go off the trail 200 feet and away from the rivers and springs. This also holds true for your animals. Clean up after your pet. Bring a leash and use it if necessary; some areas require that you do.

It's a wonderful thing to introduce children to wilderness activities. However, as with any outdoor activity, particularly ones involving water, and often very hot water, close supervision is necessary. This is a great opportunity to teach children to respect nature and others.

No-Nos: Sex–No! Glass–No!

Everything in Moderation: Alcohol (follow posted signs and local ordinances; use common sense).

Rub-a-dub-dub: While some springs actually use a bathtub as a soaking pool, they are not the place to wash yourself, your clothes, or your cooking utensils. Soap, shampoo, detergent, and toothpaste really mess up the water.

It's Mine: Some of the hot springs in the book are on private property, and sometimes it is necessary to cross private land to get to a spring. Be particularly courteous when encountering these situations if you want to be able to continue to use these lands. Close all gates you need to open, stay on marked trails and roads, leave it cleaner than when you found it, and, if stated, ask permission before entering the area or the springs. Behave responsibly so that the springs will remain open.

CAUTION
NATURAL HOT SPRINGS

- Water temperatures vary by site, ranging from warm to very hot . . . 180°F.

- Prolonged immersion may be hazardous to your health and result in hyperthermia (high body temperature).

- Footing around hot springs is often poor. Watch out for broken glass. Don't go barefoot and don't go alone. Please don't litter.

- Elderly persons and those with a history of heart disease, diabetes, high or low blood pressure, or who are pregnant should consult their physician prior to use.

- Never enter hot springs while under the influence of: alcohol, anti-coagulants, antihistamines, vasodilators, hypnotics, narcotics, stimulants, tranquilizers, vasoconstrictors, anti-ulcer or anti-Parkinsonian medicines. Undesirable side effects such as extreme drowsiness may occur.

- Hot springs are naturally occurring phenomena and as such are neither improved nor maintained by the Forest Service.

CARING FOR THE OUTDOORS

This is an enthusiastic testimonial and an invitation to join in supporting the work of the US Forest Service, the National Park Service, and the several State Park Services. At all of their offices and ranger stations we have always received prompt, courteous service, even when the staff was busy handling many other daily tasks.

Nearly all usable primitive hot springs are in national forests, and many commercial hot spring resorts are surrounded by a national forest. Even if you will not be camping in one of their excellent campgrounds, we recommend that you obtain official Forest Service maps for all of the areas through which you will be traveling. Maps may be purchased from the Forest Service regional offices listed below. To order by mail, phone or write for an order form:

web site: www.fs.fed.us

Rocky Mountain Region   303 275-5350
(Eastern Wyoming, Colorado)
740 Simms St., Lakewood, CO 80401

Intermountain Region   801 625-5605
(Southern Idaho, Utah,
Nevada, and Western Wyoming)
324 25th St., Ogden, UT 84401

Southwestern Region   505 842-3292
(Arizona, New Mexico)
333 Broadway SE, Albuquerque, NM 87102

Pacific Southwest Region   707 562-8737
(California, Hawaii)
1323 Club Dr., Vallejo, CA 94592

When you arrive at a national forest, head for the nearest ranger station and let them know what you would like to do in addition to putting your body in hot mineral water. If you plan to stay in a wilderness area overnight, request information about wilderness permits and camping permits. Discuss your understanding of the dangers of water pollution, including giardia (back country dysentery) with the Forest Service staff. They are good friends as well as competent public servants.

Leave No Trace

Plan ahead: Whenever you travel into the wilderness areas be sure to leave word with friends as to your exact destination. Read the signs at the trailhead for any new information and where they have a registration book, use it. In case you do get lost, search and rescue teams will have a start in locating you. Know the regulations for the area you are entering.

Take a good orienteering class and know basic first aid. Carry a compass and purchase a topo map for the area.

Watch the weather: Always check with the local authorities before you start out.

High elevations: Acclimate yourself before you hike. Drink plenty of water. If you experience any symptoms such as dizziness, severe headaches, etc., head back down.

Don't cut switchbacks: A little less time to your destination is not worth ruining fragile vegetation. In areas with no trails, try to walk on firm surfaces and avoid cutting a new trail.

Respect: archeological, historical, or natural items. It's against Federal law to remove them. Don't go into old mining structures as they are unstable and dangerous.

Camping: Select a previously used campsite. Camp away from the trails and at least 200 feet from lakes and streams. Keep campsites small and focus on areas without vegetation. Avoid places where impacts are just beginning.

Clean up: Set up camp, wash dishes, and bathe at least 200 feet from water (this is especially necessary near hot springs). Use biodegradable soap or no soap; soil and pine needles or dry sand make great scouring pads for dishes. Separate leftover food and bag it to take back. Scatter gray water away from water sources and camp sites. Don't bury trash (animals dig it up).

Campfires: Try to avoid building campfires in high-use areas where wood is scarce. If you do build a fire, use existing fire rings and make sure to burn all remaining pieces of wood and charcoal down to white ashes. Soak with water and crush any remnants. Or better yet, bring a small gas stove.

Bury human waste: Dig six-inch-deep holes at least 200 feet from camp, trails, and water. Carry out toilet paper in doubled plastic bags (wild animals will dig up buried paper).

Skip Hill

Whether camping in the desert or the mountains, or sharing a hot spring where some are clothed and some are not, respect for the environment and for each other is the key to a successful time in the wilderness which you can repeat over and over.

Pack it in, pack it out: Avoid burning trash. To do so takes an intense fire, almost always leaving bits and pieces that will not burn. Don't bury trash. Animals, time, and erosion will unearth it.

Leave the area cleaner than when you found it.

Leave No Trace is a non-profit organization dedicated to inspiring responsible outdoor recreation by teaching and promoting minimum impact practices. They offer for sale items relating to this philosophy to help you maintain and protect our open spaces and wildlands. I encourage you to get their brochures for the specific area (e.g., Rocky Mountains, Sierra Nevada) you will be hiking in before you go. Their web site is www.LNT.org, and their phone is 800 332-8100.

Phil Wilcox

> ### THE SEVEN PRINCIPLES OF LEAVE NO TRACE
>
> Plan Ahead and Prepare
> Travel and Camp on Durable Surfaces
> Dispose of Waste Properly
> Leave What You Find
> Minimize Campfire Impacts
> Respect Wildlife
> Be Considerate of Other Visitors

NEVADA

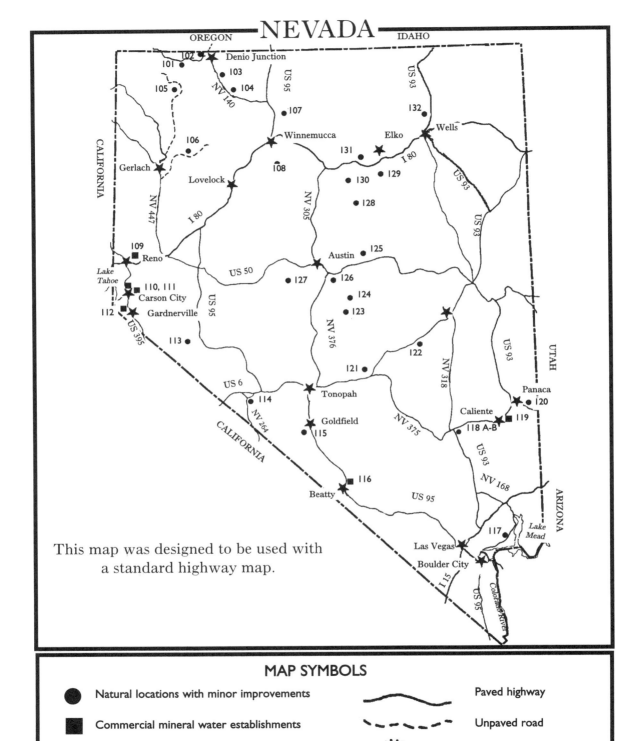

OREGON   IDAHO

101   102 Denio Junction   103   104
105   NV 140   107   US 95   US 93   132
CALIFORNIA   106   Winnemucca   131   Elko   Wells
Gerlach   Lovelock   108   130   129   I 80   US 93
NV 447   I 80   NV 305   128   US 93
109 Reno   Austin   125
Lake Tahoe   110, 111   US 50   127   126   124
Carson City   US 95   123
112 Gardnerville   NV 376   122
113   121   NV 318   US 93   UTAH
US 6   114   Tonopah   Panaca
NV 264   Goldfield   NV 375   Caliente   120
CALIFORNIA   115   118 A-B   119
116   US 93   NV 168   ARIZONA
Beatty   US 95   Lake Mead
117   Colorado River
This map was designed to be used with   Las Vegas
a standard highway map.   Boulder City   I 15   US 95

MAP SYMBOLS

●	Natural locations with minor improvements	Paved highway
■	Commercial mineral water establishments	Unpaved road
□	Tap water resorts and rental locations	Hiking trail

Chris Andrews

101   VIRGIN VALLEY WARM SPRING

● **In the Sheldon Wildlife Refuge**

A charming, gravel-bottomed, warm pond adjacent to a small campground in the high desert foothills near the Nevada-Oregon border. Elevation 5,100 feet. Open all year, subject to snow blocking the road. Small fee for soaking.

Natural mineral water emerges from the pond bottom (and is piped from other nearby springs) at 89°. The rate of flow maintains pond temperature at approximately 85°, depending on air temperature and wind speed. A cement pad and ladder into the pond have been installed and the bank between the pond and the bathhouse has been reinforced. No chemical treatment of the water is necessary. Bathing suits are required. The pool and facilities are handicap accessible with assistance.

Natural hot water continually flows through two indoor showers and to an outside pump for washing. The campground is equipped with chemical toilets. Free camping is available. Services are twenty-seven miles away in Denio.

Directions: On NV 140, 27.5 miles west of Denio Junction and 10 miles east of the Cedarville Road Junction, watch for a road sign to Virgin Valley, Royal Peacock Mine. Go south on the gravel road 2.5 miles to campground.

GPS: N 41.85318 W 119.00230

102   BOG HOT SPRINGS

● **Near the town of Denio**

A large, sandy-bottom ditch carrying hot mineral water to an irrigation pond. Located on brush-covered, flat land just below the Nevada-Oregon border. Elevation 4,300 feet. Open all year.

Natural mineral water flows out of several springs at 122°, is gathered into a single man-made channel, and gradually cools as it travels toward the reservoir. A dam with spillway pipe has been built at the point where the temperature is approximately 105°, depending on air temperature and wind speed. Water flows profusely through the pipe as it fills the two-foot deep soaking pond. Around the dam, brush has been cleared away for easy access and nearby parking, but it is possible to soak in the ditch farther upstream if a warmer water temperature is desired. Clothing optional is probably the custom at this remote location.

There are no services available, but there is an abundance of level space on which overnight parking is not prohibited. It is almost fourteen miles to a restaurant, store, service station, motel, and RV hookups in Denio Junction.

Directions: From Denio Junction, go west on NV 140 9.2 miles, turn right and drive north 4 miles on gravel road to a pond on the left. At .4 miles past the pond turn left and drive 100 yards to ditch and turn around area.

GPS: N 41.92168 W 118.80131

Chris Andrews

Photos by Chris Andrews

This part of the world seems to have found the perfect way to recycle old bathtubs.

103 HOWARD HOT SPRING

● **South of Denio Junction**

Small soaking tub one mile off Highway 140 on a barren plateau between Denio Junction and Winnemucca with a view of rolling hills on both sides. Elevation 4,200 feet. Open all year; wet weather could make road impassable.

Natural mineral water exits the earth at 135° and flows across the ground. At a spot where the water has cooled to 108°, there is an old porcelain bathtub with pipes carrying the hot water to a log and rock pool which tends to be filled with algae. Bring a shovel and wire brush. Clothing is optional.

There are no restrictions against camping at the spring. All services are eighteen miles away in Denio Junction.

Directions: From Denio Junction, head south (toward Winnemucca) on Hwy 140 for 17 miles. Just past mile post 49, turn left on a dirt road. Continue 1 mile; take the left fork and then a right fork through a gate, staying on the main road for .25 miles. Spring is visible on the right.

Coming from Winnemucca, turn right just past the sign reading "Denio Junction 20 miles."

GPS: N 41.72134 W 118.50554

104 DYKE HOT SPRING

● **South of Denio Junction**

Old porcelain bathtub set in a ravine against the hills on the western side of the Quinn River valley with hills to the west and broad vistas across the valley to the east. Elevation 4,000 feet. Open all year.

A small natural mineral water stream with a slight sulfur smell flows out of the hills at 150° and is carried by a plastic pipe into the old bathtub. To control the temperature in the tub, remove the hot water pipe and allow the water to cool down. If tub water is dirty, empty tub and refill. Clothing is optional even though the tub is near the road. Traffic is seldom a problem.

Overnight camping is not restricted. All services are thirty-nine miles away in Denio Junction.

Directions: From Denio Junction, drive south on Hwy 140 about 26 miles (9 miles south of road to Howard Hot Spring). Just past mile post 41, turn onto Big Creek Rd. (Sign says "Dyfurrena Ranch and Photo Gallery.") Go 7 miles to "T" and turn left onto Woodward Rd. Pass ranch on left (2 miles) and take first left (another 2 miles). Park at obvious pullout and walk a few yards back toward the road and tub, which is hidden in the ravine.

GPS: N 41.56699 W 118.56652

Chris Andrews

105   SOLDIER MEADOWS

● **North of the town of Gerlach**

Delightful, deep pond located in the middle of a large meadow with a beautiful view of the surrounding desert and nearby Calico Mountains. Near High Rock Lake in the Black Rock Desert of northwest Nevada. Elevation 4,500 feet. Open all year; may be difficult to reach during winter storms. Spring and fall are best times.

Mineral water seeps up through the bottom of this natural, two-foot deep, sand and stone pond. A wooden ladder leads into the pond from a small wooden deck. Water temperatures range from 90-102°, depending on air and wind conditions. A second, small squishy-bottom pond at about 100° is about half a mile away, surrounded by alkali desert. The apparent local custom is clothing optional.

The hot springs are located on the private property of Soldier Meadows Guest Ranch and Lodge, a private working ranch and bed and breakfast. (For reservations: PO Box 67, Likely, CA 96116, 530 233-4881. www.soldiermeadows.com.) There are no services available, but the owners do not mind anyone using the springs. Please close all gates and camp outside the ranch fence and posted areas. It is sixty-two miles to a service station and mini-mart in Gerlach. It is recommended that you get gas in Gerlach.

There is also a landing strip if you want to fly in.

Soldier Meadows ranch dates back to 1865. You can join the cattle drive or you can dig for opals and explore the wonders of the desert and the great outdoors.

Directions: From Gerlach, take Hwy 34 north and east for 12.2 miles. Turn right on Soldier Meadows Rd. (mostly good gravel surface) for 50 miles. Bear left toward Summit Lake and first Soldier Meadow sign (Humboldt County Road 217). Turn left. At .5 miles from the sign follow the dirt road that veers off to the left for .2 miles to the white alkali meadow and small pond. Or, continue straight from the sign for 1 mile to the big pond on the right.

Note: There are numerous other hot springs on the road to High Rock Lake, but a four-wheel drive vehicle is recommended since the road is rough.

GPS: N 41.37989 W 119.18140

Phil Wilcox

Stephanie Ensign

You are welcome to use this spring which is located on private property. However, please do not camp on the property. BLM land is very close to the springs and you can camp there.

106   TREGO HOT DITCH

●   **Northeast of the town of Gerlach**

A hot ditch next to Western Pacific railroad tracks. Located in the Black Rock Desert with a backdrop of the Pahsupp Mountains. Elevation 4,000 feet. Open all year.

Natural mineral water bubbles up out of the ground by the railroad tracks at 120° and cools gradually as it flows toward a small man-made dam. Wooden stairs lead into the water where the water temperature varies greatly depending on air and wind conditions and may be as cool as 80°. Clothing is optional, but pools can be seen from the tracks and trains pass frequently.

No services are available, but overnight parking is not prohibited. It is twenty miles to a service station and mini-mart in Gerlach.

Directions: From Gerlach, go 3.5 miles south on Route 447. Turn left on gravel County road 48 (sign to Winnemucca, 96 miles). Continue 17 miles and turn left toward railroad radio antenna. Continue 1 mile and turn right at the first fork, left at the second, and right at the third (antenna on left). Take the next left toward the railroad track (pool not visible) and continue on a one-lane, sandy, dirt road for .3 miles up a gradual slope. Bear left across clearing with campfire rings, toward railroad tracks. Pool and ditch are on the right.

Note: There are rumors to the effect that on the way back to Gerlach, about three miles on your right, there is another pool. Check it out.

GPS: N 40.7712 W 119.1165

107   PARADISE VALLEY HOT SPRINGS

●   **North of the town of Winnemucca**

Perched above the Little Humboldt River this desert hot spring is well worth the trip. Open all year; accessible only during the dry season.

Natural mineral water boils up through a small caldera and is piped from the source to a galvanized soaking tub. Clothing optional. The tub is handicap accessible with assistance.

There are no services available at this spring which is on private property. No camping at the springs. You can camp on the nearby BLM land. Minimal supplies can be found in the town of Paradise Valley, an old, unique farming village worth the visit in itself. All other services are about thirty-five miles away in Winnemucca.

Directions: Head 22 miles north on US 95 from Winnemucca and follow the signs east to Paradise Valley, about 18 miles. Go through the town, making a right at the north end, crossing over the bridge and following the signs to Chimney Reservoir. At 11.5 miles from town is another sign saying "Chimney Reservoir, 14 miles." .8 miles beyond the sign is a road turning right. This goes to a turnout and parking area. Make sure you close the gate after entering from the main road, otherwise you may wind up sharing your soak with a herd of cattle.

GPS: N 42.421 W 117.388

Chris Andrews

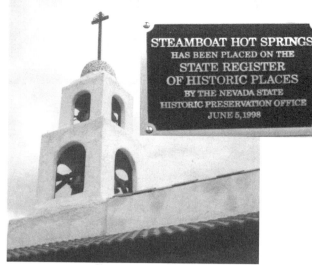

STEAMBOAT HOT SPRINGS HAS BEEN PLACED ON THE STATE REGISTER OF HISTORIC PLACES BY THE NEVADA STATE HISTORIC PRESERVATION OFFICE JUNE 5, 1998

Photos courtesy of El Dorado Hot Springs

108   KYLE HOT SPRINGS

●   Near the town of Mill City

Two stock tanks with crystal-clear water located on a barren mountainside in the East Humboldt Range overlooking a scrub-covered valley with a magnificent 360-degree view. Elevation 4,500 feet. Open all year.

High-sulphur-content mineral water flows out of the ground at over 110°. Hot sulphur dioxide steam comes out of a nearby vent. A plastic pipe carries water from the source to the first six-foot round galvanized stock tank where it measures 104°. A hose carries the overflow to the adjacent six-foot stock tank where water temperature measures around 80°. Clothing optional. The tubs are handicap accessible with assistance.

There are no services available and no shade, but overnight parking is not prohibited. There is a truck stop/restaurant/mini-mart along I-80 in Mill City (twenty-six miles) for gas, provisions, RV park, and laundromat. All other services are fifty-three miles away in Winnemucca.

Directions: From Mill City, exit 149 on Hwy 80, proceed south on Hwy 400 approximately 15.6 miles. Turn left at Kyle Hot Springs sign and drive 9.7 miles on a gravel road. Bear left at the fork at 9 miles and proceed toward the white hill with a corral at the bottom. The spring is on top of the knoll; you can drive right to it.

GPS: N 40.40708 W 117.88485

Note: Since this was originally written reports have come in that a drilling operation has drastically reduced the water flow to the tubs and the water is murky and too cool to soak.

109   STEAMBOAT VILLA HOT SPRINGS SPA

■   16010 S. Virginia St.   702 853-6600
Reno, NV 89511
www.steamboatsprings.org

Historic spa location designated a state historical site. Completely renovated, the lobby looks like a Mexican mansion. Copious amounts of steam billow up from what looks like a mountain, but is actually a tufa mound more than 500 feet high. Elevation 4,500 feet. Open all year.

Natural mineral water reaches the surface of a hot well across the street at temperatures above 204°, is cooled in holding tanks and fills seven indoor tiled tubs. Each private room has a stained glass window. There is also an outside tub and a geothermal steam room where bathing suits are required.

Several modalities of therapeutic massage, and body wraps with a mud formula are offered. T'ai chi, yoga, and aerobics classes are available. Gift shop. Membership plans available. No children under fourteen.

Location: On Hwy 395, 1 mile south of the Mt. Rose intersection at Rhodes Rd.

Phil Wilcox

110   BOWERS MANSION
4005 US 395 North   702 849-1825
Carson City, NV 89704

A Washoe County Park with extensive picnic, playground, and parking facilities, in addition to a large modern swimming pool. Elevation 5,100 feet. Park open all year; pools open Memorial Day to Labor Day. There is a charge for using the facilities.

Natural mineral water, pumped from wells at 116°, is combined with cold well water as needed. The swimming pool and children's wading pool are maintained at 80°. Both pools are treated with bromine. Bathing suits are required. Pool and picnic facilities are A.D.A. handicapped accessible.

There are no services available on the premises. Tours of the mansion are conducted from Mother's Day to the end of October. It is four miles to restaurants, motels, service stations, and RV hookups in Carson City.

Directions: Go 10 miles north of Carson City on US 395. Watch for signs and turn west on side road, 1.5 miles to location.

Phil Wilcox

111   CARSON HOT SPRINGS
1500 Hot Springs Rd.   775 885-1455
Carson City, NV 89706   888 886-7848

Completely remodeled older hot springs with swimming pool and nine large private rooms, each containing a sunken tub comfortable enough for six people. Located in the northeast outskirts of Carson City. Elevation 4,300 feet. Open all year.

Natural mineral water flows out of the ground at 121°. Air spray and evaporative cooling are used to lower the water temperature when pools are drained and refilled each day. No chemicals or city water is added. The outdoor swimming pool temperature is maintained at 98° in the summer and 102° in the winter. Pool temperatures in the individual rooms, can be controlled as desired, from 95-110°. Bathing suits are required in the swimming pool, and are optional in the private rooms.

A complete restaurant and bar with banquet facilities, limited number of motel rooms and a bed and breakfast in a refurbished 1860s home are available on the premises. Dancing on the weekends. RV park. Massage by appointment. Credit cards accepted. It is one mile to a store and service station.

Directions: From US 395 at the north end of Carson City, go east on Hot Springs Rd. 1 mile to springs.

Left: If there are too many kids in the outside pool you can rent an individual room at *Carson Hot Springs* for a bit more privacy.

112   WALLEY'S HOT SPRINGS RESORT SPA

PO Box 26   775 782-8155
2001 Foothill Rd.
■   Genoa, NV 89411

Tastefully restored 1862 spa and luxury hotel located twelve miles east of Lake Tahoe at the foot of the Sierra Nevada. Elevation 4,700 feet. Open all year.

Natural mineral water flows from several wells at temperatures up to 160° and is then piped to the bathhouse and to six outdoor cement pools (two with jets) where the temperatures are maintained from 96-104°. The cement swimming pool uses bromine-treated creek water and averages 80°. Bathing suits required in the outdoor pools. Handicap accessible.

Overnight accommodations are available. The main building is a two-story health club with separate men's and women's sections, each containing a sauna, steambath and weight training equipment. Massage is also available in each section. Facilities include dining rooms and bars. Visa, MasterCard, and American Express are accepted. It is seven miles to a store, service station, and RV hookups. Phone for rates and reservations.

Photos by Jayson Loam

In refurbishing *Walley's* the new owners carried on the tradition of relaxed elegance that was the signature of the original resort built in 1862.

113   WALKER WARM SPRINGS

●   **Southwest of the town of Hawthorne**

Cottonwood trees line the river and tall grasses hide a beautifully constructed rock tub up against a hillside in the Nevada desert about 150 yards from the East Walker River. Elevation 4,375 feet. Open all year to high-clearance vehicles only.

Natural mineral water flows directly into a spotless rock and concrete soaking pool, five-feet by eight-feet, two-feet deep, and capable of holding five or six close friends. A rock bench runs along one side of the pool. There is an attached foot washing pool with a plumbed drain. The water at the source comes in at between 110-120°. Check water first before getting in. The only way to cool off the hot water is to haul buckets of cold water from the river. Clothing optional.

Unofficial camping at the springs. Good fishing. All other services twenty-two miles away in Hawthorne.

Directions: Four miles south of Hawthorne on NV 359, turn right (west) on Lucky Boy Pass Rd. Consider this point 0. Cross the mountain pass, drive beneath two power lines, and turn right (north) at 18.7 miles on East Walker Rd. At 26.8 miles turn left on dirt road. At 28.7 turn right on a really rocky rod. Bear left at 29.1 miles. Pass a mine at 30.2 miles and the river is at 31.3 miles. Turn left and follow the river upstream another .4 miles to the springs on the left side of the road near the hill.

Source maps: *NV Gazetteer, Aurora* 15 min.
GPS: N 38.4910 W 118.9797

Pitch your tent and settle in to enjoy the rocky cliffs, sage brush, and deep river canyons, and maybe a fish or two for dinner.

Photos by Chris Andrews

114   FISH LAKE HOT WELL

● **Near the town of Dyer**

A cement-lined soaking pool on the edge of a barren desert wash in Fish Lake Valley, approximately half way between Reno and Las Vegas. Winter is most beautiful, with snow-capped peaks encircling the valley. Elevation 4,800 feet. Open all year.

Natural mineral water emerges from a well casing at 105° and at a rate of more than fifty gallons per minute. The well was discovered in the 1880s when ranchers were drilling for oil. The well casing is surrounded by a six-foot by six-foot cement sump that maintains a water depth of four feet above a gravel bottom. From there it flows into a large, 102° cement soaking pool that can easily hold ten to twelve people. A three-foot wide cement walk surrounds the pool, with cinder block and wooden benches on three sides. Overflow goes into a large man-made swimming hole stocked with a variety of large goldfish where water temperature measures 95°. Then the water flows into a second pond at 85° and into a third cooler pool. Posted signs say no nude bathing, but the custom seems to be clothing optional at your own discretion, depending on the people present. The pool is handicap accessible with assistance.

There is an abundance of level space for overnight parking. Facilities include a fenced-off area around the tub and pools, metal barbeque stands, campfire rings, and trash receptacles. Signs about not trashing or vandalizing the area reflect the feeling that this is now a heavily used party and camping site. Please help keep it clean.

Directions: From the junction of NV 264 and NV 773, go 5.7 miles south on NV 264 to a gravel road on the east side of the highway. Follow this for 7 miles to a fork, then bear left for .1 mile to the springs. The gravel road is subject to flash-flood damage and should not be attempted at night.

Source maps: USGS *Davis Mountain* and *Rhyolite Ridge* (well not shown on map).

GPS: N 37.8600 W 117.9837

The county is doing its best to keep *Fish Lake* open—please do your best to help.

Phil Wilcox

115   ALKALI (SILVER PEAK) HOT SPRING

● **Near the town of Goldfield**

Two remote, brick-lined soaking pools at the edge of a salt flat in the remains of an abandoned turn-of-the-century hot springs resort with stunning views of the high Sierra to the west. Elevation 5,000 feet, Open all year.

Natural mineral water flows out of the ground through a flow pipe at 115°. On one edge of the source spring, volunteers have used bricks to build two large (four-six person) soaking pools in which the temperature is controlled by diverting or admitting hot water as desired. Wooden steps lead to the pools, and pieces of old carpet are around for sitting or sunning. Trash cans are available to collect the party trash. The apparent local custom is clothing optional.

There are no services on the premises, but there is plenty of level ground on which overnight parking is not prohibited. It is eleven miles to a store, service station, and motel in Goldfield.

Directions: From the town of Goldfield (27 miles south of Tonopah) drive north on US 95 for 4 miles and look for a sign to "Alkali/Silver Peak" on the west side of the highway. Turn west and drive 6.8 miles on a paved road to a power substation. A large abandoned swimming pool is near the road, just past the power station. Follow the channel 50 feet up the hill toward the station to the soaking pools. The hot springs is on the south side of the road. This area can be very muddy after rain or snow so stay on the pavement.

116   BAILEY'S HOT SPRINGS
■   Box 387   775 553-2395
       Beatty, NV 89003

An older hot spring, rich in railroad history, now primarily an RV park with three large indoor, hot mineral water soaking pools. Located in the high desert country just east of Death Valley National Monument. Elevation 3,500 feet. Open all year.

Natural, crystal clear, odorless mineral water emerges from the ground at 110° and bubbles up through the gravel bottoms of three indoor soaking pools that used to be railroad water reservoirs. Flow rates are controlled to maintain different temperatures in the three pools, approximately 98-101°, 103-105°, and 105-108°. The rate of flow-through is sufficient to eliminate the need for chemical treatment of the water. Bathing suits are optional in the private-space pools. Pool use is included in the overnight RV fee, and pools are available on a day-use basis to tent campers and the general public for a small fee.

Facilities include seventeen tree-shaded, full hookup RV spaces with picnic area and barbeque pits, showers, restroom, and a lawn for tent camping. No credit cards accepted. It is five miles to a store, cafe, and service station.

Directions: From the only traffic signal in Beatty, go 5.5 miles north on US 95. Watch for the large sign on the east side of the road.

Phil Wilcox

117   ROGERS WARM SPRING

● **Near the town of Overton**

A refreshing warm pond and shady picnic oasis, complete with palm trees, on the barren north shore of Lake Mead in the Lake Mead National Recreation Area. Elevation 2,000 feet. Open all year.

Natural mineral water at approximately 90° flows directly up through a gravel bottom into a 100-foot-diameter pool at a sufficient rate to maintain the entire three-foot deep pool at approximately 80°. Hundreds of gallons per minute flow over a cement and rock spillway in a series of small waterfalls. Bathing suits would be advisable at this location. With assistance, wheelchairs could enter the pond. Signs suggest keeping your head out of the water.

Middle and bottom photos by Phil Wilcox

There are restrooms and three shaded picnic benches. Overnight parking (after 10 PM) is prohibited. It is eight and one-half miles to a store, restaurant, and service station in Overton, and five miles to a very nice campground at Valley of Fire State Park.

Directions: From the intersection of US 93 and NV 147 in the city of Henderson, go northeast on Lake Mead Dr. At the intersection with Northshore Rd. (NV 169), follow Northshore Rd. northeast toward Overton. Rogers Warm Spring is 4 miles beyond the Echo Bay Marina turnoff.

Alternate Directions: When approaching from the north, take the I-15 exit Logandale/Overton. Turn east on NV 169 to Lake Mead National Recreation Area and continue south for 27 miles to the Rogers Spring sign.

GPS: N 36.378 W 114.443

Chris Andrews

Justine Hill

Even though the water is only warm, *Crystal Springs* was included as a nice place to cool off while driving in summer in the middle of the hot Nevada desert.

118 A ASH SPRINGS

● **North of the town of Alamo**

Natural warm-water swimming holes formed in deep channels under the shade of ash and cottonwood trees, surrounded by barren desert foothills. Elevation 4,000 feet. Open all year.

Hundreds of gallons per minute of natural mineral water flows out of several springs on Bureau of Land Management (BLM) property and gradually cools as it runs into a soaking pool, fifteen-feet to twenty-feet across and quite deep. The water is approximately 92°. A separate spring feeds a nearby rock, brick, and cement pool where water temperature measures 98°. Bathing suits are a good idea.

Facilities include a picnic area, firepits, trash collection, and level BLM land for parking with a two hour limit. No overnight camping. "R Place," a service station, restaurant, store, campground, and RV park, is open across the highway twenty-four hours a day. Do not enter any marked, private land.

Directions: From Las Vegas, drive 90 miles north on US 93 to Alamo. Continue 4 miles on US 93 to Ash Springs Resort on the right (east) side of the highway. Continue north beyond the end of the resort property fence and turn right on a narrow dirt road for 100 yards to the camping/campfire area and adjoining soaking pools.

118 B CRYSTAL SPRINGS

● **Near Ash Springs**

A real oasis has been created by warm water pouring through a wide irrigation spout into an overgrown pool just off "Extraterrestrial Highway" near Nellis Air Force Base. Elevation 4,000 feet. Open all year.

Spray rises from the profuse flow of 75° water as it is funneled through the irrigation spout into a broad pool where it seeps into the shrubbery along the banks. The spring and pool are located behind a barbed wire fence with paths leading to the running water. Although it is near the highway, the water is not visible to the few motorists who pass by, so bathing suits are optional.

There are no services or facilities. Level areas along the highway may be used for overnight parking. Most services can be found approximately seven miles away at "R Place," across from Ash Springs.

Directions: Drive approximately 100 miles north from Las Vegas to the intersections of US 93 and NV 375. Go west .5 miles to an area of shade trees and greenery. Walk 20 yards south to the spring

119   CALIENTE HOT SPRINGS MOTEL

Box 216   702 726-3777

■   Caliente, NV 89008

Primarily a motel, with some hot-water facilities. Located on the edge of Caliente in beautiful Rainbow Canyon, one hundred and fifty miles north of Las Vegas. Elevation 4,400 feet. Open all year.

Natural mineral water flows from a spring at 115° and is piped to three indoor, family-size, newly retiled soaking pools in which hot mineral water and cold tap water may be mixed as desired by the customer. No chemical treatment is necessary because soaking pools are drained, cleaned, and refilled after each use. Soaking pools may be rented by the public on an hourly basis; pools are free to motel guests.

There are six rooms with kitchenettes and a hydrojet tub using hot mineral water and cold tap water. Major credit cards are accepted. A restaurant, store, and service station are located within a few blocks.

Justine Hill

A sign at *Panaca Springs* says: "The large and constant flow of sweet warm water from this spring makes possible the desert oasis of Meadow Valley. First noted by Manley's Death Valley party of 1849. Dependent on these spring waters, Mormons built the first permanent settlement in southern Nevada at Panaca in 1864. For 30 years this water was used for all domestic purposes."

120   PANACA WARM SPRINGS

●   North of Panaca

A large, warm swimming hole maintained by the town of Panaca, located on BLM land surrounded by low mountains and ranch land in the high desert of eastern Nevada near the Utah border. Elevation 4,742 feet. Open all year.

Natural warm springs flow out of the mountain and through a marsh into a large dammed pond which is as deep as five and one-half feet near the dam, and varies in temperature from 78-80°. A five-step ladder leads into the pond. Once a year the pond is drained and cleaned by the town. The water is clean, but there is a lot of broken glass in the surrounding area. There are no clothing requirements; however, the spring is right along a heavily traveled, unpaved road.

Overnight parking is not prohibited. Gas, a store, and a mini-mart are available in Panaca and auto service and a restaurant are five miles away at the Highway 93 junction.

Directions: In Panaca turn north off Main St. to Fifth St. Follow the straight dirt road for .3 miles to the spring.

GPS: N 37.807 W 114.380

121   WARM SPRINGS

●   East of Tonopah

A hot, sandy-bottom ditch pool formed in a channel that originally fed a large outdoor swimming pool surrounded by barren, nearly treeless high desert. Elevation 5,400 feet. Open all year. At this time there are no soaking pools and the trench is very shallow.

Natural mineral water at more than 120° emerges from the ground and flows down a trench with white calcium deposits on both sides. The water flows through a wide pipe under the road forming a channel. When the water emerges on the south side of US 6, the foot-deep channel measures 104° and gradually cools as it follows NV 375 for nearly a mile before disappearing into the terrain. Bathing suits are suggested since the pools are right along the road, even though traffic is sparse.

No services are available.

Location: Warm Springs is on US 6 at the intersection of US 6 and 375.

122 LOCKE'S SPRING

● **Southwest of Currant**

Narrow, shallow irrigation ditch surrounded by rangeland near Humboldt National Forest in the high desert of Nevada near the Utah border. Elevation approximately 6,000 feet. Open all year.

A two-foot wide, shallow irrigation ditch with 80° water has been dug between the rangeland brush on both sides of US 6 near Blackrock Station. The ditch is filled with moss and surrounded by tall grass. As the ditch is right along the highway, bathing suits are recommended if you decide to soak.

There is nothing available on the premises, but services at Blackrock Station include gas, a store/mini-mart, and a telephone.

Directions: Located along US 6, 22 miles southwest of Currant, approximately halfway between Ely and Tonopah.

If you happen to be driving along this road *Locke's Spring* is nice to know about, but it is not worth a special trip to see.

Justine Hill

123 DIANA'S PUNCH BOWL

● **Southeast of Austin**

Volcanic crater filled with very hot water whose overflow forms a wide body of water for soaking. Elevation 6,700 feet. Open all year.

Natural mineral water at 183° runs down from Diana's Punch Bowl forming a hot creek about five miles wide, allowing the water temperature to cool down to the low 100s at the far end of the creek. Several dams have been built along the waterway providing areas to soak, many at least waist-high. Clothing optional. Very difficult handicap access.

There are no services on the premises, but there is a lot of flat, unposted area to camp overnight. Toquima Campground is sixteen miles away. All other services are forty-six miles away in Austin.

Directions: From the intersection of US 50 and NV 376 go .25 miles south on 376. Bear left on a gravel road. Consider this point 0 on your odometer. This is FS Road 001. At 14.4 miles pass the road to your left, and at 17.8 miles pass Toquima Campground. At 24.2 miles bear right at a major fork in the road. At 24.5 you'll pass through a ranch yard, bear left. Bear right at the fork at 28 miles. At 32.7 miles turn left on a small dirt road toward a large conical butte a couple of miles away. This butte is Diana's Punch Bowl. It is worth a hike up to the top to see the spring inside. A road goes around to the right to the springs (about .5 miles).

GPS: N 39.0304 W 116.6667

This hot water ditch was formed by the overflow from *Diana's Punch Bowl.*

Chris Andrews

It's no smoking and no camping at *Pott's Ranch Hot Spring.*

Photos by Chris Andrews

124   POTT'S RANCH HOT SPRING

● **Southeast of Austin**

A watering tank large enough for four set into the hillside with views of the high desert of the Monitor Valley, surrounded on both sides by the Toiyabe National Forest. Elevation 6,700 feet. Open all year.

Natural mineral water comes out of the source spring at 113° and is piped to an eight-foot round cattle tank and bathtub. Water temperature is adjusted by diverting the hot water pipes. Local volunteers have built a small wood deck and bench and help keep the area quite clean. Clothing optional. Handicap accessible with assistance.

There are no facilities out here so be prepared with everything you need as the nearest supplies are forty-three miles away in Austin or ninety miles away in Tonopah. The Toquima Campground is thirteen and one-half miles away.

Directions: See directions to Diana's Punch Bowl on the previous page. The directions are the same until you come to the fork at the 28 mile odometer reading. To get to Pott's bear left at 28 miles and then left at the cattle guard. At 30.4 pass an old ranch house on the left. At 30.8 bear right and the spring is at 31.3.

GPS: N 39.0798 W 116.6400

125   BARTINE HOT SPRINGS

● **West of the town of Eureka**

Soaking pool located on a tufa mound in the middle of the high desert. Elevation 6,100 feet. Open all year; weather dependent. (The spring is on-again, off-again, depending on the water table.)

Natural mineral water enters a concrete box about four feet square by two feet deep filled with 107° clear, clean water via a well casing set in the middle and is piped to a four-foot by eight-foot oval soaking pool that is often in need of repair. No cold water is available so temperature can only be controlled by diverting the pipe that goes into the pool. Clothing optional. Handicap accessible with assistance.

Unofficial camping at or near the springs. All services are twenty-two miles away in Eureka.

Directions: .4 miles east of mile marker EU 12 on US 50 turn north on Three Bars Rd. Travel 2.3 miles then turn right on the power line road. Travel another 1.4 miles, then bear left .1 mile to the spring on the tufa mound.

Source map: *USGS Bartine Ranch* (15 minute).

GPS: N 39.5579 W 116.3605

126   SPENCER HOT SPRINGS

● **Southeast of the town of Austin**

A group of volunteer-built soaking pools on a knoll with a view of barren hills and snow-capped mountains. Elevation 5,700 feet. Open all year.

Natural mineral water flows out of several springs at 122°, then through a shallow channel down the slope of the knoll. Volunteers have dug a small, three-foot deep, sand-bottom soaking pool next to this channel. The temperature is 104°. A wooden slat deck has been built near the soaking pool. Volunteers have also installed a large metal stock tank downhill for soaking in 107° water. A second stock tank has been installed about one-quarter of a mile to the north where the water is about 112°. Water temperature is controlled by inserting or removing the pipe or hoses carrying the hot water. Clothing optional is the apparent local custom.

There are no services available, but there is a limited amount of level space on which overnight parking is not prohibited. A steel fire pit has been built near the metal soaking tank, and there are several large bins for trash collection. Please do your part to keep this location clean.

Directions: From the intersection of US 50 (12 miles east of Austin) and NV 376, go 400 yards south on NV 376 and turn left onto FS road 001 with a sign saying Monitor Valley. Continue on a gravel road about 5.5 miles southeast and take the first left after the power lines. Follow this road 1.1 miles to the springs which are on the west face of the knoll.

GPS: N 39.3304 W 116.8548

Highly recommended by Skip Hill, the author of *The Hot Springs Gazette* as "*the* place to stay" when exploring the hot springs in this area—and there are quite a few.

Photos by Chris Andrews

Photos by Skip Hill

127 RAINBOW HOT SPRINGS

● **Southwest of the town of Austin**

Named by those inveterate hot-springers, Skip Hill and Evie Litton, for the rainbow in the sky as they came across this hot springs in the middle of nowhere. Open all year; weather dependent.

Natural mineral water from one of many springs measuring a 197° is piped down to three bathtubs where the cold water in one of tubs (from a different spring) is used to cool the soaking tubs to a comfortable temperature. Clothing optional.

All services about forty miles back in Austin.

Directions: Go west from Austin on US 50 for about 2 miles and take the turnoff SR 722 to Ione, Reese River, and Gold Venture Rd. going south. After about 34 miles and just past mile marker LA 6 is the turnoff to Hendrix's Smith Creek Ranch. In another 6.9 miles a barely visible dirt road going toward the dry lake can be seen to the right. The hot springs are on a mound directly in front of you and about .25 miles away. The area is somewhat marshy and it was easier to walk to the springs than risk being stuck.

GPS: N 39.18.94 W 117.3295

128 WALTI HOT SPRINGS

● **South of the town of Elko**

Another of the desert hot springs. Surrounded by cottonwood trees, this one is located on the Gund Ranch which is owned and operated by the University of Nevada, Reno and open to the public. Open all year. Check at the ranch before using the springs.

The source of the natural mineral water flows out of the ground at 160° and flows into a large pond at least a couple of hundred feet long, forty-feet to fifty-feet wide and deep enough to dive into. The water temperature in the pond varies from one end to the other. A bench and deck are all the amenities provided.

No camping permitted.

Directions: From US 50, east of Austin and between Austin Summit and Bob Scott Summit, take the Grass Valley Rd. heading north. It starts out paved but after about 4 miles, turns to a good gravel road. Continue north, following the signs to Gund Ranch for almost 38 miles until you see the ranch on your left. Be sure and check in before proceeding to the springs.

Skip Hill

129   RUBY VALLEY (LAKES) HOT SPRINGS

● **South of the town of Elko**

Series of natural hot spring pools located in the spectacular high desert near Ruby Lake National Wildlife Refuge on the east side of the Ruby Mountains with views of Humboldt National Forest. Elevation approximately 7,000 feet. Open all year; may be impassable during heavy rains.

Hot, 122° water emerges up through the ground at various spots on a grassy knoll just outside the border fence of the Wildlife Refuge into several pools where water temperatures range from 106-122°. The area around the springs is a marshy bog, and even with several wooden planks which have been set down as walkways, you still sink into the marsh. Clothing optional.

There are no facilities and no shade, but plenty of flat areas (BLM land) away from the marshy hot springs where you can park overnight. The nearest town is Jiggs (thirty-six miles away) where you can purchase gas, and food.

Directions: Ruby Valley can be reached from US 93 (drive west), from I-80 east of Elko (drive south) or from I-50 (drive north). Follow signs along these highways to Ruby Valley National Wildlife refuge. From Elko, drive south on excellent paved NV 228 for 36 miles to Jiggs. Continue until the pavement ends and the road becomes unpaved Harrison Pass Rd. which crosses Humboldt National Forest at Harrison Pass (elevation 7,248 feet). The road is not maintained in winter. On the east side of the mountain, Harrison Pass Rd. ends at a wide gravel road. Turn left for .3 miles, then right onto a one-lane dirt road. At 3.5 miles bear right at the fork and follow the fence around the wildlife refuge. At .3 miles go right when the road forks. The hot springs are on a knoll surrounded by dark green bullrushes which are visible from the refuge.

GPS: N 40.1512 W 115.2445

130   CRESCENT VIEW HOT SPRINGS

● **Southeast of the town of Crescent Valley**

A variety of stock tanks and bathtubs on a remote sagebrush-covered hillside overlooking the Crescent Valley. Elevation 5,300 feet. Open all year; cars may have problems if roads are wet.

Natural mineral water from a hillside spring in piped and channeled through troughs to an eight-foot stock tank, several bath tubs, and one tub in an old aluminum trailer. The source temperature is 185°. Water temperature is controlled by diverting the piped hot water. Clothing optional.

There is unofficial camping at or near the springs which is on BLM land. Limited services are fifteen miles away in Crescent Valley.

Directions: At the south end of the town of Crescent Valley turn east at the cattle guard and drive 6 miles to an A-frame house and hot pool (this place used to be available to the public, and may be if you ask permission). From the A-frame continue another 7.4 miles to a "T" in the road. Turn left and drive another 1.3 miles, turn right and drive 1.1 miles to the spring.

Source map: *USGS Frenchie Creek* (15 minute).

GPS: N 40.3161 W 116.4342

Chris Andrews

Photos by Chris Andrews

131 DRY SUZIE (HOT SULPHUR) HOT SPRINGS

● **Northeast of the town of Carlin**

A shovel and a new tub would make this spring which comes out of a hillside in the rolling hills of the high desert a great place to soak. Elevation 5,000 feet. Open all year; high-clearance vehicles recommended.

Natural mineral water flows out of a hillside at 145° and is piped to a small plastic pool. There is also a stock tank that may be used with a tarp, as vandals have shot numerous holes in the tank. With a little work you could also create a hot shower. The only way to cool the water in the tubs is to divert the incoming hose. Clothing optional.

Unofficial camping at or near the springs is allowed. All other services are nine miles away in Carlin.

Directions: Get off I-80 at exit 282 and consider this point 0. Travel north on a good gravel road. At 1.6 miles bear right, then turn right onto a dirt road heading up a hill. At 1.8 miles you'll cross a creek washout. Continue up a steep hill, go down the other side and up another hill. At 3.2 miles there is a cross road, continue straight. From here you may see some darker green vegetation a mile ahead and to the left. This is the thermal area. At 4.1 miles the road skirts around the fenced thermal area and the gate to the springs is at 4.7 miles.

Source map: *USGS Huntsman Ranch* (7.5 minute)
GPS: N 40.7659 W 116.0425

132 TWELVE MILE HOT SPRINGS

● **North of Wells**

Very large soaking pool formed by a rock and concrete wall at the base of a large hill. Located in a small canyon near Bishop Creek. Elevation 5,000 feet. Open all year; roads may not be passable and fording Bishop Creek may be dangerous in wet weather or times of high water.

Natural mineral water flows out of the rocks directly into a large, clean, gravel-bottom pool about twelve feet wide, ninety-feet long and approximately three-feet deep, making it one of the biggest hot soaking pools at 104° that we've ever found. While the apparent local custom is clothing optional, keep a suit handy on the weekends.

All services, except level ground for overnight camping, are back in Wells.

Directions: Consider the intersection of 6th St. and Lake Ave. in downtown Wells as point 0. Turn northeast on Lake Ave. Cross the railroad tracks and turn left on 8th St. Continue across Wells Ave on what is now a dirt road. One mile further the road is again paved. Continue north. At 9.7 miles and just past 2 farmhouses the road curves sharply west. Turn onto the dirt road that comes off to the right and continue straight on this road to the main pool at 11.7 miles. (There is a large steel and wood bridge approximately .1 mile before the spring.) The road in is very rough and a very high clearance vehicle is suggested.

Grandma's Farmhouse B&B was recommended as a good place to stay. Phone: 775 752-3065.

Note: There are hot water seeps along the banks lining Bishop Creek where other pools could be built.
GPS: N 41.24283 W 114.94816

UTAH

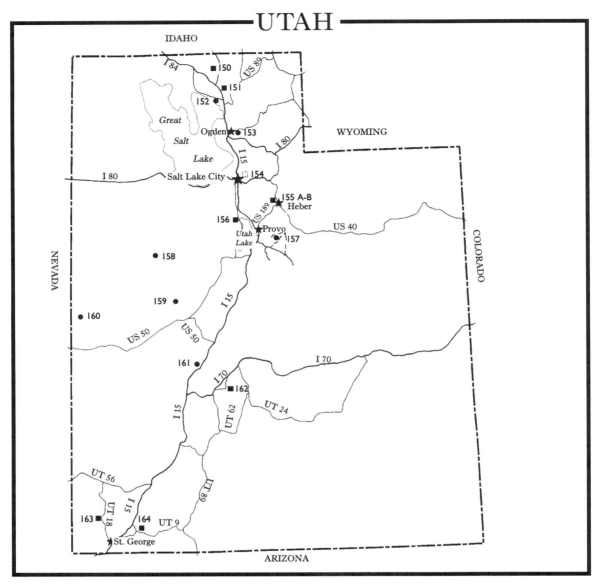

This map was designed to be used with a standard highway map.

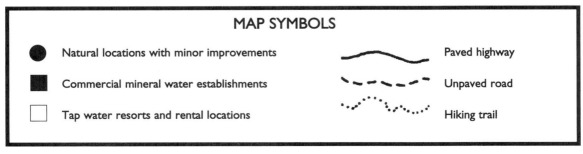

MAP SYMBOLS

⬤ Natural locations with minor improvements

◼ Commercial mineral water establishments

☐ Tap water resorts and rental locations

〰️ Paved highway

- - - Unpaved road

⋯ Hiking trail

Crystal Hot Springs has been a commercial venture since 1901. The Native Americans, Chinese and Japanese who helped build the nearby railroad certainly didn't have the opportunity to choose among the five different pools with varying temperatures and water slides were undreamed of.

150	BELMONT SPRINGS
	Box 36 801 458-3200
	Fielding, UT 84311

Modern, commercial plunge with RV park and golf course in a large northern Utah valley. Elevation 4,300 feet. Open April through October; scuba park open during winter.

Natural mineral water flows out of artesian wells at 125° and is piped to four outdoor pools, all of which are treated at night with minimal chlorine that burns off by day. The large swimming pool is maintained at 93°, a hot tub soaking pool at 106°, and two hot tub jet pools at 106°. Bathing suits required. Limited handicap accessibility.

Locker rooms, two picnic areas, a golf course, overnight parking, tent camping, RV hookups, a scuba diving park, and a tropical fish farm which also raises red-claw lobsters are on the premises. A cafe, store, service station, and motel are available within ten miles. Scuba instructors and classes are welcome. No credit cards. Directions: From the town of Plymouth (exit 394) on I-15, go 1 mile south and watch for resort sign.

Jayson Loam

In addition to the swimming and soaking pools, there is a 35-foot deep scuba pond open all year.

151	CRYSTAL HOT SPRINGS
	8215 North Hwy 38 801 547-0777
	Honeyville, UT 84314 435 279-8104
	www.jsandrbgraphics.com/crystal springs

Small, historical resort featuring one of the world's largest side-by-side hot and cold springs. The property includes spacious, tree-shaded lawns for picnics and camping. Elevation 4,700 feet. Open all year.

Natural mineral water flowing out of a hot spring at 140° and a cold spring at 52°, is piped to an Olympic-size swimming pool, a "soaker pool" large enough to swim in, three outdoor hydrojet pools, the mineral pool, a lap pool and the catch pool for the two waterslides. The pools are filled on a flow-through basis requiring a minimum of chlorine treatment. Various pools on the premises range from temperatures of 85-105°. Bathing suits are required. Facility is handicap accessible.

Locker rooms, seasonal snack bar, large overnight camping area and RV hookups are available on the premises. It is two miles to a store and fifteen miles to a motel. Visa, American Express, and MasterCard accepted.

Directions: From I-15, take the Honeyville exit. Go one mile east on UT 240 to UT 38, then 1.7 miles north to the resort on the west side of the highway.

152 INDIAN SPRINGS (STINKY SPRINGS)

● **West of the town of Brigham City**

The latest structure is an architectural delight compared to the previous long history of hastily erected tents. Alongside a highway in the flat country north of the Great Salt Lake. Elevation 4,000 feet. Open all year.

Natural mineral water flows out of a spring at 118°, through a culvert under the highway, and into the cement soaking pits. Temperature within each pool is controlled by diverting the hot water flow as desired. In recent years, volunteers have kept the surrounding party trash to a minimum, but the water does have a sulfur dioxide smell. Be sure to keep the flaps open to provide sufficient air circulation. The apparent local custom is clothing optional within the structure.

There are no services available on the premises.

Directions: From I-15, take exit 368 and travel 2.4 miles west to the town of Corinne. Bear left at the fork and travel a little over 6 miles to the springs. The springs are on the south side of the road shortly before you reach Little Mountain, a rocky hill on the north side of the road.

GPS: N 41.5761 W 112.2337

153 OGDEN HOT SPRINGS

● **East of the city of Ogden**

Small, primitive hot springs at the river's edge, located in a beautiful river gorge in Ogden Canyon. Elevation 4,800 feet. Open all year, subject to annual flooding.

Natural mineral water flows out of a spring at 130° and through a pipe and hoses to a volunteer-built, rock and mud pool at 107°. The water continues flowing into a rock and cement-bottomed pool at 101°. The sides have been built up to prevent the entrance of river water. The temperature is controlled by diverting the hoses when desired. The apparent local custom is clothing optional, even though the highway is visible.

There are no services available on the premises.

Directions: Exit I-15 in Ogden at SR 39 (12th St.) and go east 4.9 miles to the mouth of Ogden Canyon. Park on either side of the road just after passing under suspended water pipe. Short trail downstream to spring starts at mile 9 green marker. (If pulling a trailer, go 1 mile farther upstream to a turnaround and come back to park.)

GPS: N 41.2359 W 111.9242

154 WASATCH SPAS
3955 S. State St.   801 264-TUBS
❏   Salt Lake City, UT 84107

Private hot tub rentals, plus spa sales and service, on a main street in Salt Lake City.

Four indoor rooms and one out-of-doors area enclosed by a beautiful redwood gazebo are for rent to the public by the hour. Temperatures are set at 102° and tubs are treated with bromine. Major credit cards are accepted. Phone or email (hottubs@aros.net) for rates, reservations, and directions.

Courtesy of The Homestead

155 A   THE HOMESTEAD

■   700 N. Homestead Dr.   435 654-1102
    Midway, UT 84049   800 327-7220

The only warm water scuba site in the continental US has been added to this upscale, historic, destination resort specializing in leisure vacations and group meetings, with extensive access to summer and winter sports and recreation. Elevation 5,600 feet. Open all year.

A 110-foot tunnel has been hollowed out of the tufa crater's north side, providing access to scuba divers, snorkelers, swimmers, and mineral bathers to enjoy the 96° water.

Natural mineral water flows from a tufa-cone spring at 96°. The water temperature is boosted, and the water is piped to one small outdoor mineral bath that averages 100° and is not treated with chemicals. All other pools use chlorine-treated tap water. The large outdoor swimming pool is maintained at 85°, the indoor hydrojet pool at 102°, and the indoor lap pool at 90°. There is also a dry sauna available. Pool use is available to registered guests and pool members. Bathing suits are required.

Locker rooms, dining rooms, a pub, an eighteen-hole championship golf course, hotel rooms, suites, condominiums, and bed and breakfast are available on the premises. During the winter there is snowmobiling, skiing, sleigh rides, and guided trail rides; during the summer there is golf, tennis, trail rides, and mountain biking. Special dive packages offered. It is two miles to a store, service station, and RV hookups. Major credit cards accepted.

Directions: From Heber City on US 189, go west on UT 113 to the town of Midway and follow signs to the resort.

155 B   MOUNTAIN SPAA RESORT

■   800 North Mtn. Spaa Lane   435 654-0807
    Midway, UT 84049   435 654-0721

Historic, rustic resort located in beautiful Heber Valley, one mile from Wasatch Mountain State Park. Elevation 5,700 feet. Open from Memorial Day to Labor Day on Thursday, Friday, and Saturday.

Natural mineral water flows from cone-shaped tufa craters at 120° and is piped to two pools. The outdoor swimming pool, with kiddie slide and large deck area, is maintained at 86-98°. The indoor swimming pool, built inside a large crater, maintains a temperature of 87-103°. Both pools are drained twice weekly, disinfected, and refilled.

Guest house, cabins, soda fountain, snack bar, game room, locker rooms, lawn and picnic area, overnight camping, and RV hookups are available on the premises. Banquet room and pavilion facilities available for large groups. Visa and MasterCard are accepted.

Directions: From Heber City on US 189, go west on UT 113 to the town of Midway. Turn north on River Rd., go .7 miles to 600 North in Midway, and follow signs to the resort.

Jayson Loam

The building in the background houses the swimming pool, which is built in a large natural crater.

156   INLET HOT SPRINGS PARK

● **Southwest of Lehi**

A large pool, on state-owned property, on the north edge of Utah Lake surrounded by willows. Near the old site of the the Saratoga Resort, which is now a subdivision. Elevation 4,200 feet. Open all year.

Natural mineral water flows directly into a sandy-bottomed soaking pool, about eighteen-feet by fifty-feet, and two-feet to five-feet deep. There are other smaller pools in the area, dependent on volunteer diggers. Water temperature ranges from 100-107°. Clothing optional with caution.

There are no services on the premises but camping is available in several state parks in the area and it is five miles to all other services in Lehi.

Directions: Starting the the intersection of UT 73 (Main St.) and Center St. in downtown Lehi, travel 2 miles west on UT 73. Turn left (south) on 9550 West and travel 2.9 miles until you see a small parking area on the left. This is just past the intersection of 9550 West and 6800 North. Follow the trail 150 yards east to the spring.

GPS: N 40.3531 W. 111.8997

Note: Located on state land. Park regulations prohibit alcohol and animals. Regularly patrolled by the sheriff. Posted notice: May be nude bathers present. Please respect the rights and feelings of others.

Diamond Fork Hot Springs is indeed the jewel in Utah's crown. The best hot spring in the state offers three hot soaking pools and a spectacular waterfall.

157   DIAMOND FORK HOT SPRINGS
(also known as Fifth Water Canyon)

● **Spanish Fork (South of Provo)**

Three delightful rock pools in a beautiful canyon at the end of an easy hike, with a flowing creek and a large waterfall. Elevation 5,800 feet. Open all year.

Natural mineral water flows out of the ground at 125° and depending how rocks have been moved along the creek, combines with creek water to cool the higher pool to a comfortable temperature. The lower pool receives the overflow from the upper pool and is slightly cooler. The third pool is across the creek and is quite hot when the creek is low, but it cools some when creek water is high and flows over into the pool. The apparent local custom is clothing optional.

There are no services on the premises, but overnight camping is not prohibited at the trailhead and at the many pull out spots along the creek. Bring water and supplies with you.

(Directions on next page.)

Phil Wilcox

Directions: The road to Diamond Fork is expected to be closed until 2004. Alternate route: Take exit 263 off I-15 and head east through Springville to South Canyon Rd. which turns into East Canyon Rd. Use the right fork at Hobble Creek and follow the road to the three-way intersection at the top of Diamond Fork Canyon. Continue straight (right) and go west on Diamond Fork Canyon Rd. to Three Forks parking area. Cross bridge and start up trail. Stay straight and do not turn right over the second bridge. Cross the bridge over the creek. After 1 mile, proceed another 1.5 miles slightly uphill on a well-maintained trail along Fifth Water Canyon to the springs and waterfall. Expect it to take you at least 1 hour on the trail each way. Watch your children carefully as there are rattlesnakes in the area!

GPS: N 40.0827 W 111.3180

Chris Andrews

Chris Andrews

The two bathtubs that were there originally have rusted out. You'll have to bring your own if you want to soak.

158   WILSON HEALTH SPRINGS

● **Northwest of Delta**

You will need to bring your own tub to soak at this spring which is located on the salt flats near a very large hot source pool in the high Utah desert at the south edge of the Wendover Bombing and Gunnery Range. Elevation 4,500 feet. Open all year although roads are not maintained.

Natural mineral water at 120° flows through two channels dug out of the clay directly into channels on the ground. There is no way to control the hot water except by letting it cool as it heads away from the source, so be careful. Clothing optional.

There are no facilities on the premises but lots of places for unofficial camping nearby. All services are located ninety-five miles away in Delta or 120 miles away in Wendover.

Directions: From Delta, travel northeast on US 5 to UT 174. Turn left and travel northwest approximately 80 miles following the signs to the Fish Springs National Wildlife Refuge. Continue past the ranger station another 4.9 miles and turn right near an old abandoned bus. The spring is on a small, 8-foot high butte, approximately .25 miles from the main gravel road. The roads can become a muddy quagmire during the rainy season.

Source map: USGS *Fish Springs NW* (spring not on map).

GPS: N 39.90650 W 113.43021

Don't forget to bring a water-proof flashlight to explore the forty-foot long cave beneath the waterfall.

Photos by Chris Andrews

159   BAKER HOT SPRINGS

● **Northwest of Delta**

Concrete soaking pools and a great place to relax are all that remain of an old resort located in the high desert in western Utah. Elevation 4,600 feet. Open all year although roads are not maintained.

Natural mineral water flows out of a spring at 122° into an earthen channel which directly feeds the three five-foot by eight-foot soaking pools. Each pool has a set of stairs leading down into the two-foot deep tubs. Cold spring water runs through a parallel channel and can be piped to each tub to cool the water to a comfortable temperature. Clothing optional. Handicap accessible with minimal assistance.

There are no facilities available on the premises but there is plenty of open land which can be used for camping. All services are twenty-seven miles away in Delta.

Directions: From the junction of US 6 and UT 174 (10 miles northeast of Delta) drive west on 174 for 19.3 miles. Turn right on a good gravel road and drive 7.1 miles. Turn right into springs parking area.

GPS: N 39.6105 W 112.7304

160   GANDY WARM SPRINGS

● **South of Gandy**

Refreshing warm waterfalls, caves and a large pond to soak in makes this a must on a warm day. At the base of a large volcano-shaped butte in the high Utah desert, not far from the Utah-Nevada border. Elevation 5,300 feet. Open all year although roads are not maintained.

Natural mineral water flows from a spring at over 4,400 gallons per minute at a temperature of 82°. The warm water flows through a large creek to fill the sandy-bottom swimming hole which is two-feet to four-feet deep. Temperatures range between 78-82° depending on winds and air temperature. While the local custom seems to be clothing optional, it is a good idea to have a suit handy in case you need one. Handicap accessible with assistance.

There are no facilities available on the premises but there is plenty of open land which can be used for camping. Basic services are available in Baker, NV forty-two miles away. All services can be found in Delta, UT 114 miles away.

Directions: From US 50 and US 6, 50 miles east of the Utah-Nevada border, turn north on a gravel road towards Gandy, UT. Travel 28.5 miles and turn left (west) on another dirt road. (There's a small pump house on the east side of the road.) Reset your odometer to 0. At 1.3 miles bear right, at 1.9 miles bear left, at 2.4 miles bear left, and at 2.6 miles bear right. Spring is at 2.7 miles. Make sure you are heading towards the volcano-shaped butte.

GPS: N 39.4599 W 114.0371

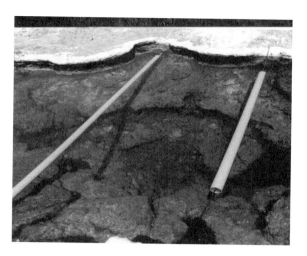

These pipes, strung across the pool, allow you to hold on to something as you gently bob around in this very deep pool.

Photos by Chris Andrews

161   MEADOW HOT SPRINGS

● **South of Provo, near Meadow**

Delightful large pool, formed from travertine or mineral deposits, with ample sitting room on underwater stone ledges. Located in the pasture lands of Utah with unobstructed views of the Pahvant Mountain Range. Elevation 4,800 feet. Open all year.

Natural mineral water flows up through the bottom of a beautifully clear, room-size pool at 100°. Heavy ropes pulled through PVC pipe are anchored across the pool, allowing you to remain on the surface while viewing the clear, deeper portions of the pool. The apparent local custom is clothing optional.

There are no facilities on the premises, but overnight parking is not prohibited. It is six miles to a store in Meadow.

Directions: From I-15 (south of Provo) take exit 158 at Meadow. From Meadow on the east side of I-15, go south on Hwy 133 for 1.6 miles, turning right (west) on the gravel road .5 miles south of mile marker 6. Head straight west for 5 miles to the end of the road. Spring is about 200 yards south.

GPS: N 38.8646 W 112.5033

Steve Heerema

Unfortunately there is no way in black and white to show the clarity of the water and the depth of the beautiful colors in this pool. Help keep this one clean so that it will remain open.

El Dorado Hot Spring

162 MYSTIC HOT SPRINGS OF MONROE

■

575 East First North
Monroe, UT 84754

888 527-3286

www.mystichotsprings.com

One hundred thirty-three acres, adjoining a national forest, allows for sightings of bald eagles and visits to Indian ruins, and overlooks the Sevier Valley with spectacular mountain views. Elevation 5,200 feet. Open all year.

Natural mineral water flows at 200 gallons per minute out of a spring at 168°, cooling as it flows across the mountains into two soaking pools where the temperature ranges from 100-112°. A huge travertine mound engulfs seven bathtubs offering a soak for one or two people. The water then flows on to the natural tropical fish ponds. Bathing suits are required due to local customs.

Biking and hiking trails, picnic area, camping, full RV hookups, pioneer cabins, tepees, and a sweat lodge are available on the premises. An ongoing concert program is presented for your enjoyment. Check the web site for current schedule. It is a short walk to the large and colorful Red Hill Spring. A service station is within four blocks. Soaking is available for day use or free with overnight stay. Cash or checks only.

Directions: From the town of Richfield on I-70, go 6 miles south on US 89, then 3 miles on UT 118 to the town of Monroe. Follow signs to the resort.

163 VEYO POOL

■

287 East Veyo Rd.
Veyo, UT 84782

435 574-2300

Located at the bottom of a deep canyon in the high Utah desert. Cottonwood trees, 100-feet high, form a canopy to protect the pools from the summer heat. The largest rock climbing park in the United States is located on the property. Elevation 4,600 feet. Open May 1 to Labor Day.

Natural mineral water flows out of an artesian well at a temperature of 85° and flows over a rock waterfall into the newly redone outdoor swimming pool that is ozonated. The 85° water also fills a shallow, 140-foot long pond for the kids. Bathing suits are required. Management will provide any assistance needed for handicapped visitors.

Locker rooms, snack bar, restaurant, camping sites, a sand volleyball court, and a picnic area are available on the premises. It is one mile to a store and service station, eight miles to overnight camping and RV hookups, and twelve miles to a motel. Credit cards are accepted. Call to reserve camp sites and picnic areas.

Directions: From the city of St. George on I-15, go 19 miles north on UT 18 to the town of Veyo and follow signs to the resort.

Courtesy of Veyo Hot Springs

164 PAH TEMPE MINERAL HOT SPRINGS RESORT

825 North 800 East   435 635-2879
Hurricane, UT 84737
www.realestatehotboard.com/pahtempe

Located in the spectacular Virgin River Canyon, eighteen miles from St. George and twenty miles southwest of Zion National Park. Elevation 3,000 feet. Open all year; reservations encouraged.

Natural mineral water flows up from the earth and into newly constructed soaking pools at approximately 106°. Much of the time there are also natural pools in the river. There is one shaded, outdoor swimming pool that averages 94° and does not require chemical treatment. Bathing suits are required, alcohol and tobacco are prohibited. Some areas are handicap accessible.

A bed and breakfast with nine charming rooms, some with private baths, and a central dining facility is available, as are two cabins with private baths. Camping and RV hookups are available. A retreat center is located on the premises for reunions, weddings, and special seminars. A vegetarian breakfast is served daily. Massage, facials, yoga, and other therapy classes are offered. Visa, MasterCard, and approved checks are accepted.

Directions: From St. George: Take I-15 to exit 16 (Zion National Park, the Grand Canyon). This ramp will merge into UT 9. Continue on UT 9 through the town of Hurricane and turn right onto Enchanted Way located just before a large bridge spanning the Virgin River. Follow the paved, winding road down to the gate.

From Zion National Park: Stay on UT 9 through the town of LaVerkin. Turn left onto Enchanted Way and follow the directions as above.

Note: Advance reservations are encouraged. Please call for additional information.

Photos by Chris Andrews

Natural soaking areas located along the river, including a place to get a mud bath offer guests at *Pah Tempe* multiple choices of hot natural mineral water soaks. Be sure to stop there on the way to Zion National Park.

COLORADO

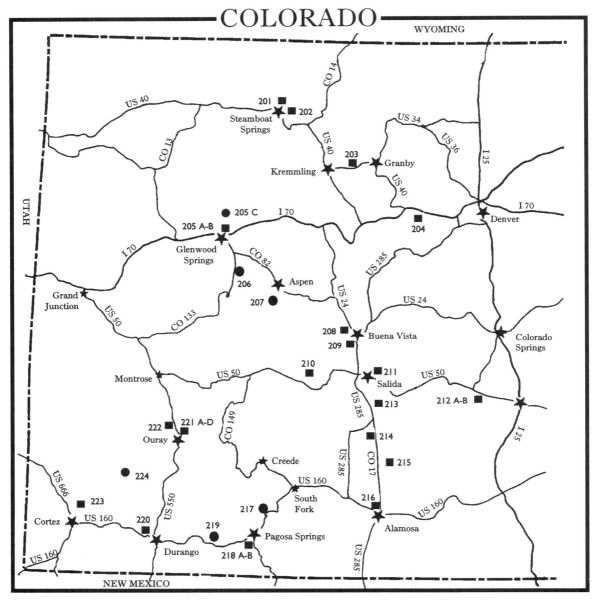

This map was designed to be used with a standard highway map.

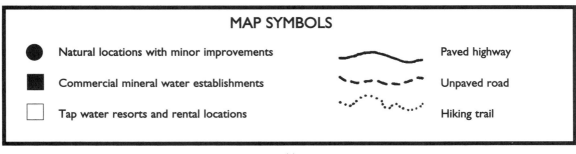

MAP SYMBOLS

- ● Natural locations with minor improvements
- ■ Commercial mineral water establishments
- □ Tap water resorts and rental locations

- ～ Paved highway
- – – Unpaved road
- ⋯ Hiking trail

201 STRAWBERRY PARK HOT SPRINGS

PO Box 77332   970 879-0342

Steamboat Springs, CO 80477

A beautiful aspen-covered valley in the Routt National Forest provides a perfect setting for a unique hot spring that manages to retain a maximum of primitive naturalness while providing improved services for a variety of hot spring enthusiasts. Adults only after dark. Elevation 7,500 feet. Open all year.

Natural mineral water flows out of many hillside fissures at 146° and cools as it is channeled into a series of creek bank, rock and masonry pools with sandy bottoms where it is combined with creek water to provide a range of soaking temperatures from 100-105° in the upper pool down to 85° in the lower pool. Continuous flow-through in all pools eliminates the need for chemical treatment. A separate pool with heated changing area is for rent by the hour. Bathing suits are required during the day (10 AM until dark), optional at night. No one under eighteen is allowed after dark. Handicap access with assistance.

An 1890s railroad caboose, along with five rustic cabins, six overnight camping spaces, and two gypsy wagons offer a variety of accommodations. There is no electricity, but a phone is available for emergencies. Catered private parties are available on the premises. Massage is also available. A tepee is used as a changing room and there is a full bathhouse. It is seven miles to all other services. No credit cards are accepted.

Directions: From US 40 in the town of Steamboat Springs, go north on 7th St. and follow "Hot Springs" signs, turning left on Amethyst Rd., continuing 7 miles to the resort at the end of County Road 36. The steep grades and winding roads are not recommended for trailers. Four-wheel drive is required on all vehicles during the winter season. Phone for hours, rates, reservations, and transportation from Steamboat Springs.

Note: It is well worth the expense of the shuttle during the winter months, as the roads are narrow and very slippery, resulting in accidents and possible closure of the road during the winter. Also, if you need to be towed out, it is very expensive.

Above photos by Phil Wilcox

Bill Pennington from *El Dorado Hot Spring* in New Mexico enjoying a soak during an early snow storm.

Courtesy of Steamboat Springs

Even before these springs were "discovered" by James Crawford they were known by the Ute Indians as Medicine Springs.

202 STEAMBOAT SPRINGS
HEALTH AND RECREATION ASSOC.
PO Box 1211   970 879-1828
Steamboat Springs, CO 80477
www.steamboathotsprings.com

Large community pool, diving board, hot pools, a 350-foot water slide, and sauna situated near the city center. Elevation 6,700 feet. Open all year.

Natural mineral water flows out of a spring at 103° and is piped to five pools that are treated with bromine and ozone. The soaking pools are maintained at a temperature of 101°, the water slide pick-up pool at 90°, and the large lap pool at 80°. Two large outdoor soaking pools, one with jets, are maintained at 102°. Bathing suits are required. Pools are handicap accessible.

Facilities include locker rooms, saunas, snack bar, weight room, cardiovascular equipment and tennis courts. Exercise classes, massage, and child care are available on the premises. It is three blocks to a cafe, store, service station, and motel and two miles to overnight camping and RV hookups. Visa and MasterCard are accepted.

Location: On the north side of US 40, at the east edge of the city of Steamboat Springs.

Whatever the weather there is no excuse with all of the different pools offered not to be able to find one either inside or out that fits the day or evening perfectly. You can even get a hot shower at the Ute Cave Pool. The springs have been in continuous operation for the last 140 years.

Top and photo on right courtesy of Hot Sulphur Springs
Bottom photo by El Dorado Hot Spring

203 HOT SULPHUR SPRINGS

PO Box 275   970 725-3306
Hot Sulphur Springs, CO 80451
www.hotsulphursprings.com

Lots of wood, stone and nature in a resort setting on ninety scenic acres with a view of the Continental Divide, close to winter and summer sports. Elevation 7,600 feet. Open all year.

Natural mineral water flows out of a spring at 123° and is piped to a variety of twenty different pools and private baths where temperatures vary from 98-112°. The outdoor swimming pool is open May to October and maintained around 80°. There are three warm pools for children under sixteen with paying adults—all other pools are adults only. Fifteen outdoor soaking pools and one solarium pool are maintained at 100-108° on a flow-through basis that eliminates the need for chemical treatment. There is now a new lap therapy pool. The outdoor Ute Cave Pool has a "do it yourself" massage waterfall. Two indoor pools in private spaces rent by the hour, and there are two indoor pools in separate men's and women's bathhouses. Temperatures in these pools are 108°. Bathing suits are required. Handicap accessible. All pool areas are quiet areas. Suits required only in public areas.

Accommodations include an 1840s renovated mining cabin, a few 40s deco rooms and seventeen other lodging units. No phones or TVs, in the rooms. The main lodge has fourteen rooms for massage and other spa amenities. There is a conference room available for up to thirty people. A free campground on the river is located adjacent to the property. It is three blocks to a cafe, store, and service station, and seventeen miles to RV hookups. Credit cards accepted.

Directions: From US 40 in the town of Hot Sulphur Springs, follow signs north across the bridge to the resort.

Courtesy of Hot Sulphur Springs

Photos by Marjorie Young

In addition to this tropical indoor setting under a dome, there are outdoor soaking pools and a special area for mudbaths.

204 INDIAN SPRINGS RESORT

302 Soda Creek Rd.   303 567-2191
Idaho Springs, CO 80452
www.IndianSpringsResort.com

Popular historic resort with geothermal caves just off I-70 in the Arapaho National Forest. Elevation 7,300 feet. Open all year.

Natural mineral water flows out of three underground springs at 120°. Within the men's cave are three walk-in soaking pools ranging in temperature from 104-112°. Within the women's cave are four similar pools. There are four private-space outdoor soaking pools and eleven private indoor tubs that are large enough for couples or families. Temperatures are approximately 106-108°. All of the above pools operate on a flow-through basis; a minimum of bromine is added. A minimum of bromine is also used in the large, landscaped indoor pool, which is maintained at 96° in winter and 90° in the summer. Bathing suits are required in the swimming pool and prohibited in the caves. Handicap access is difficult.

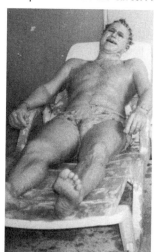

Mud baths, locker rooms, massage, additional spa services and spa packages, dining room, rooms in the hotel, inn and lodge, overnight camping, and RV hookups are available on the premises. It is five blocks to a store and service station. Credit cards accepted.

Directions: From I-70, take the Idaho Springs exit to the business district, then follow signs south on Soda Springs Rd. to resort.

Relaxing while the mud dries.

205 A   GLENWOOD HOT SPRINGS LODGE AND POOL

PO Box 308   970 945-6571

■   Glenwood Springs, CO 81601

www.hotspringspool.com

A very large commercial resort, called by many "the grandaddy of them all," near the center of town on the north bank of the Colorado River. Elevation 5,700 feet. Open all year.

Natural mineral water flows out of the spring at 122°. The water is cooled by heat exchangers and supplies four pools. All pools are pre-treated with ozone and are treated with chlorine. The 104° therapy pool uses pure untreated spring water that turns over the entire pool contents every hour. The one-hundred-foot-long outdoor soaking pool has eight bubble jet therapy chairs. The two-block-long (405 foot) swimming pool is maintained at a temperature of 90° in summer and 93° in winter. It has a sand/charcoal filtration system that fills the entire pool four times per day. Water is further purified by a high-tech ozonator system for water clarity. The summer-only kiddie pool is kept at 92°. A private athletic club is available for walk-ins and includes a water jet indoor therapy pool maintained at 102° and treated with bromine. The club also has a steam room, sauna, weight room, and four racquetball courts. Bathing suits are required everywhere. The entire facility is handicap accessible.

Changing facilities, rental swimsuits and towels, a deli, sport shop, miniature golf course, massage, a particularly nice gift shop, and a 107-room lodge are available on the premises. It is one block to a store and service stations and two miles to overnight camping and RV hookups. All major credit cards are accepted.

Snow on the mountains and a nip in the air doesn't discourage people from swimming in the world's largest outdoor hot springs pool (over two blocks long). Recreational activities abound in the area during all seasons.

Seniors relax comfortably in the warm water while the kids take a shower in the "mushroom" rain forest.

VAPOR CAVE

Courtesy of Yampah Spa

205 B   YAMPAH SPA AND VAPOR CAVES
709 E. 6th   970 945-0667
■   Glenwood Springs, CO 81601

Natural underground geothermal steam baths located in historic, natural vapor caves whose use dates back to the time of the Ute Indians. Elevation 5,700. Open all year.

Natural mineral water creates vapor that emerges at 125° within three caves and maintains the caves at 112-115° year around. All caves are coed, and bathing suits are required. There are also two private-space hydrojet pools filled with tap water, treated with bromine, and maintained at 104°.

Changing facilities, massage, beauty salon, and a full range of health and beauty treatments including facials, herbal wraps, body scrubs, body mud, and massage are available on the premises. It is three blocks to a cafe, store, service station and motel and five miles to overnight camping and RV hookups. Credit cards are accepted.

Marjorie Young

In a dry year there is often barely enough water to soak, and what there is has great amounts of green algae floating in it. In a good year it is a great place to soak, mud bath included.

205 C   SOUTH CANYON HOT SPRINGS

●   West of Glenwood Springs

Natural mineral water flows out of the ground at 118° cooling to approximately 107° as it flows into a large squishy-bottom pool up the hillside across from the creek. The area is not currently fenced or posted, and there is no recent pattern of harassment. The local custom is clothing optional.

There are no services on the premises but all major services can be found a couple of miles away in Glenwood Springs.

Directions: From Glenwood Springs take I-70 to the South Canyon exit 111, cross the Colorado River, cross the railroad tracks, and go up canyon .6 miles. Park along the west bank at a pull out. Several easily visible trails head downhill towards the creek. Depending on which one you take, you will either need to scramble up a pile of rocks or cross over the creek via a log and make a short climb up the hill to the pool. The ground is very slippery due to seeps and rain can make the climb very treacherous.

GPS: N 39.552 W 107.412

A second pool at *South Canyon* provides a bit of a warm waterfall experience.

Steve Heerema

Penny Hot Springs has become a great family attraction on a hot summer day.

Debbie Johnson

206   PENNY HOT SPRINGS

● **North of the town of Redstone**

Primitive, riverbank hot spring pools offering lovely views of the surrounding hills, seasonally flooded by high water. Elevation 8,000 feet. Open all year (subject to flooding).

Natural mineral water flows out of a spring at 133° and drops directly into the Crystal River. Between annual high-water washouts, volunteers build rock and sand pools in which hot mineral water and cold river water can be mixed to a comfortable temperature. Because the location is close to the highway, bathing suits are strongly recommended.

There are no services on the premises. All services are within three miles in the historic mining town of Redstone.

Directions: From Glenwood Springs, as you head toward Redstone, on the east side of CO 133, .8 miles south of mile marker 56, there is a small parking area (with no trees) on the east side of the highway next to the river. It is 12.8 miles on CO 133 after you make the turn off Hwy 82. A short, obvious trail goes down to the pools, visible from the embankment.

GPS: N 39.227 W107.224

207   CONUNDRUM HOT SPRINGS

● **South of the town of Aspen**

One of the most beautiful remote springs surrounded by spectacular Rocky Mountain scenery in a designated Wilderness Area of the White River National Forest at the end of a difficult nine-mile, one-way trail. Elevation 11,200 feet. Open all year, subject to weather conditions.

Natural mineral water flows out of a spring at 120° and is piped into three volunteer-built rock and sand pools, three-feet to four-feet deep with temperatures around 100° in the lower pools. The largest pool will accommodate at least a dozen hikers. This spring is off a popular trail and often very crowded during the summer. Clothing optional.

It is a nine-mile, rugged, uphill hike from the trailhead, although you can camp along the trail. You should not, however, camp within 100 feet of the springs. Be sure to observe good wilderness camping practices and keep the area pristine. It is twenty miles to all other services.

The weather can change from minute to minute. Be sure to obtain information about current conditions at a White River National Forest ranger station before attempting the trip.

Directions: From Aspen take CO 82 northwest about .25 miles. Turn left at Maroon Creek Rd. (FS 102) and immediately split left on Castle Creek Dr. Continue 5 miles and turn right on Conundrum Rd. Drive 1.1 miles to the Conundrum Creek trailhead parking lot. (Stay off surrounding private area.)

USGS: *Hayden Peak, Maroon Bells.*
GPS: N 39.012 W106.891

Debbie Johnson

208 COTTONWOOD HOT SPRINGS INN

18999 County Rd. 306   719 395-6434

Buena Vista, CO 81211   800 241-4119

www.cottonwood-hot-springs.com

A small, relaxing country inn nestled in a high mountain canyon, surrounded by the San Isabel National Forest in the highest mountain range in the continental US. Location in Colorado's "Banana Belt" means 345 days of sunshine. Close to summer and winter recreation. Elevation 8,550 feet. Open all year. No kids after dark.

Odorless natural mineral water flows out of a spring at 130° and is gravity fed into the entire facility, feeding five beautiful, natural, rock-lined soaking pools, each cabin's individual private tub, and three outdoor private hydropools (adults only, clothing optional) at 100-106°. All pools, including a cold plunge, operate on a flow-through basis that requires no chemical treatment. The mineral water is so pure that it is used as tap water throughout the resort. Bathing suits are optional within the fenced private spas. All pools are available to the public for a day-use fee. Registered guests need to pay extra only for the private tubs. The two new pools are handicap accessible.

Twelve rooms with private baths are located on the second floor of the main lodge. There are three rustic, creekside cabins, each with natural rock tub, and one three-bedroom cottage with a private tub on its deck. (Two-day minimum stay is required in cabins and cottage during high season.) Camping tepees and a dormitory are also available. There are no TVs or phones in any of the rooms. Available for your enjoyment are the community room, library, and kitchen. The community room is also available for group meetings, seminars, work shops, reunions, and special events. Meals can be arranged for groups, or the kitchen can be leased

Surrounded by the highest mountain range in the continental US, unlimited recreational activities are available in the area, such as hiking, fishing, mountain climbing, horseback riding, skiing, golfing, sightseeing, ghost towns, and some first-class water for white water rafting and kayaking.

for your use. All forms of massage, including watsu water therapy, and herbal body wraps are available. Major credit cards are accepted. It is five and one-half miles to all other services. Phone or write for rates and reservations.

Directions: From US 24 in Buena Vista, go west 5.5 miles on CO 306, the road to Cottonwood Pass. Watch for resort signs on the right side of the road.

Lynn Blackwell

Two brand new pools are beautifully decorated with paintings by Lynn Blackwell. These pools will be used for watsu therapy besides offering a wonderful soak.

You can often find more people soaking in the warm water in Chalk Creek than up in the pools.

The source of the hot water that fills the swimming and soaking pools pictured below is the wishing well in this shelter.

209   MOUNT PRINCETON HOT SPRINGS

■

County Road 162   719 395-2361

Nathrop, CO 81236   888 395-7799

www.mtprinceton.com

Large, modern resort between Leadville and Salida, surrounded by San Isabel National Forest. Elevation 8,500 feet. Open all year.

Natural mineral water flows out of a spring at 132°. Odorless and tasteless, this water is used in all pipes. Three outdoor swimming pools are maintained at temperatures between 80-82° and are treated with chlorine. A regulation lap pool is kept at 86° and a soaking pool between 99-103° which is partially covered. All pools are available to the public for a fee and free to registered guests (extra fee for waterslide). The hot mineral pool and the slide are open only during the summer. There are several natural spots for soaking down in Chalk Creek which are accessible from the resort. Bathing suits are required. Some facilities are handicap accessible.

Locker rooms, restaurant, hotel rooms, picnic area, saddle horses, carriage rides, fishing, and hiking are available on the premises. Skiing and river rafting are close by. A conference center/party room is available for large groups. It is five miles to all other services. Major credit cards are accepted.

Directions: From US 285 in the town of Nathrop, go west 5 miles on CO 162 to resort.

210   WAUNITA HOT SPRINGS RANCH

■

8007 County Road 887   970 641-1266

Gunnison, CO 81230

Very attractive American-plan guest ranch surrounded by Gunnison National Forest. Elevation 9,000 feet. Open all year; groups of fifteen or more, two-night minimum during winter.

Natural mineral water flows out of several springs at 175° and is piped to a swimming pool and to geothermal heating units in the buildings. The swimming pool is maintained at 95° and operates on a flow-through basis, so only a minimum of chlorine treatment is needed. A hot tub is maintained between 100-105°. Pool use is reserved for registered guests, with a minimum stay of six days by prior reservation only. Bathing suits are required. Limited handicap accessibility.

Guest ranch services, including rooms, meals, saddle horses, and fishing pond are available on the premises. Heat and domestic hot water come directly from their spring. No credit cards are accepted.

Directions: From the town of Gunnison, go 19 miles east on US 50. Turn left on County Road 887 and follow signs 8 miles north to the ranch. Gunnison is served by several airlines and free pickup can be arranged.

Debbie Johnson

211 SALIDA HOT SPRINGS
410 West Rainbow Blvd.   719 539-6738
Salida, CO 81201

Modernized, indoor municipal pool, hot baths, park, picnic area, and playground. Elevation 7,000 feet. Open all year; summer and winter hours.

Natural mineral water flows out of Poncha Springs at 150° and is piped five miles to Salida. The large indoor swimming pool is maintained at a temperature of 100-104°, the lap pool is maintained at 90-92°, and a shallow baby pool at 96°. All pools are treated with chlorine. There are six private indoor soaking pools that are drained and cleaned after each use. The water temperature is controlled by the customer. An extensive warm-water program for people afflicted with arthritis is offered as well as boating instruction for moving-water safety in kayaks, canoes, and rafts. Bathing suits are required everywhere except in private soaking pools. Handicap accessible with assistance.

Locker rooms are available on the premises. It is less than five blocks to all other services. No credit cards.

Directions: From the junction of US 50 and US 285, go 3.5 miles east on US 50. Look for signs on the north side of the street.

One of the six private, indoor soaking pools you can rent if the noise in the big pool gets to be too much.

Debbie Johnson

212 A THE WELL
1 Malibu Blvd. Hwy 50 West 719 372-9255
Penrose, CO 81240   800 898-9355

Funky, rustic buildings with a large, hot mineral water swimming/soaking pool located in the high desert country in a broad valley called the Banana Belt of Colorado, with sunshine 350 days a year. West of Pueblo and Colorado Springs. Elevation 5,200 feet. Open all year; closed Tuesdays.

Artesian well water at 108° emerges from a depth of 2,000 feet and flows through a pipe at 325 gallons per minute, showering into a large, oval-shaped, seventy-foot cement pool, three-feet to five-feet deep. Pool temperature is maintained at approximately 98-100° in winter and 94° in summer and is controlled by the amount of aeration. No chemicals are added to the water, which remains clear due to CO_2 that bubbles into it. The pool is drained and cleaned once a week. Clothing or no clothing is entirely optional (no street clothing allowed in the pool).

Facilities include overnight RV and tent sites (no hookups), modern bathhouse, cabana building with soft drink machine, and volleyball. Massage is often available. No cameras, radios, or pets are allowed, and no glass of any kind in the pool area. Handicap accessible with assistance. Non-members are welcome to use the facilities as well as members, who receive discounted day-use and overnight fees. It is one and one-half miles to a motel, restaurant, gas station, and market in Penrose. Cash only.

Directions: From the junction of US 50 and CO 115 (36 miles southwest of Colorado Springs, 27 miles west of Pueblo), drive west for 1 mile to the second highway crossover. The Well is visible on the south side of the street.

This beautiful pool is just the right temperature all year round and the warm, friendly people make this a great place to spend the day.

212 B DESERT REEF BEACH CLUB

PO Box 503   719 784-6134

Penrose, CO 81240

A small, remote, recreation club located east of Florence, Colorado. The club has grown up around a geothermal well in the desert foothills south of Colorado Springs. Elevation 5,200 feet. Call for current open days and hours.

Natural mineral water flows out of an artesian well at 130° and is piped to a dramatic large pool where the water flows in over a waterfall on a flow-through basis so that no chemical treatment of the water is necessary. Flow rate is adjusted to maintain pool temperature within a comfortable range for soaking through all seasons. Bathing suits are optional. Not handicap accessible at this time.

There is a landscaped lawn area for sunning and picnicking, and cold drinks are available on the premises. A large greenhouse in which plants are raised is also used as a meeting room or shelter. Regulation-size sand volleyball court and horseshoe pits are provided for your enjoyment. Visa and MasterCard are accepted. It is two miles to all other services. Interested guests need to phone during business hours for information on guest passes, rates, and directions.

I had a great time "vamping" with this wonderful sculpture, just one of the many on the grounds.

Spectacular views, multiple pools, cabins, and places to camp are augmented by the wonderful hospitality of the hosts and the friendly attitude of the people who belong.

213 VALLEY VIEW HOT SPRINGS

PO Box 65   719 256-4315
Villa Grove, CO 81155

A series of wonderful pools at a clothing optional resort offering relaxation as its primary activity, are situated on the west slope of the Sangre De Cristo Mountains. Elevation 8,700 feet. Open all year (closed December 1-25).

Natural mineral water flows out of numerous springs scattered across the hillside. The outdoor swimming pool is maintained at 85° year round. Next to the swimming pool is a concrete hot tub with 104-106° water. The swimming pool area is handicap accessible. There are five gravel-bottomed, rock-lined soaking ponds built right over several springs. The largest of these is a short distance uphill from the swimming pool and keeps a temperature of 96° year round. Two smaller ponds also keep this temperature. In one of the pools the water enters the pond through a pipe, which provides a nice massage when you sit under it. At the top of a steep trail (and well worth the hike for the great view you will get) are two more ponds; these vary in temperature from 80-105° depending on the volume of snow melt or rain. There is a small wood-fired sauna with a cold plunge pool inside. A new electric sauna is under construction. All the pools and ponds are supplied on a flow-through basis so no chemical treatment is needed. Clothing is optional everywhere on the grounds. Watch for poison ivy.

A communal lodge with kitchen, six cabins, and tent spaces scattered through the woods are available for rent. It is twelve miles to all other services in Villa Grove. Credit cards accepted.

Note: This is primarily a membership facility, with the premises reserved for members and their guests on holidays and weekends. The public is welcome to visit during the week. Write or phone first for full information.

Directions: From the junction of US 285 and CO 17, take the gravel County Road GG due east 7 miles to the location.

Upper left photo by Marjorie Young
Other photos by Debbie Johnson

The clean lines of the spa building echo the peaks of the Sangre De Cristo Mountains in the background.

During summer months when it is too hot to soak in the direct sun, there is a pool under the pagoda to provide protection but still allow for the view.

214 MINERAL HOT SPRINGS SPA
■ 28640 County Road 58 EE 719 256-4328
Moffat, CO 81143

A beautifully appointed, sparkling clean spa located in the north end of the San Luis Valley with spectacular views of sunsets and moonrises over the Sangre De Cristo Mountains. Elevation 7,747 feet. Open all year for day use. Call for hours.

Natural mineral water flows from several main springs at temperatures ranging from 90-140°, providing outdoor soaking pools with sufficient flow through to require no chemical treatment and to keep water at optimal temperatures. The tower pool, under the old water tower, is five feet deep. There are two other shallower soaking pools maintained at 102-108°. All pools are tiled and protected by glassed-in decks, providing wonderful views. The bathhouse includes private individual tubs with controllable temperatures. Bathing suits required. Some areas are handicap accessible.

Locker rooms, a sauna, massage, wraps and spa treatments, a shop, snack foods and beverages, a gallery of local artisans, gardens, and picnic area are all available on the grounds. Towels, robes and slippers are for rent. A separate pool and deck area is available for groups and private parties. Overnight facilities are planned for the future, and several small rural inns and bed and breakfasts are within a half-hour drive. Credit cards accepted. It is six miles to all other services.

Location: On Colorado 17, 1 mile south of the junction with US 285, 50 miles north of Alamosa, and 30 miles south of Salida.

Photos top and bottom courtesy of Mineral Hot Springs. Middle photo by Barbara Hanson. Bottom right by Marjorie Young.

During the early 1930s oilmen struck hot water instead of black gold. Hope they enjoyed the soak.

Photos by Debbie Johnson

215 SAND DUNES SWIMMING POOL
1991 County Road 63   719 378-2807
Hooper, CO 81136

Expansive views of the Sangre de Cristo Mountains and the Great Sand Dunes Monument surround a hot well swimming pool and baby pool which creates an oasis in the middle of chico bush country. Elevation 7,600 feet. Open all year; hours vary (closed Thursday for cleaning).

Natural mineral water comes up from a 4,200-foot, free flowing artesian well and is piped to a fifty-foot by one-hundred-foot swimming pool with two diving boards and an attached shallow baby pool. The water registers 118° as it enters the main pool and maintains a temperature range between 98-103° depending on the season. A continuous flow through keeps the pools clean although a small amount of chlorine granules are added to the pool at closing during the summer. An enclosure at one end of the pool provides protection from the weather. Bathing suits required. Parking spaces, cement entry and sidewalks make the area handicap accessible.

Showers, dressing rooms, a full concessionary, suit and towel rentals are available on the premises. It is three and one-half miles to a restaurant, gas and convenience store in Hooper. A motel is located approximately ten miles south at the Great Sand Dunes National Monument exit. Campgrounds and RV hookups are available at the Great Sand Dunes, thirty miles away, and at San Luis State Park, twenty miles away on Sand Dunes Monument Rd. Credit cards accepted.

Directions: From Alamosa on CO 17 go 1 mile north of Hooper and turn east. Continue 1.5 miles and turn north 1 mile to the pool.

216 SPLASHLAND HOT SPRINGS
Box 972   (summer) 719 589-6307
Alamosa, CO 81101

Large, rural, community-owned plunge in the center of a wide, high valley. Elevation 7,500 feet. Open Memorial Day through Labor Day (closed Wednesday); call for hours.

Natural mineral water flows out of a spring at 106° and is piped to a large outdoor swimming pool that maintains a temperature of approximately 94° and to a wading pool for toddlers. The water is treated with chlorine. Swimming lessons offered. Bathing suits are required.

Locker rooms, suit, towel and toy rentals, and a snack bar are available on the premises. It is one mile to a cafe, store, and service station and two miles to all other services. No credit cards are accepted.

Location: On CO 17 1 mile north of Alamosa.

Justine Hill

Martin Rosenthal

A soak in either pool would feel great after the long, grueling hike to get to *Rainbow*. The spring is nicknamed Rainbow because of the mineral deposits left by the hot water as it cascades over the rocks into the pools.

217   RAINBOW (WOLF CREEK PASS) HOT SPRINGS

● **Northeast of the town of Pagosa Springs**

A primitive riverside hot spring at the end of a very rugged five-mile hike in the Weminuche Wilderness, northwest of CO 160. Elevation 9,000 feet, with a 1,000-foot elevation gain from the trailhead. Open all year (subject to flooding). Hard to reach during winter (this is avalanche country).

Natural mineral water flows out of a spring under a rock and cascades down the side of a bluff leaving a rainbow-colored pattern formed by the minerals. It fills two shallow, rock log and mud pools at the east edge of the San Juan River. The smaller upper pool will hold about three people, the larger lower pool about a dozen. A high rate of geothermal flow maintains a temperature of more than 100° in these pools. A third sandy-bottom, twelve-inch deep pool is approximately one-hundred yards upriver. Water at 106° bubbles up from the bottom into this rock and mud pool. This pool is useable only during the low water months of July and August. Proximity to the river makes cooling off easy. Clothing is optional.

There are no services available except pack-in camping areas scattered along the trail. Two national forest campgrounds are located one and one-half to two miles before the trailhead. Three miles before the trailhead is a trailer park with hookups, showers, propane, cabins, outfitters for horseback riding, fishing, and snowmobile tours. It is seventeen miles from the trailhead to all other services in Pagosa Springs. A park ranger spends the summer at the springs.

Directions: From the eastern end of Pagosa Springs, at the junction of CO 160 and CO 84, drive northeast on CO 160 for 14 miles to a national forest sign for West Fork Rd., Trailhead, FS 648. Turn left (north) and drive 3 miles, passing two national forest campgrounds to a parking area and trailhead, following signs for Rainbow Trail. The trail begins with a short steep climb up a 4WD road through Born Lake Ranch. Stay on the trail; you are on private property. After passing a sign saying "Hot Springs 4 miles," bear left when the trail forks. Cross the first of three bridges over the creek after passing a sign for "Weminuche Wilderness." When the trail forks after the third bridge, take the left fork up a very steep trail. Rainbow Trail is marked by red-painted horizontal steel bars extending from trees. At the junction with Beaver Creek Trail, continue on Rainbow Trail. It is approximately 1 mile from here to the springs. After crossing several small rivulets, the trail ascends to a large clearing with fallen logs and campfire rings. The hot springs are just below to the left at river level and are visible at the foot of a rocky bluff. There is no official trail down to the pools.

To reach the pool upriver, continue on the trail through the camping area and down into a meadow where the trail is at river level. The pool is across the river from a seep in the rocks and can be reached by rock-hopping during low water.

Note: Allow three to four hours for the hike in, and about half that time to hike out. Weather changes very rapidly in this area. It is a good idea to check with the San Juan Natio al Forest, Pagosa Ranger District, 970 264-2268.

Source map: *San Juan National Forest*.
GPS: N 37.511 W 106.945

Marjorie Young

Courtesy of The Spa Motel

THE LEGEND OF PAGOSA SPRINGS

The Great Pagosa Springs is the largest and hottest known geothermal pool in the world. Its depth has been measured to 850 feet without touching bottom. The main spring puts out water at 153°.

"Pahgosa" is the name given the spring by the Ute Indians and means boiling water. Legends tell of a terrible illness that fell upon the Utes. No matter what the medicine men did, the Utes continued to die. In a last desperate attempt to appease the Great Spirit they built a gigantic bonfire along the banks of the San Juan River. They danced and sang around the bonfire until they dropped into an exhausted sleep. When they awoke they discovered a large pool of boiling water where their fire had been. After drinking the water and bathing in it they were cured.

A monument now stands on the site of the bonfire. The minerals from the water have formed a giant tufa mound. Steam rises continually from the mound.

In 1881, Pagosa's first public bathhouse was built near the springs. Today, the Visitors Information Building near the springs is a replica of the 1888 bathhouse.

During the winter you can explore the great outdoors on a snowmobile or ski at Wolf Creek Ski area, only twenty miles away. During the summer bring your fishing rod, bicycle, and hiking boots.

Owned and well taken care of for over forty years by the Giodano family, the property is adjacent to Reservoir Hill with hiking and biking trails.

218 A   PAGOSA SPRINGS POOL (THE SPA MOTEL)
■   317 Hot Springs Blvd.   970 264-5910
Pagosa Springs, CO 81147
www.thespaatpagosasprings.com

A nicely maintained motel with swimming pool (dating back to 1938) refurbished bathhouse and massage buildings with indoor hot tubs. Located across the San Juan River from downtown Pagosa Springs. Elevation 7,100 feet. Open all year.

Natural mineral water is pumped from a well at 130° and piped to the swimming pool and bathhouse. The hot water is recycled through the river. The outdoor swimming pool is maintained at 95° in winter and 88° in summer. Two indoor soaking pools in separate men's and women's sections are maintained at 108°. The outdoor hot tub is maintained at 106°. All pools have continuous flow-through, so only minimal chemical treatment is necessary. Each of the two bathhouse sections also has its own steambath. Bathing suits are required in the outdoor pools. Facilities are free to motel guests and open for a fee to the general public. The outdoor pool is handicap accessible with assistance.

Rooms and RV park with full hookups are available on the premises along with a nicely decorated massage building where ten therapists offer many massage modalities, facials, chiropractic, and reflexology. It is less than three blocks to all other services in town. Feel free to bring snacks, but no glass. Credit cards accepted.

Directions: In Pagosa Springs on US 160, turn south at Hot Springs Blvd. Watch for motel and pool on your left.

No matter what the season or time of day, the view down the San Juan River from the pools placed along the river and set into the travertine hillsides is beautiful. You can even swim in the river and then climb back into the pools to warm up.

218 B   THE SPRING INN
PO Box 1799   970 264-4168
165 Hot Springs Blvd.   800 225-0934
Pagosa Springs, CO 81147
www.pagosasprings.net/springinn

Lush flower beds accent this resort inn as multiple pools set along the river and into the hillsides offer opportunities for a relaxing soak as you watch the water rushing down the adjacent San Juan River. Elevation 7,100 feet. Open all year.

Natural mineral water flows out of a spring at 155° and is piped to fifteen rock and cement pools of varying sizes and temperatures from 95-112°, all about three-feet deep, some sculpted into the gently sloping hillside overlooking the San Juan River, several along the paths, and a few along the river bank. A submerged boardwalk with a rope handrail leads you through a large, warm fishpond to a secluded pool located below a tufa mound. All pools have continuous flow-through, so no chemical treatment is necessary. Bathing suits are required. Two of the pools are handicap accessible.

Facilities include suites and motel rooms, massage, a Zen bookstore, sundecks with lounge chairs, and a hike and ski shop. Dressing rooms with showers and lockers are available for day use. Sidewalks are heated geothermally as are the hot water sources at the inn. Other services are within three blocks. Major credit cards accepted.

Directions: Turn south off of Hwy 160 onto Hot Springs Blvd. Cross the San Juan River bridge. The Inn is on the right, just past the Visitor Information Center. Phone for rates and reservations.

The three pictures on the right are of various pools found at *The Spring Inn.* The view across the river into the town is particularly lovely in the evening.

219 PIEDRA RIVER HOT SPRING

● **West of Pagosa Springs**

A series of shallow primitive pools in a beautiful mountain setting in the San Juan National Forest. Elevation 7,400 feet. Open all year, subject to flooding, mud, and snow.

Natural mineral water at about 110° flows up from the bottom of several ankle-deep, volunteer-built, rock and mud pools on the east bank of the Piedra River. Within fifty yards along the east riverbank are additional pools that need to be scooped out before you can soak. The local custom is clothing optional.

No services are available on the premises. There is pack-in camping in the surrounding national forest. It is about seven miles to a campground, cabins, and outfitters for pack trips at the junction of US 160 and FS 622. Three miles east of this junction, at Chimney Rock, are a cafe, gas station, laundry, and store.

Directions: From US 160, 21 miles west of Pagosa Springs, 40 miles east of Durango, and just east of the Piedra River, turn north onto First Fork Rd., FS 622, marked with a national forest access sign. Follow FS 622, a one-lane dirt road (can be muddy) for 6.7 miles to a marked intersection with Sheep Creek Trail (left) and Monument Park Rd. (right). Turn left and park at the clearing and Sheep Creek trailhead. Hike down the steep, rocky trail for about 1 mile to where it widens into a meadow with an old steel cable bridge over the river. Do not cross the bridge; turn right and follow the trail north along the river for approximately 1 mile. The trail, which has been above the river, crosses tiny Coffee Creek, then drops down to a clearing at river level with fallen trees and logs. A sign points to "Hot Springs," to which someone has added "along the river."

Note: The ascent back up to the parking area is fairly strenuous along the steep, rocky trail.

Source map: *San Juan National Forest.*
GPS: N 37.313 W 107.344

Tall shade trees and beautiful flowers surround the various pools and lawn area at *Trimble Hot Springs.*

220   TRIMBLE HOT SPRINGS
6475 County Road 203
Durango, CO 81301   970 247-0111
www.trimblehotsprings.com

Restored historic resort in the scenic Animas River Valley, below the La Plata Mountains. Elevation 6,500 feet. Open all year.

Natural mineral water flows out of a spring at 120° and is piped to the outdoor pools where it is treated with ozone. The Olympic-size swimming pool is maintained at 82°, one of the hydrojet pools is maintained at 100-102°, and the other is maintained at 108-110°. Bathing suits are required. Facilities include dressing rooms, a workshop and party room perfect for private parties and wedding receptions, snack bar, picnic area, and a fully equipped apartment. A new spa area with a beautiful new soaking pool has just been completed. Massage and other body/skin treatments, aqua aerobics, and yoga classes are available on the premises. It is one mile to a bed and breakfast inn and six miles to all other services. Major credit cards accepted.

Directions: From the city of Durango, go 7 miles north on US 550, then west 100 yards on Trimble Lane to the springs.

Photos by Debbie Johnson

221 A   OURAY HOT SPRINGS POOL
PO Box 468   970 325-4638
Ouray, CO 81427

Large, city-owned swimming pool and fitness center. Elevation 7,800 feet. Open all year.

Natural mineral water flows out of several springs at 150° and is cooled as needed to supply three large outdoor pools. The shallow soaking pool is maintained at 100°; the deep swimming and diving pool is maintained at 80°; and the therapy pool is maintained at 105°. All pools have continuous flow-through with a filtration system. Bathing suits are required. There are rails at the pools and the guards are able to help anyone who might need assistance.

Locker rooms, snack house, fitness center, and swim shop with suit rentals are available on the premises. All other services are within six blocks. Visa and MasterCard are accepted.

Location: The entire complex is easily visible on the west side of US 550 in the town of Ouray.

The pool was originally built in 1926 by a group of volunteers who then decided to build the bathhouse the following year.

Barbara Hanson

Location: Located on the corner of 6th Ave. and 5th St. in the town of Ouray, 2 blocks east of Main St. (US 550). Follow signs.

The private Lorelei pool pictured below is beautifully landscaped and includes a hot spring waterfall. Intimate enough for two and large enough to accommodate a wedding or other special event.

221 B WIESBADEN HOT SPRINGS SPA & LODGINGS

625 5th St. 970 325-4347
PO Box 349 (mailing address)
Ouray, CO 81427
www.geocities.com/wiesbadenspa

Charming mountain resort built to complement the spectacular canyon area of Uncompahgre National Forest. Elevation 7,700 feet. Open all year.

Natural mineral water flows from three springs at temperatures ranging from 108-130°. All pools operate on a flow-through basis, requiring no chemical treatment. The outdoor swimming pool ranges from 99° to 102°. The soaking pool in the natural vapor cave is maintained at 108-110°, considered a challenge well worth meeting. Bathing suits required. Handicap accessibility is limited to one pool and the private pool.

A 105° flow-through soaking pool done completely in natural stone is supplied by a hot-spring waterfall in a private area called "The Lorelei." In this beautifully landscaped 1,200-foot area, which may be rented by the hour, suits are optional. Space can be rented for parties, weddings, etc.

Continually flowing hot water runs under the buildings producing heat to warm the individually decorated rooms, some with fireplaces and some with kitchens. Using AVEDA products, massage, facials, body polishing, herbal body wraps and dry brushing are available. With advance notice you can also receive La Stone therapy, mud wraps, acupressure and reflexology. It is only two blocks to downtown. Credit cards accepted.

Top photo courtesy of Weisbaden Hot Springs Spa
Photo on right by Marjorie Young

The place to be for the fabulous views and a bit of privacy is the very top pool, one flight of steps up from this pool.

221 C BOX CANYON LODGE AND HOT SPRINGS

45 3rd Ave.   **970 325-4981**

Ouray, CO 81427

email: bcm@mii.com

Modern, comfortable lodge at the base of 13,000 foot mountains. Situated in a quiet off-highway location adjacent to Box Canyon Falls and the Uncompahgre River. Elevation 7,800 feet. Open all year.

Natural mineral water flows from a spring at 140° and is gravity fed to four outdoor, continuous flow-through redwood tubs requiring no chemical treatment. The four hydrojet tubs are situated on redwood decks that are terraced up the mountainside behind the lodge, offering spectacular views of the city and surrounding mountains. Temperatures in the tubs range from 103-108°. Use of the tubs is reserved for registered guests and bathing suits are required. Major credit cards are accepted.

Several geothermal springs, varying in temperature from 138-156°, are located on the property. In addition to using these springs for the soaking tubs, both the bathing and drinking water is heated via heat exchangers, and, during the winter months, the entire lodge is heated using this natural resource.

Location: Two blocks west of US 550 on 3rd Ave.

221 D BEST WESTERN TWIN PEAKS MOTEL

125 3rd Ave.   **970 325-4427**

Ouray, CO 81427

www.bestwestern.com/twinpeaksmotel

Modern, motel in a picturesque mountain town. Elevation 7,700 ft. Open April through October.

Natural mineral water flows out of a spring at 156° and is piped to two pools. The outdoor swimming pool is maintained at 82°, the outdoor waterfall soaking tub at 106°, and the indoor soaking pool at 104°. Pools are reserved for the use of registered guests. Bathing suits are required. There are railings on the pools making them handicap accessible. Jeep rentals available. Major credit cards accepted.

Location: One block west of US 550 on 3rd Ave.

In addition to two outdoor pools, one for soaking and one for swimming, there is also an indoor whirlpool tub. All the pools use natural mineral water.

Orvis is one of those places where those with suits–and those without–are tolerant of each other. It's worth a night's stay in the comfortable, clean rooms to experience this pond early in the morning with the steam rising above it, and to enjoy a soak under the stars.

222   ORVIS HOT SPRINGS
■ 1585 County Road #3   970 626-5324
Ridgway, CO 81432

Small and charming rustic lodge with multiple geothermal pools offering a mellow, relaxed soaking experience, located in a wide mountain valley. Elevation 7,000 feet. Open all year.

Mineral water flows from several springs at temperatures ranging from 112-127° and is piped to a variety of tubs and pools, all of which operate on a flow-through basis requiring no chemical treatment. All pools are available to the public for day use as well as to registered guests. Earth berms and fencing have been added, making the entire grounds clothing optional. Large trees will provide shade from the hot summer sun.

There are four private rooms with tiled soaking pools that have a water temperature of 102-108° and are drained and cleaned every day. Immediately adjoining the sauna building is one outside soaking pool built of stone, which has a water temperature of more than 110°. There is one large, indoor cement soaking pool (three-feet deep, twenty-five feet in diameter) that has a temperature of 101°. There is also one large, excavated soaking pond (six-feet deep, thirty-feet in diameter) that has hot mineral water continuously flowing in from the bottom and the sides. This enlarged natural hot spring maintains a year-round temperature of 103-105°. A cold soaking pool now adjoins this pond. Clothing is optional in all pools including the twenty-five foot indoor soaking pool after dark. Two yurts will provide a quiet space for massage. Beverages, snacks and "stuff" will be sold in the new lobby.

Facilities include six lodge rooms which share two baths. Room rates include unlimited use of sauna and pool facilities. Visa and MasterCard are accepted. It is less than two miles to the town of Ridgway and eight miles to Ouray for all other services. Phone for rates, hours, reservations, and directions.

This pool, located right outside the sauna, is 110°.

223   RICO HOT SPRING

● **South of Telluride**

On the bank of the Dolores River on the west slope of the beautiful Uncompahgre Mountain Range. Springs originally used by the miners as they dug out the silver and gold for which this region became famous. Elevation 8,300 feet. Open all year; weather dependent.

Natural mineral water at 107° is piped through PVC pipes into a commercial hot tub where the water registers 103° before it spills into the river. Changing benches, a campfire circle, and trails have been established over the years by volunteers who also keep this place free of litter. There is no way to cool the water in the tub, but you can cool yourself by a quick dip in the adjacent river. Clothing optional.

All services available in Telluride, about thirty minutes away. Campgrounds nearby.

Directions: Take Hwy 145 south from Telluride to the village of Rico. Turn left on the gravel road immediately after crossing the Dolores River bridge and proceed .3 mile. Turn left on the small road leading to the small metal building next to the mine ponds. Take the short trail to the tub and river.

Important Note: Because of the proximity to the mines the water is rich in copper-colored minerals resulting in a bright orange coating on the tub and a deposit of "heavy metals." People have been soaking there without incident for many years, but you should make up your own mind.

The "Old Wild West" never had it this good. Period-piece cabins have been "rustically" restored, one cabin with its own hot tub. The source spring pool, covered by a large tepee, is reached by climbing down a ladder. The outdoor pond is glorious, no matter what the temperature.

224 DUNTON HOT SPRINGS

■

PO Box 818   970 882-4800
Dolores, CO 81323
www.duntonhotsprings.com

An authentic nineteenth century mining town whose cabins, barns and other building have been painstakingly restored now functions as an upscale destination resort for corporate retreats or rentals to individuals and families. Located between Telluride and Cortez, in the beautiful San Juan Mountains of Southern Colorado. Elevation 8,900 feet. Open all year.

Several natural mineral springs are found on the property at temperatures around 106°. A wonderful soak can be had in a large natural outdoor pool with views of 14,000 foot peaks covered in snow year-round. A tepee has been erected over the source spring pool, accessed by climbing down a ladder. The Dunton Bath House offers a large tub, a fireplace, a cold dip, and stunning views. One of the fully restored log cabins has its own private soaking tub in the bedroom. One rental unit is fully handicap accessible.

Ten log cabins, one three-bedroom house, a bunkhouse with ten beds, and two tepees which can function as additional bedrooms are available for rent. Capacity of the resort is thirty-four people based on double occupancy and two lofts for the kids. Rentals include three meals a day prepared by a master chef, and enjoyed in the former Dunton Bar and Saloon, where rumor has it that Butch Cassidy and the Sundance Kid enjoyed local hospitality after robbing the bank in Telluride. An open-air chapel located near the thirty-five-foot Dunton Falls is the perfect setting for outdoor weddings. Outdoor activities include horseback riding, mountain biking, fly fishing, hiking, ice climbing, river rafting, back country skiing, snowshoeing, and helicopter skiing directly out of Dunton. Massages available. Up-to-date communication facilities include fiber optic phone service and internet access.

Phone or use the web site for further information.

Photos courtesy of Dunton Hot Springs

TEXAS

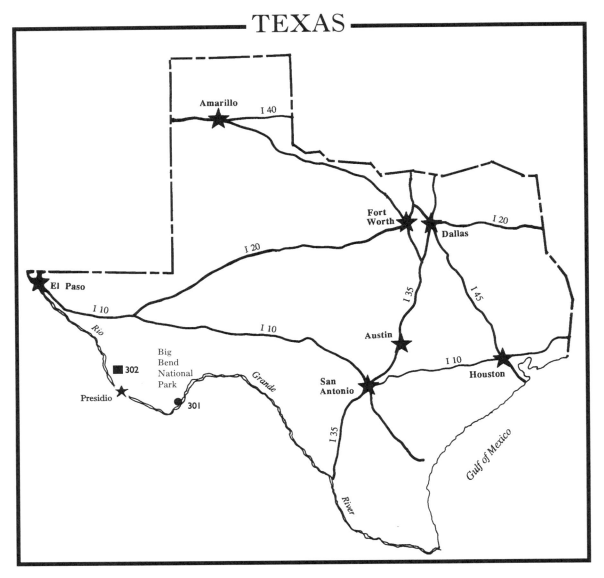

This map was designed to be used with a standard highway map.

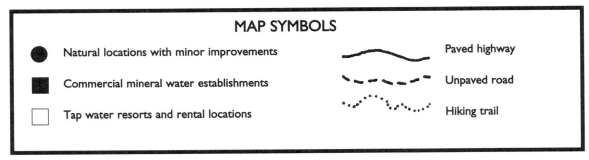

MAP SYMBOLS

Natural locations with minor improvements

Commercial mineral water establishments

Tap water resorts and rental locations

Paved highway

Unpaved road

Hiking trail

Kent Wilson

301 LANGFORD (BOQUILLAS) HOT SPRING

● **Big Bend National Park, Texas**

Historic masonry hot pool in the ruins of an old resort on the banks of the Rio Grande. Located near the Rio Grande Village Campground in Big Bend National Park. Elevation 1,800 feet. Open all year.

Natural mineral water flows out of the ground at 105° into a large, shallow stone and concrete soaking pool a few feet above river level. Following the rains, and when the river level rises above four feet the springs become submerged. So, bring a shovel as it is up to you to dig out the tubs. Swimming in the river is not recommended because of pollution and currents. Bathing suits are required.

There are no services on the premises. It is six miles to a store, service station, overnight camping, and RV hookups, and twenty-eight miles to a motel and restaurant.

Directions: From Big Bend National Park Headquarters, drive 16 miles toward Rio Grand Village Campground. Turn right at hot springs sign, then drive 2 miles on dirt road to the end and walk .25 miles downriver to hot spring. The last mile of dirt road is very narrow and not accessible by motor home or large campers.

Source map: *Big Bend National Park.*
GPS: N 29.178 W 102.953

Lynn Foss

A guide to Indian pictographs is available at the trailhead. Be sure to see the colorful murals which still decorate the inside of the old resort hotel rooms.

El Dorado Hot Spring

Courtesy of Chinati Hot Springs

302 CHINATI HOT SPRINGS

915 229-4165

■ **East of Ruidosa**
e-mail: hotsprings@brooksdata.net

Historic oasis in the Chihuahuan Desert just below the Chinati Mountains in the northern Big Bend region of Texas. Elevation 3, 500 feet. Open all year.

Natural mineral water comes out of a spring at 109° and is piped to three private rooms in a bathhouse, each with a one to two-person tub, and a larger creekside outdoor pool. The tubs are drained and refilled after each use, so no chemical treatment is necessary. In fact, the water is so pure it is used as tap water on the premises. The major chemical concentrations in the water are lithium and arsenic (healthy minerals in small amounts).

Current facilities include the bathhouse, several rustic adobe cabins, and a ranch house. There are also grassy areas for camping and for picnics. It is fifty miles to Presidio and the nearest available service station or grocery store. A series of outdoor group baths, food service, a retreat facility with additional accommodations, a healing center, and individual retreat cabins are planned for the future

Write or phone first for information, rates, and reservations, or visit www. synchronicity-found.com.

This property is in the middle of a very primitive and beautiful section of the country characterized by deep canyons and distinctive geology. Nearby are the Big Bend Ranch Park, Big Bend National Park, and Chinati Peak (for which the hot springs is now named).

Directions: From Presidio take US 170 north through the small town of Ruidosa. In less than a mile you will see a cattle guard across the highway and a sign on the right saying "Hot Springs Road" and "Chinati Hot Springs." Turn right. You are now on the road leading to the hot springs. It is about 7 miles to the gate (on the left) which is always open. Continue to the office on the right. Do not park on the grass. You can park in the road or pull in on the driveway if there is room. There should be signs along the way to help. You should plan on about an hour from Presidio to the hot springs (approximately 50 miles).

It is possible to come directly from Marfa to the hot springs along Pinto Canyon Rd. (#2810), but the road is very rough after the pavement ends and that area is generally deserted. It may be 15 minutes less travel time, but it is probably not worth the wear and tear.

GPS: N 30.038 W 104.598

The brick building (above left) is one of the places you can stay. The door (picture below) leads to one of the the private baths. Spring water rises and is gathered in a reservoir behind the post at the corner of the porch roof.

HISTORY OF THE CHINATI HOT SPRINGS

(Information taken from the bulletin published by the Tangram Corporation, 1701 River Run Rd., Ste. 800, Fort Worth, TX 76017.)

Indians, early settlers, soldiers and area residents from both sides of the border have used the healing waters for hundreds of years.

Mr. and Mrs. W. L. Kingston acquired the volcanic springs in 1898. They built the original cabins and bathhouse in 1936 making the "Kingston Hot Springs" available to the public. The resort was closed in May 1990 when it was sold to Donald Judd, a local artist, who purchased the property for private use only.

Richard Fenker and the Tangram Corporation purchased the property from Judd's estate in April, 1997, and are currently restoring it for general use. The springs were formerly known as Kingston Hot Springs or Ruidosa Hot Springs.

The hot spring plans ultimately call for use by scientists and students in many disciplines. It also will be linked with organizations interested in the Big Bend area and used as a retreat facility or a center for study.

Upper left: El Dorado Hot Spring
Upper right: Kent Wilson
Lower right: Courtesy of Chinati Hot Springs

NEW MEXICO

This map was designed to be used with a standard highway map.

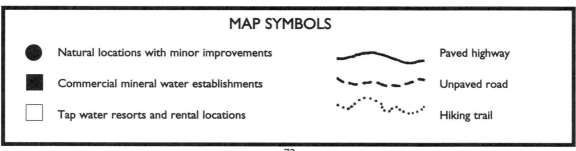

MAP SYMBOLS

● Natural locations with minor improvements

■ Commercial mineral water establishments

□ Tap water resorts and rental locations

〜 Paved highway

- - - Unpaved road

····· Hiking trail

Each of the pools at the resort has its own specific concentration of minerals.

Photos by Debbie Johnson

401 OJO CALIENTE RESORT

■ Box 468   505 583-2233
Ojo Caliente, NM 87549
www.ojocalientespa.com

Rustic adobe resort, originally built in the early 1900s, has been remodeled in a Spanish motif. Located in the foothills of Carson National Forest, forty-six miles north of Santa Fe. Elevation 6,300 feet. Open all year.

Natural mineral water flows out of five different springs with different temperatures and mineral contents. An outdoor, sandy-bottom, iron mineral water soaking pool is directly over the source of the spring, with a pool temperature up to 105°. An indoor soda pool has piped in water measuring up to 104°. The sun beating on the roof creates a natural steam room, and a sign inside indicates "Quiet Zone." Taps are available at both pools for a drink of the healing mineral water. The outdoor swimming pool and spa contain traces of arsenic with cold water added to maintain a year-round temperature of 85° in the pool and 106° in the spa. For the eighteen-and-older crowd there are three new geothermal mineral and mud pools. The iron and soda pools have continual flow-through and are drained three to four times a week, requiring no chemicals. The swimming pool is treated with chlorine. Children are limited to the big and little arsenic pools. A private arsenic tub can be rented with access afterwards to the other mineral pools.

There are separate men's and women's bathhouses, and one that is coed. Water temperatures in the indoor tubs can be adjusted by adding cold water. Bathing suits are required in all the pools except in the indoor tubs. Two indoor tubs are handicap accessible, as are all the pools.

Massage, sweat wraps, herbal wraps, salt glows, and herbal facials are offered. Towels and bathing suits can be borrowed. The bathhouses have showers, lockers, and dressing areas. Also available is a conference room for retreats, conferences, and clinics, a dining room, lodging in the adobe hotel or cottages, a camping area, a fully connected, thirty-site RV campground, a gift shop, and volleyball and shuffleboard courts. Major credit cards accepted.

Directions: From Santa Fe, go 46 miles north on US 285. Watch for signs.

The adult-only area has a mud pool that makes your skin feel wonderful.

Debbie Johnson

This area is also very popular with the local anglers.

402 A   BLACK ROCK HOT SPRINGS

● **West of the town of Arroyo Hondo**

Two mud-bottomed rock pools located on the west bank of the Rio Grande Gorge, just a few feet above river level. Elevation 6,500 feet. Open all year; pools may not be open until summer, and the road is subject to flooding.

Natural mineral water flows up through the bottom of the inland pool, maintaining the pool temperature at 97° except when high water in the river floods the pool. The adjacent pool, closer to the river, is much cooler due to more mixing with river water. The apparent local custom is clothing optional.

There are no services available except pit toilets near the John Dunn Bridge. This is also the staging area for kayaking and float trips down the river. It is three miles to a store, cafe, service station, etc. in Arroyo Hondo, and nine miles to RV hookups near Taos. Note: Unpaved roads may become impassable during wet weather.

Directions: From the blinking light at NM 522 in Arroyo Hondo, take either County Road B-002 at Herb's Lounge and Mini-Mart just north of the river or County Road B-005 just south of the river. At .2 miles they join. Continue for .7 miles to where the pavement ends. Bear left over a tiny bridge. At .1 mile bear right, and continue .1 mile farther on. You are now on a two-lane gravel road above the south bank of the Arroyo Hondo River. At .4 miles since you entered the two-lane road, cross a bridge over the tiny creek and bear right. (The very rough road to the left heads toward Stagecoach [Manby] Hot Springs.) Drive for 1 mile, cross another bridge over the river, and .1 mile farther, cross the John Dunn bridge, a steel bridge over the Rio Grande where the Arroyo Hondo River merges. Just past the bridge are pit toilets and a swimming beach to the right. To get to the hot springs, turn left after the bridge and head uphill. Park at the flat clearing in the horseshoe of the turn and walk straight ahead on a path that leads down to the pools near the river, approximately .25 miles (a 5-10 minute walk).

Just south of the springs, remains of rocky walls are visible where a bridge used to span the river on the route. The very steep old stagecoach road can be seen from the parking clearing. Look across the gorge for a route that cuts diagonally in switchbacks down to the river.

402 B   STAGECOACH (MANBY) HOT SPRINGS

● **Southwest of the town of Arroyo Hondo**

Three shallow, sandy-bottom rock pools at river's edge, near the ruins of a bathhouse that was an old stage-coach stop on the east bank of the Rio Grande Gorge. Elevation 6,500 feet. Open all year; subject to road flooding.

Natural mineral water flows out of the ground at 97° directly into the one-foot deep rock pools, which are large enough for three to four people. The lower pool is only slightly above low water in the river, so the temperature depends on the amount of cold water seeping in. Two larger, shallow 80° pools are a few feet away near a sandy beach. The apparent custom is clothing optional.

There are no services available except a port-a-potty in the upper parking area, but overnight camping is not prohibited on the sandy beach. Overnight parking is also not prohibited in the flat parking clearing and surrounding areas at the top of the trail. It is nine miles to a store and service station in Arroyo Hondo. Note: Unpaved roads may become impassable during wet weather.

Directions: The suggested route begins at the blinking light (a landmark from which locals give directions) north of Taos and south of Arroyo Hondo where NM 64 heads west toward the Rio Grande Bridge and the Taos Municipal Airport. Follow NM 64 from the blinking light for 4.1 miles (.3 miles west of the airport). Turn right (north) onto Tune Dr., an unpaved, graded two-lane road that has a posted speed limit of 25 mph. Bear left at the forks at .2 miles, .3 miles, and another .2 miles. The last fork has a sign indicating "Manby." Go .2 miles to a large parking clearing. A wide path leads down from the southwest end of the parking clearing to the springs. An obvious trail goes down from the ridge to river level; it is very gradual and not strenuous (a 15-20-minute walk).

Source maps: USGS *Arroyo Hondo.*
GPS: N 36.508 W 105.722

Debbie Johnson

Marjorie Young

403 A   SAN ANTONIO HOT SPRINGS

● **North of the town of Jemez Springs**

A gem of a hot spring with a series of rock-edged pools built against the hillside of San Diego Canyon in the stunning wooded setting of the Santa Fe National Forest. Elevation 8,000 feet. Open May to October due to weather conditions.

Natural mineral water flows in at the low 100s, directly into the rock and cement upper pool, then cascades over rocks and through pipes into two lower pools. People have scooped out just enough of the silty, rocky bottom in the lower pools to create places deep enough to soak up to your waist. The upper pool is somewhat deeper.

There are no services available. However, if you like to fish, the river at the base of the parking lot is a good place to do it. All services are in La Cueva at the junction of NM 4 and NM 126, or eleven miles south in Jemez Springs.

Directions: From the intersection of NM 4 and NM 126, follow NM 126 to FS 376 north (3.8 miles), which will be on the right. Take FS 376, a deeply rutted dirt road, 5 miles. The parking area is down to the right. After you park, cross the wood bridge and follow the fairly obvious trail uphill for approximately 10 minutes to the pools. Someone has put round reflection markers on the trees along the trail which you can use if you have very good eyes. The trail is quite steep and can be very slippery if wet.

GPS: N 35.938 W 106.646

Camping overnight gives you a chance to soak in all of the pools at *McCauley Hot Spring*, including the large one above and one of the smaller ones, below.

Photos by Erica Janes

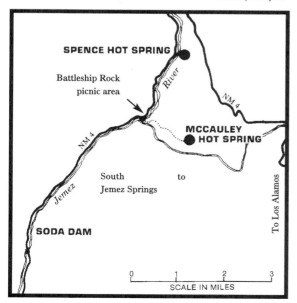

403 B   MCCAULEY HOT SPRING

(see map)

● **North of the town of Jemez Springs**

Very large, shallow, warm pool whose waters flow down into several deeper, smaller pools in a gorgeous mountain clearing. Elevation 7,300 feet. Open approximately May through October due to weather conditions.

Natural mineral water flows out of the ground at 95° directly into a two-foot deep pond, forty-feet in diameter. Pool temperature measures between 85-90°, depending on air and wind conditions. A second, rock and log pool, three-feet deep, is approximately fifty feet downhill in the creekbed runoff, where water cascades into two separate places in the pool, accessed by a log and rock bridge. From here it falls down to another pool, four-feet to five-feet deep where the temperature is a degree or two cooler. The apparent local custom is clothing optional.

There are no services on the premises, except level areas for pack-in camping. It is three and one-half miles to a store, gas, restaurant, and lodge in La Cueva at the intersection of NM 4 and NM 126, five miles to a campground and AYH youth hostel, ten miles north to San Antonio campground and seventeen miles to RV hookups.

Directions: From the ranger station at the north end of Jemez Springs, go 4 miles north on NM 4 to Battleship Rock picnic area, which is open 6 AM to 10 PM only. A day-use fee is charged. Starting from the firepit gazebo in the picnic area, follow FS trail 137, called East Fork Trail. Just past the gazebo, the trail immediately forks. Follow the right fork along the river. Stay on the main trail (despite many spurs) that gradually ascends in switchbacks. Hike approximately 2 miles until you hear the gurgling creek, which is runoff from the warm spring. A large clearing with campfire rings is off to the right just before you reach the pond. This trail is moderately strenuous, especially at this altitude. Alternate directions: At the intersection of NM 126 and NM 4, turn right, staying on 4. Go 5 miles and park at Jemez Falls campground and hike in the 2 miles to the springs from the marked trail head.

GPS: N 35.820 W 106.627

Chris Andrews

There are no services available. It is one and one-half miles from the north end of the parking area to a store, gas, restaurant and lodge in La Cueva at the intersection of NM 4 and NM 126, five miles to a campground, seven miles to an AYH youth hostel, and seventeen miles to RV hookups. Services are also located south of the pools in Jemez Springs.

Directions: From the town of Jemez Springs, go 7 miles north on NM 4 to a large parking area on the east side of the highway 2 miles past "Battleship Rock Picnic Area." From the town of Los Alamos, drive west on NM 501 to the intersection in La Cueva with NM 126 and NM 4. Then go south on NM 4 for 1.5 miles to the large parking area on the east side of the road. From the parking area, a rocky clearing is visible across the river to the northeast. The trail begins at the south end of the parking pull out. A sturdy wooden footbridge across the Jemez River replaces a log crossing. The trail continues up a steep slope to the springs. The parking pullout is posted "No parking from sundown to sunup." During snow and rain, the slope can become very slippery.

GPS: N 35.849 W 106.627

403 C SPENCE HOT SPRING
(see map on previous page)
● **North of the town of Jemez Springs**

A unique group of several sandy-bottom pools on a steep hillside with a spectacular view of surrounding mountains. Located in the Santa Fe National Forest on the east side of the Jemez River. Elevation 6,000 feet. Open all year.

Natural mineral water at 109° flows up through the bottom into a rock-bordered pool large enough for ten people. There is a pipe for draining and cleaning. A series of pipes send the water to two pools just below, which have gradually cooler temperatures. The first is a shallow, one-foot deep sandy-bottom pool between huge boulders with a 100° water source inside a cave. The second is smaller and cooler. Air temperature and wind affect the temperature in these shallow pools. There is also a pipe here for draining and cleaning.

Hike uphill for fifty feet, cross a clearing, then follow the runoff around some large boulders uphill and to the left of the three lower pools for two other pools.

Another pool is about two hundred feet straight uphill from the lower pools. Hike across the clearing and continue uphill, following the runoff. This primitive knee-deep, squishy-bottom, sand and rock pool is large enough for two to three people. The water source which flows out between the rocks measures 109°. The apparent local custom is clothing optional.

Barbara Hanson

Thanks to the many volunteers who show up at *Spence Hot Spring* to help keep this very special place with its many pools and beautiful water in pristine condition. There has been some discussion about closing the pools because of inappropriate behavior—please do your part to make sure this does not happen.

Debbie Johnson

A great place to spend a few days relaxing, both at *Giggling Star* (one of the few places to stay anywhere that has its own hot water pond), and at the three really great natural hot springs in the Jemez area. The cabins are really fixed up beautifully and there is fishing right down at the river.

404 A   GIGGLING STAR RIVERFRONT CABINS
040 Abouselman Loop (Box 60)

505 829-9175

■   Jemez Springs, NM 87025
www.sulphurcanyon.com/giggle

Delightfully restored cabins and a wonderful hot soaking pond under the cottonwoods are situated along the Jemez River. Located off the main road through town. Elevation 6,300 feet. Open all year.

Natural mineral springs which once fed the original bathhouse built in the mid-1800s now fills a large stone, river rock, and flagstone pool surrounded by natural vegetation. The water comes out of the source in the pump house at 138°. The temperature of the pool ranges between 102-108°. One time per month the pool is drained and scrubbed with chlorine. Clothing optional after dark.

Three cabins are available for rent: Double Dipper (two bedrooms, kitchen, fireplace); Little Dipper (one bedroom, kitchen, fireplace); and Skinny Dipper (refrigerator and sleeping loft). Restoration was carefully done with hand-painted tiles, claw-footed bathtubs, and hand-crafted furniture. The back porches of the cabins overlook the river, hot springs, and canyon walls. Easy access to the Jemez Mountains, a national recreation area, and several natural hot springs. All other services are a short walk into town. Credit cards accepted. Advance reservations suggested.

Marjorie Young

Giggling Star is conveniently located one and one-half hours from the Albuquerque airport and a little less than two hours to Santa Fe.

404 B BODHI MANDA ZEN CENTER
MOTEL AND HOT SPRINGS
Box 8   505 829-3854
■ Jemez Springs, NM 87205

A four-unit motel a few minutes stroll away from the riverbank hot pools. Operated by the Bodhi Manda Zen Center and located in the town of Jemez Springs. Elevation 6,300 feet. Closed between September and December 15 for retreats.

Natural mineral water flows out of the ground at 169°, then into three rock and sand soaking pools where natural cooling results in varying temperatures. The pools are two-feet to three feet deep. The river next to the pools serves as a cold plunge. Bathing suits are required. Call first if you wish to use the pools. No drop-ins, please.

It is one block to a store and cafe and seven miles to a service station. Phone ahead for current information, rates, directions, and reservations.

Courtesy of Jemez Springs Bath House

Justine Hill

404 C JEMEZ SPRINGS BATH HOUSE, INC.
062 State Hwy 4 (Box 112) 505 829-3303
■ Jemez Springs, NM 87205
www.jemez.com/BATHS

A pleasant, well-maintained bathhouse located in the park on the main street of Jemez Springs. Elevation 6,200 feet. Open all year.

Natural mineral water flows out of a city-owned springs at 155-185° and is piped to a cooling tank and then to the bathhouse. There are eight private rooms, each containing a one-person bathtub. Curtains can be pulled aside so that couples can soak next to each other. A private outdoor cedar tub is available to groups of up to six. Cool and hot mineral water are mixed to provide the desired water temperature. Tubs are drained and refilled after each use, so no chemical treatment of the water is necessary. Clothing is optional. Children under five are not permitted in tub areas. Indoor tubs and facilities are handicap accessible.

Massage, wraps, facials and other beauty services are available on the premises, as is a store selling local crafts, beauty supplies, cold drinks, and snacks. Towels can be rented. It is one block to a store, lodgings, and restaurant, and ten miles to a service station. Major credit cards accepted. Phone for rates, reservations, and directions.

405 TEN THOUSAND WAVES

❏ PO Box 10200   505 982-9304
Santa Fe, NM 87504

A beautiful health spa recreates the feel of a Japanese hot spring resort in the mountains above Santa Fe. Located three and one-half miles up Artist Road (Ski Basin Road) with desert and mountain views.

Six privately enclosed outdoor tubs, with waterfalls, decks, and cooling rooms and one indoor tub with two balconies are available. Four of the areas include saunas, and one includes a steam room. A communal wood tub and sauna large enough for twenty-five people and a separate women's pebble-bottomed communal tub with sauna are also available. Suits are optional in the coed communal tub until 8:15 PM, and optional at all time in the women's communal tub. No chlorine is used in any of the tubs. Instead a purification method of ultraviolet light, ozone, copper/silver ions, and hydrogen peroxide is used. The tubs are maintained at a temperatures of 104-106°. Several massage rooms, tubs and houses are handicap accessible.

Eight charming lodging suits are available for rent nearby. Kimonos, sandals, soap, shampoo, towels, and hair dryers are provided and bathing suits can be rented. A juice and snack bar is in the lobby. Various health treatments are offered, including the newly added pagoda massage and Japanese nightingale facial. Still available are aromatherapy, herbal wraps, salt glows, watsu (in-water massage), East Indian cleansing treatments, and other facials. Visa, MasterCard, and Discover Card are accepted. Be sure to phone for reservations.

These pools are on the grounds of the United World College. Officials request that you keep the area clean, respect the bathing suit requirement, and keep noise levels down. Please do your part so that the college will continue to allow the pools to remain open to the public.

406 MONTEZUMA HOT SPRINGS

● **Northwest of the town of Las Vegas**

The once-abandoned ruins of a major turn-of-the-century hot springs resort bathhouse. Located just across the Gallinas River on the property of the lavish Victorian "Montezuma's Castle," now Armand Hammer's United World College. Elevation 6,450 feet. Open all year.

Natural mineral water flows out of several artesian springs at 94-113° into three clusters of concrete soaking pools of various sizes and depths up to six feet, resulting in a wide range of temperature choices. Continuous flow-through (fifteen gallons per minute) eliminates the need for chemical treatment of the water. Volunteers are fastidious about keeping the pools clean, draining and scrubbing them every two weeks. One cluster of pools (the hottest) has been newly redesigned, sculpted, and landscaped into the hillside; a second group of two pools is near a coffin-looking concrete block; the third sit near the old bathhouse. The whole area around the pools can be very wet and marshy. The pools are just steps from the road. Bathing suits are required.

There are no services available on the premises. It is six miles to a store, cafe, service station, etc. in Las Vegas.

Directions: From I-25 take exit 65 W in Las Vegas, cross over I-25, turn right on Business 25 to Mills Ave. Turn left on Mills for 1.5 miles to Hot Springs Rd., marked with a sign to Montezuma and United World College. Turn right (this is NM 65) for 5 miles until you see the castle on the hill. A sign along the right side of the road on the metal guard rail indicates "Hot Springs Baths." Park along the shoulder of the road. Several openings in the fence lead to railroad tie steps down to the pools. The five indoor pools are now fenced and closed. The outdoor pools are open to the public year-round at no charge.

Courtesy of Marshall Hot Springs

TRUTH OR CONSEQUENCES

The hot springs at Truth or Consequences produce two and one-half million gallons of water per day, have the largest mineral water table in the Southwest, and boast the highest mineral content in the United States.

These were the sacred springs of the Apaches, and Geronimo speaks of spending a peaceful year in the area. Artifacts indicate high usage by the earlier Mimbres Indians. The springs were known to the Spanish as Ojo Caliente de Las Polomas (Hot Springs of the Doves). The crystal clear water is also good for drinking (no unpleasant odor or taste). The town itself sits on the banks of the Rio Grande, just below Elephant Butte, the largest freshwater lake in the region, offering boating, sailing, and some of the best bass fishing around.

If you haven't visited this area in a while, you will be pleasantly surprised to find that while the area has retained its uniqueness, it also offers such amenities as golf courses, a museum, restaurants, and many small shops.

Many of the indoor tubs at the various bath houses could easily be handicap accessible.

407 A ARTESIAN BATH HOUSE AND TRAILER PARK
312 Marr   505 894-2684
■ Truth or Consequences, NM 87901

Five single-size and three family-size ceramic tubs at an average water temperature of 108°, are available for rent by the hour. Tubs are refilled for each use so no chemicals are necessary. Each room contains a bench and cold shower.

RV hookups, tenant laundry, and public showers are available on the premises, plus massage by appointment. No credit cards are accepted.

407 B CHARLES MOTEL AND BATH HOUSE
601 Broadway   505 894-7154
                           800 317-4518
■ Truth or Consequences, NM 87901
www.globaldrum.net/sierra_newmexico/spa

Nine individual baths are cleaned and refilled for each bather, eliminating the need for chemicals. While the hot water comes in at temperatures between 108-111°, cold water is available to cool the water. Following the soak, the bather can be wrapped in a sheet and then a wool blanket. There is also a hot tub on the roof which seats four-to-six people and provides fabulous views.

Twenty apartment-style motel units, totally remodeled to reflect the period of the 40s, are available for rent nightly or weekly. Massage, reflexology, ayurvedic work, clay packs, facials, and acupuncture are available. Art gallery and gift shop.

407 C FIREWATER LODGE
309 Broadway   505 894-3405
■ Truth or Consequences, NM 87901

The renovations on an older adobe villa are nearly complete, offering bed and breakfast accommodations. Large tubs using the hot mineral water are available in the bigger private rooms. Renting a smaller room includes unlimited use of the private hot mineral bath area where temperatures in the tubs range between 108-111°. One tub and both bathrooms are handicap accessible.

A bakery/cafe is on the premises and massage, acupuncture, and reflexology are available.

Photos by El Dorado Hot Spring

407 D HAY-YO-KAY HOT SPRINGS
300 Austin Ave.   505 894-2228
■ **Truth or Consequences, NM 87901**

Oldest continuously operated bathhouse in town, complete with a unique and interesting cactus garden to enjoy. Elevation 4,300 feet. Open all year; limited hours May through September.

Natural mineral water fills a large pool (ten feet by twenty feet) at 105° in a handsome wooden structure, formerly part of the original bath house. Individual springs fill three smaller tubs for one to two people and two tubs which will accommodate up to six. All of the tubs are indoors, have gravel bottoms, and are three-feet deep. Temperatures range between 101-107°. No chemical treatment is necessary. Each pool is in a private room with tile floors and benches. Suits are optional in the private spaces.

Massage therapists and reflexologist on call. A separate spring source for drinking water is provided. All services are available in town. Reservations suggested.

407 E INDIAN SPRINGS NATURAL
FLOWING POOLS, WATER HOLE #1
218 Austin St.   505 894-2018
■ **Truth or Consequences, NM 87901**

Motel units, some with kitchenettes available on a daily, weekly or monthly basis; includes use of baths.

Photos by El Dorado Hot Spring

Courtesy of Marshall Hot Springs

407 F MARSHALL HOT SPRINGS
311 Marr   877 894-9286
■ **Truth or Consequences, NM 87901**
www.marshallhotsprings.com

Hot mineral water flows continuously through five gravel-bottom private pools that are six feet square and four feet deep. All pools are in private rooms with benches for resting, and are beautifully decorated with ancient Mimbres Petroglyphs on the walls. The water is not chemically treated and there is a hand pump for drinking water in the seventy-five year-old wooden bathhouse, built over the only hot mineral drainage canal in the continental US. Water temperatures range from 105-111°.

A variety of overnight accommodations including a fully furnished vintage studio and two vintage trailer are available, along with a cabin, and two other rooms equipped with kitchens. Includes unlimited use of the pools. Therapeutic massage and several other modalities are offered along with on going various forms of movement classes. A lovely patio offers shade, a fountain, and a picnic area. A seminar and retreat area is also available.

Mud holes to soak your feet are just some of the amenities provided at this growing health spa.

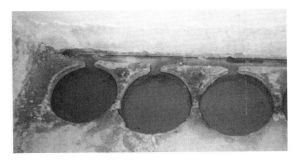

Courtesy of Riverbend

407 G   RIVERBEND HOT SPRINGS
     (affiliated with Hosteling International)
     100 Austin   **505 894-6183**
■   **Truth or Consequences, NM 87901**
     www.riolink.com/~rivrbnd

Three outdoor soaking tubs on a deck overlooking the Rio Grande with a view of Turtleback Mountain. Elevation 4,300 feet. Open all year.

Natural mineral water at 114° is pumped up from a well and cools as it flows through pipes to the soaking tubs. A three-foot deep, five-feet by seventeen-foot former bait tank is divided into three tubs, each one a degree or two cooler than the last with temperatures ranging from 104-107°. The pools, which are nicknamed "Hot Minnow Baths," are filled twice daily, morning and evening, for registered guests who may use them free of charge. The pools are drained after each use, so no chemical treatment is necessary. Non-guests may rent the tubs during the day. Bathing suits are required

Men's and women's dormitories with a shared kitchen, two private units with kitchenettes that will sleep two to four people, a family unit for two to ten people, tepee camping, a pontoon houseboat and a number of RV spaces are available. Laundry, cold drinks, barbecue, local merchant discounts, and morning bakery goods for dormitory guests are offered. Also available is massage therapy, canoeing, hiking, swimming, and hosted tours. All other services are within five blocks.

Directions: From the north, take exit 79 off I-25. Drive 1.5 miles to the only traffic light and turn left at Third St. Go 1 block, then take an immediate right on Cedar. Drive three long blocks to the stop sign, pull through past park and river. Road curves at 100 Austin, hot springs on left. From the south on I-25 take exit 75 and go 3 miles downtown past the Baptist Church to fork on Broadway. Stay right and go under sign for park. Go 1 block to river, turn right and go 1 short block to hot springs on right.

One of the beautiful Mimbres petroglyphs from *Marshall Hot Springs* who has similar designs decorating the walls of their rooms.

408 FAYWOOD HOT SPRINGS

165 Highway 61   505 536-9663
HC 71 Box 1240
Faywood, NM 88034
www.faywood.com

In Southwestern New Mexico, halfway between Deming and Silver City, adjacent to City of Rocks State Park, lies a true desert oasis with large trees and parklike surroundings, creating a charming, natural, rustic atmosphere. Elevation 5,000 feet. Open all year.

Natural mineral water flows downhill from the top of a tufa dome at 130° into over a dozen outdoor stone and concrete soaking pools in a naturally beautiful desert setting. The various pools have temperatures from 100-110°. There are both public and private pools and some pools are reserved for overnight guests only. In the private tubs the user can control the water temperature. Many of the pools have moveable sun shades which are retracted at night for stargazing. The water is pure enough to be used for drinking and was bottled and sold for many years. There are both clothing-required and clothing-optional public pools. Handicap access with assistance.

Cabins, tent and RV sites, travel trailers, and a tepee are available for overnight accommodations. Massage therapy is also available. A new café, museum, gift shop, and gallery are planned for the near future. (Phone for the status of construction.) It is fifteen miles to a store.

Directions: From Silver City, take Hwy 180 south about 25 miles, turn left (east) on Hwy 61 and go about 2 miles from the intersection of 180 and 61. A sign and the entrance are on the left. From Deming, take Hwy 180 north for 24 miles, turn right on Hwy 61 and proceed about 2 miles from the intersection.

The choice is yours! The upper pool is a public pool which means you may get to meet some other interesting soakers. The pool pictured below is a private pool for rent by the hour or possibly reserved just for you when you stay overnight in one of the cabins or other available accommodations.

Photos courtesy of Faywood Hot Springs

● **North of Silver City**

Rock soaking pools on the edge of the Gila River located below streams of hot water cascading from the face of the cliffs above and, depending on river level, in overhangs along the river's edge. Elevation 5,200 feet. Open all year; accessible only during low water flow.

Natural mineral water flows out of many rock fissures at 102°, twenty feet to forty feet above river level, and runs across a steep slope before dropping directly into the pool at the river's edge. During low water, three pools are found under the edge of the rocks, with hot water dripping from the ceiling at temperatures ranging from 98-101°. Clothing is optional.

There are no services at the location. Camping is permitted at the Forks Campground where the trail starts and all other services can be found one and one-half miles north at Gila Hot Springs.

Directions: From the trailhead at Forks Campground, 1.5 miles south of Gila Hot Springs follow the trail 1.5 miles south along the east bank of the main fork of the Gila River. You will need to cross the river 10-12 times. The trail can be very slippery and difficult when wet. Check with the Forest Service about the need for a permit and conditions on the river.

Lynn Foss

410 A   GILA HOT SPRINGS VACATION CENTER

■ **Gila Hot Springs, Rte. 11   505 536-9551**
Silver City, NM 88061

An all-year vacation center providing multiple services, located in the middle of the Gila National Forest. Elevation 5,000 feet. Open all year.

Doc Campbell's Post offers a country store with groceries, snack bar, ice, gas, fishing and hunting licenses, supplies, gifts, laundromat, showers, and most important, knowledgeable advice about the area. Arrangements can be made for wilderness pack trips, fishing and hunting trips, youth group trips, drop camps, and pack stock for backpackers. Reservations for lodging are also made here. Credit cards are accepted at the store.

Lodging includes a spacious apartment with kitchenette, and a completely furnished trailer all using natural hot springs water for drinking, showers, and baths. The RV park has hot and cold taps at all hookups. Hot springs water can be hooked up to your trailer, or you can use the RV Park showers and hot tub. A picnic pavilion offers grill and fire ring, plus a children's playground.

Note: Allow two hours for the forty-four mile drive from Silver City along scenic route NM 15, a two-lane mountain road which twists and winds through the Gila National Forest.

410 B GILA HOT SPRINGS—RIVER CAMPGROUND

Shady, primitive area with hot pools beside the river. Natural mineral water flowing at 150° from the springs on the east bank of the Gila River is piped to the riverside camping area. The first pool is quite hot at 110° and greenish-orange with algae. The other two pools cool to 105° as the water is air cooled in these shallow pools. The bathing suit issue seems to be decided by those who are camping there, although official policy is bathing suits required. Ground is fairly level, so could be handicap accessible with caution.

All that is provided are water spigots with safe drinking water, rest rooms, and trash cans. There are seven rustic campsites for tents and self-contained vehicles only.

Directions: Located right off of NM 15, the main road into the area. Watch for signs on your right (before you get to Doc Campbell's store). There is a small fee.

Ysabel Luecke

A perfect place to camp on the way to view the Gila Cliff Dwellings. If you need supplies or directions you can stop at Doc Campbell's Post just up the road. This whole area is surrounded by beautiful wilderness and is well worth a visit.

411 A MIDDLE FORK HOT SPRING

(see map)

North of the Gila Visitors Center

A series of shallow rock and sand soaking pools on the Middle Fork of the Gila River, one-half mile from the Gila Visitors Center and the Indian Cliff Dwellings. Elevation 5,800 feet. Open all year, subject to high water in the river, which must be forded twice each way.

Natural mineral water flows out of the spring on the east side of the canyon at 130°, directly into several shallow pools next to the river, where the water gradually cools as it flows through the pools. Bathing suits are advisable during the daytime.

All services are back at the Gila Hot Springs Vacation Center.

(Directions on next page.)

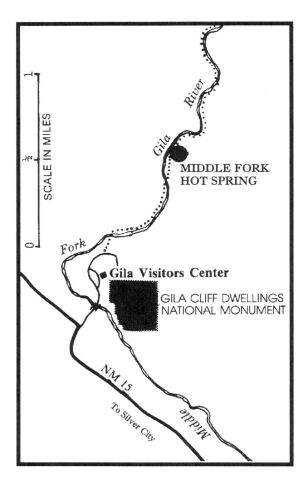

Directions: To reach the trailhead, go to the far end of the visitor center parking lot and turn right. There is a special parking area for hikers up the hill on the left. Walk down the road past the gate to the bottom of the hill. The main trail (157) continues toward the canyon, crossing the river almost immediately. The springs are on the east (right) side of the canyon after the second crossing. The water is almost always very cold and often deep. Check at the ranger station before starting out.

Note: Allow two hours for the forty-four mile drive from Silver City along scenic route NM 15, a two-lane mountain road that twists and winds through the Gila National Forest.

Photos by Ysabel Luecke

For further information contact:
The Gila National Forest Service,
3005 E. Camino del Bosque, Silver City, New Mexico 88061
505 388-8201
or
Silver City Ranger District
505 538-2771

411 B HOUSE LOG CANYON (JORDAN) HOT SPRINGS

● **Northwest of the Gila Visitors Center**

Remote, unimproved hot springs on a tree- and fern-covered hillside in the Gila Wilderness where the canyon meets the Middle Fork of the Gila River. Elevation 6,200 feet. Accessible only during low water in the river.

Natural mineral water flows out of several springs at 92° and cascades directly into a log- and rock-dammed pool large enough to hold ten people. The apparent local custom is clothing optional.

All services are back at the Gila Hot Springs Vacation Center. Check with the very knowledgeable people here about trails, etc. as they have hiked this area for years. Make sure you have sufficient supplies for whatever trip you take.

Directions: To begin the 8-mile hike, park at the Middle Fork trailhead (trail 157). Follow the trail past the locked gate and straight upstream into the canyon. The trail follows the river for 6 miles until it joins with the trail from Little Bear Canyon. There should be 14 more crossings (about 2 miles) before you reach the hot springs on the northeast side of the canyon. Continue a bit further after crossing 14 and look for a marshy area with hot water seeps. A mile farther up the Middle Fork beyond Big Bear Canyon, are more warm springs called The Meadows at the mouth of Indian Creek Canyon.

Note: A wilderness permit is required before entering this area. While obtaining your permit from the ranger at the Gila Visitors Center, check on the adequacy of your provisions and on the level of the water in the river.

Source maps: *Gila National Forest*, USGS *Woodland Park*. (Springs not shown on either map.)

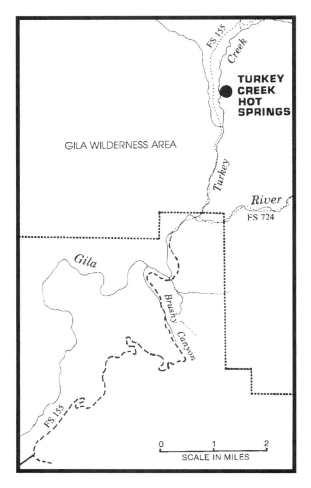

GILA WILDERNESS AREA

TURKEY
CREEK
HOT
SPRINGS

Turkey

River

FS 724

Gila

Brushy Canyon

FS 155

0   1   2

SCALE IN MILES

Directions: Starting at the end of the 4WD road, Wilderness Trail FS 724 crosses the Gila River several times before reaching Wilderness Trail FS 155, which starts up Turkey Creek Canyon. Approximately 2 miles from the trail junction, FS 155 begins to climb a ridge separating Turkey Creek from Skeleton Canyon. Do not follow FS 155 onto that ridge. (If you encounter switchbacks you've gone the wrong way.) Instead, stay to the right in the bottom of Turkey Creek Canyon, even though there is often no visible trail. Another half-mile will bring you to the first of the springs.

Source maps: *Gila National Forest, Gila Wilderness and Black Range Primitive Area*, USGS *Canyon Hill*. (Note: Springs are not shown.)

GPS: N 33.108 W 108.483

Paige Kreegel

412   TURKEY CREEK HOT SPRINGS
(see map)
● **North of the town of Gila**

Several truly primitive hot springs accessible only via a challenging and rewarding hike into the Gila Wilderness. Elevation 5,200 feet. Not accessible during high water in the Gila River.

Natural mineral water (approximately 160°) flows out of many rock fractures along the bottom of Turkey Creek Canyon and combines with creek water in several volunteer-built soaking pools. Temperatures are regulated by controlling the relative amounts of hot and cold water entering a pool. Be careful, as many of these pools are quite hot. The apparent local custom is clothing optional.

There are no services available, but there are a limited number of overnight camping spots near the hot springs. Visitors have done an excellent job of packing out their trash; please do your part to maintain this tradition. All services are seventeen miles away.

Directions and impressions from Shara Briggs and Steve Heerema, who hiked into this remote area. After a short walk on what is left of a road that has been washed away, cross the Gila River. Follow the road and cross the river two more times. Then cross Turkey Creek to reach the junction with FS trail 155. Follow this trail, which disappears in the rocky river bed at times. In approximately 2 miles there are campsites near the trail. This is a good place to camp. To reach the springs, follow the trail until you notice a faint trail leading to the right. Take this trail, which will cross a dry creek bed and continue walking upstream for .50 mile. This part of the hike is very rugged and can be slow going. Be prepared and able to cross the creek several times, climb over boulders, and crawl through a cave.

413 A SAN FRANCISCO HOT SPRINGS —MIDDLE

●   **South of the town of Pleasanton**

IMPORTANT NOTE: The (Lower) or Middle San Francisco Hot Springs are inaccessible to the general public due to the closing of the private property road.

413 B SAN FRANCISCO (BUBBLES) HOT SPRING—UPPER

●   **South of the town of Pleasanton**
(Information provided by the Glenwood Ranger Station)

A large, warm water pool and a smaller hot pool are located under a spectacular cliff on the west side of the San Francisco River's flood plain. This pool and hot springs are located two miles south of Pleasanton. Forest Service signs identifying access will get you to the trailhead for the springs. A bulletin board provides visitor information and restrictions (NO nudity!!). The hot springs, pool, and the surrounding area are a day use only recreation site, although camping is allowed for seven days south of the trailhead. Elevation 4,500 feet at the pool. High water can occur during all four seasons making the fording of the river very dangerous.

A large, warm water pool and a smaller hot pool are located under a spectacular cliff on the west side of the San Francisco River's flood plain. Natural mineral water flows up through the sandy pool bottom at approximately 106°, maintaining the larger pool at 96-100° depending on air temperature. The smaller pool maintains a higher temperature, up to 104°. The pool flushes and cleans itself during high water and flows out over a small dam. Watch out for rattlesnakes!

Directions: Near mile marker 58 on US 180 go over the cattle guard to the west and follow the dirt road (Forest Road 4229) for approximately .5 miles. The road terminates in a parking area and trailhead that includes a vault toilet and an information bulletin board. The trail starts near the bulletin board and is approximately 1.5 miles to the pools. The trail is only slightly improved and goes across the slope to the southwest and drops to a river crossing. The trail is very steep the last .5 miles, so caution and good walking boots are advised. You can see the big pool from the edge of the cliff before the steep descent. The hike can take a good hour, particularly on the return.

IMPORTANT NOTE: For the most current information, and before you set out to the springs, it is strongly recommended that you contact the Glenwood Ranger Station, Gila Nation Forest, PO Box 8, Glenwood, NM 88039. 505 539-2481 or email bodonnel@fs.fed. us.

414 FRISCO BOX HOT SPRING

●   **East of the town of Luna**

Shallow, concrete soaking pool with spectacular views, located in a scenic canyon at the end of a rough road and a rugged but beautiful one and one-half mile trail. Elevation 6,800 feet. Open all year, subject to high water.

Natural mineral water flows out of a spring at 100° and is piped to a four-foot by eight-foot by twenty-inch-deep concrete box located above river level. The apparent local custom is clothing optional.

There are no services available on the premises. There is a walk-in camping area just north across the river from the hot spring. Overnight parking is permitted on level land just east of the private property gate. It is ten miles to groceries and gasoline and twenty miles to all other services.

Directions: Start at the Luna Ranger Station to obtain current information on weather conditions, river level, and a Gila National Forest Map. From US 180 in Luna, drive north on FS 19 (signed Bill Knight Gap Road) and turn east on FS 210 (signed Frisco Box Road) to a private property gate. Pass through the gate, carefully closing it after you, and continue east until this very rough road becomes impassable. Park and hike an additional 1.5 miles east, fording the river six or more times. There is a large elevation change on the hike, and it is often quite windy so take care. On the south bank, look for a pipe and sign for Frisco Box Spring. Follow a well-worn, slightly uphill path 75 yards to the concrete box.

This trio is happy that there finally is a good path into one soaking area of upper *San Francisco Hot Springs.*

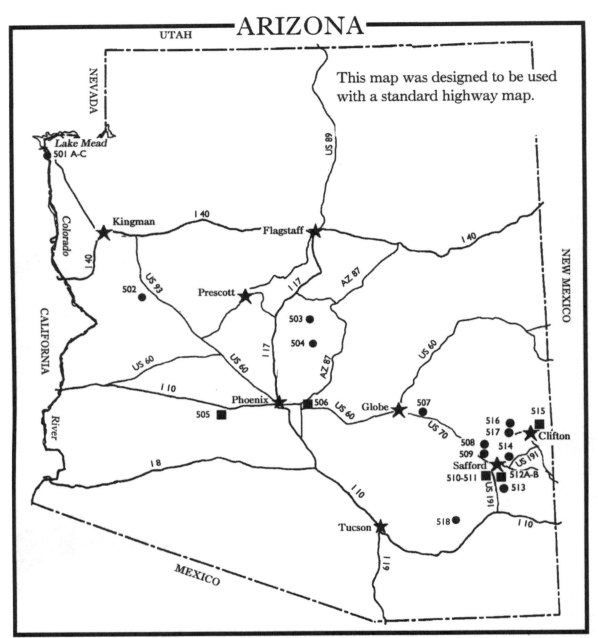

ARIZONA

UTAH

NEVADA

This map was designed to be used with a standard highway map.

Lake Mead
501 A-C

Colorado

I 40

Kingman

I 40

Flagstaff

US 89

I 40

NEW MEXICO

CALIFORNIA

US 93

502

Prescott

I 17

AZ 87

503

504

US 60

AZ 87

US 60

River

US 60

I 17

I 10

Phoenix

505

506

US 60

Globe

507

US 60

516

517

515

Clifton

508

514

509

US 191

Safford

510-511

512A-B

513

I 8

I 10

US 191

518

I 10

Tucson

I 19

MEXICO

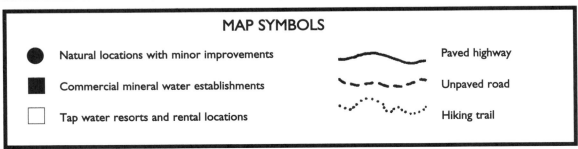

MAP SYMBOLS

● Natural locations with minor improvements

■ Commercial mineral water establishments

□ Tap water resorts and rental locations

⁓⁓⁓ Paved highway

– – – Unpaved road

········ Hiking trail

HOT SPRINGS OF THE LOWER COLORADO

Over many centuries, flash floods have carved hundreds of spectacular canyons that lead into the Colorado River. In three of these canyons, downstream from Hoover Dam, natural mineral water flows out of rocky sidewalls at temperatures up to 125°, then gradually cools as it tumbles over a series of waterfalls between sandy-bottom pools. The water is sparkling clear, with no odor and a pleasant taste. In all three of these canyons, volunteers continue to build rock-and-sand soaking pools, even though most of them are washed away every year by the floods. Elevation 800 feet. You can reach these pools all year; however, the extreme heat during the summer months may make this area unpleasant. It is also highly recommended that you check at Willow Beach regarding floods and high water during the rainy season.

Land routes to these springs range from the difficult to the impossible. Most visitors rent an outboard-powered boat at the Willow Beach Marina, which is located at mile marker 52, eight miles downriver from Arizona (Ringbolt) Hot Springs. Willow Beach also has a ramp for launching your own boat, gas for boats, and a store for supplies. There are no overnight facilities at Willow Beach. It is twenty miles to all services in Boulder City, Nevada. The access road to Willow Beach connects with US 93, fourteen miles south of Hoover Dam on the Arizona side of the river.

Rafters and kayakers can obtain a special permit from the Lake Mead National Recreation Area to put in just below Hoover Dam, float to the various hot springs, and take out at Willow Beach.

The National Park Service maintains pit toilets at the entrances to Gold Strike and Arizona Hot Springs.

Note: The amount of water being released from Hoover Dam is controlled by the Bureau of Reclamation and may change from hour to hour, substantially affecting the water level in the river. Therefore, it is important that you secure your boat or raft in a manner that will withstand such changes.

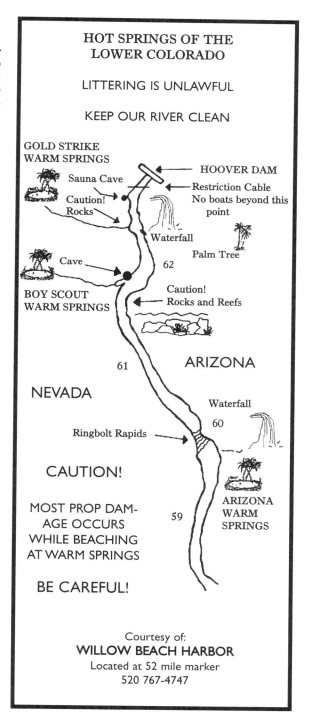

HOT SPRINGS OF THE LOWER COLORADO

LITTERING IS UNLAWFUL

KEEP OUR RIVER CLEAN

GOLD STRIKE WARM SPRINGS

Sauna Cave

Caution! Rocks

HOOVER DAM

Restriction Cable No boats beyond this point

Waterfall

Palm Tree

Cave

62

BOY SCOUT WARM SPRINGS

Caution! Rocks and Reefs

61

NEVADA

ARIZONA

Waterfall

60

Ringbolt Rapids

ARIZONA WARM SPRINGS

CAUTION!

59

MOST PROP DAMAGE OCCURS WHILE BEACHING AT WARM SPRINGS

BE CAREFUL!

Courtesy of:
WILLOW BEACH HARBOR
Located at 52 mile marker
520 767-4747

501 A ARIZONA (RINGBOLT) HOT SPRINGS

(see map)

● **Near Hoover Dam**

This is the most popular of the three hot springs because it is closest to Willow Beach and downstream from the turbulent water of Ringbolt Rapids. It is one-eighth mile downriver from mile marker 60, and two small warning buoys can be seen on a large submerged rock near the beach at the bottom of this canyon. There is no visible stream at the beach because the hot water disappears into the sand a hundred yards before reaching the river.

The long narrow canyon has beautiful rock formations and a few sections that require some scrambling ability. As you head upstream, you will often be walking in the streambed as well as climbing over sharp rocks, so be prepared with appropriate footwear. Barefoot is definitely not recommended. There is a ranger-installed metal ladder at the one major waterfall.

Source springs in the upper canyon run at 106° or more, depending on water flow, and volunteers have built a rock and sand soaking pool which can be very, very hot—be careful. The geothermal water is cooled down to approximately 95° by the time it flows over the twenty-five-foot waterfall.

There is a large amount of camping space in the lower canyon and on a dry sandy plateau just south of the canyon mouth. When you enter the canyon from the river, bear left when the trail splits inland from the beach. A pit toilet is near the camping area. This is the only spring along the river that has a practical overland route.

Hiking directions: From Hoover Dam, drive southeast on US 93 to mile post 4.2 and a dirt parking area on your right, at the head of White Rock Canyon. Follow this canyon downhill, through the wash, to the river. Then follow the edge of the river .25 miles south to the lower end of Ringbolt Hot Springs canyon and hike upstream to the springs. Distance 2.9 miles, with an 800-foot elevation change. The trail is rated moderately strenuous, so allow at least 2.5 hours each way. Watch for Bighorn sheep.

GPS: N 35.9609 W 114.7251

After landing on the beach, walk between the rocks to the hot shower and the ladder that leads you to another wonderful soaking pool at the top. If you continue through the pool at the top, you will come out on top of the rocks and have a wonderful, panoramic view.

Chris Andrews

The soaking pool pictured above can be reached by climbing up the ladder located up canyon from the landing beach.

Justine Hill

Chris Andrews

Hot water seeping out of the rocks fills this soaking pool, one of many up and down the four mile canyon.

501 B   GOLD STRIKE HOT SPRINGS

(see map)

● **Near Hoover Dam**

The beach at the bottom of this canyon is within sight of the warning cable stretched across the river just below the dam. One hundred yards up the canyon from the beach, natural mineral water flows out of cliff seeps at 109° into a series of volunteer-built soaking pools. The canyon is about four miles long with about two miles of springs creating multiple places to soak in water temperatures ranging from 98-110°.

As you head farther up the canyon, you will often be walking in the stream bed as well as climbing over sharp rocks, so be prepared with appropriate footwear.

The canyon includes several beautiful waterfalls, which can be bypassed only with some strenuous scrambling along smooth rock walls. Near the bottom of the first large falls is a sandy-bottom pool with a water temperature of 100°.

From the river, the landmark for this canyon is a pit toilet in the sandy area at the wide canyon mouth. In the river near the canyon mouth, there are some large underwater rocks that cause rapids. There are also large rocks in the shallow water close to shore, making it difficult to navigate into this canyon entrance. Space for overnight camping at the beach is very limited. If you do choose to camp, set up at the far inland edge of the sand, or the changing river levels may flood your site.

Note: Hiking overland to this spring is not recommended. It is extremely difficult and dangerous.

GPS: N 35.9995 W 114.7425

501 C   BOY SCOUT HOT SPRINGS

(see map)

● **Near Hoover Dam**

A large cave, shaped like a human ear, can be seen on the west riverbank just upstream (north) from this canyon, whose entrance is protected by a land spit that blocks visibility from the south. When coming from the north, look for the bend in the river on the left past mile marker 62. Ahead is a layered rock formation. The canyon entrance and small beach sit in front of you before the river veers left. Landing on the gently sloping sandy beach is easy, but a sudden drop in river level could leave your boat many yards from the water.

The wide sand and gravel canyon mouth has a trickle of 70° water and plenty of camping space for a group. As you head upstream, the canyon narrows. You will often be walking in the streambed as well as climbing over sharp rocks, so be prepared with appropriate footwear. Barefoot is definitely not recommended. Remains of previously constructed cement dams and pipes are visible as you walk upstream into the canyon. There are several pools and waterfalls with temperatures up to 104° in the narrow upper canyon. The apparent local custom is clothing optional.

Note: There is no safe overland hiking trail to this hot spring.

GPS: N 35.9828 W 114.7483

Chris Andrews

Photos by Justine Hill

502   KAISER WARM SPRING

● **Southeast of Kingman**
Between Wikieup and Nothing

A primitive rock and mud pool in a beautiful serene desert canyon with nearby cold creek pools. A fairly easy mile and one-half walk through a sandy canyon with minor elevation changes. Elevation 2,400 feet. Open all year, but recommended only October through April due to extreme summer heat. This area is also prone to flash floods.

Natural mineral water at about 100° bubbles up through the sandy creekbed along Warm Spring Canyon. The six to eight-person, volunteer-built pool is approximately eighteen inches deep. Runoff flows through openings in the rock and mud wall into the creek. Take along a stiff brush to remove the algae from the rocks. Approximately 150 yards further down the canyon, cold Burro Creek emerges, surrounded by large flat pink and purple sandstone boulders that are ideal for sunning. Clothing is optional.

There are no facilities at the springs. There is plenty of BLM land along US 93 where overnight parking is not prohibited. Pack-in camping is also possible on BLM land in the canyon. It is seven miles from the trailhead to Burro Creek Campground, which has rest rooms and RV dump, but no hookups. All other services are eleven miles from the trailhead in Wikieup. Fourteen miles south of the trailhead Nothing, Arizona has gas, AAA garage and towing, and the "T'Aint Much Store."

Directions: From Kingman drive 60 miles southeast on US 93, a portion of which is also I-40. After Wikieup, watch for mile markers. At .1 mile past mile marker 135, look for a gated dirt road just before the impressive Kaiser Canyon Bridge. This rocky road is the trailhead. As this is a very dangerous stretch of US 93, park well off the highway.

Hike the rough rocky trailhead just north of the bridge (close the gate). The creekbed is visible below. Hike for approximately 1.5 miles (30 minutes) until the canyon bends sharply to the left. Within 100 yards you will see warm seeps in the sandy canyon floor. Just ahead on the left is the soaking pool. Continue another 150 yards to reach the cold pools in Burro Creek. With a 4WD (high clearance vehicle) you can follow a jeep trail that leads down to within .5 to .75 miles from the springs from Cholla Rd., the third dirt road north of the bridge, .5 miles north of the bridge.

Source map: USGS Kaiser Spring.
GPS: N 34.563 W 113.497

El Dorado Hot Spring

Oscar Voss

Two different source springs feed the outside pool and the indoor pool. The entrance pictured on the right. is part of the remains of an old resort.

---

503   VERDE HOT SPRINGS

●   **Near the Town of Camp Verde**

Small cement soaking pools, all that remains of an historic resort which burned down years ago, are decorated with artwork and historic paintings, including one of the springs resort as it appeared in its heyday. Located on the west bank of the Verde River in a beautiful, high desert canyon. Elevation 2,800 feet. Open all year, subject to river level and bad-weather road hazards.

Natural mineral water flows out of several riverbank springs at 104° and into a small indoor cement soaking pool. A larger outdoor cement pool is built over another spring and averages 98°. Twenty feet below, at low-water level, are several more springs that feed volunteer-built, rock and sand pools. Fifty feet upstream from the large cement pool is a 104° pool in a riverbank cave. The apparent local custom is clothing optional. Conscientious visitors have done a superb job of packing out all trash. Please respect this tradition.

There are no services available on the premises, and it is more than twenty miles to the nearest store, service station, and market. Parking and camping are permitted only in a Forest Service campground one mile south of the Childs Power Plant. Therefore, it is a one and one-half mile hike to the river ford at Verde Hot Springs. Check at the ranger station in Camp Verde regarding road conditions and river level before attempting to reach this site.

Directions: Exit off I 17 at exit 283 (Cottonwood, Payson, Camp Verde). Turn right on Hwy 260 and follow this road through the town of Camp Verde. Just outside of town, cross over a bridge and continue approximately 6 miles. On the right hand side of the road is a sign saying "Fossil Creek Rd. Verde River" (Forest Road 708). Turn right. In about 16 miles you will come to a "Y" (it's easy to miss)–take the right fork onto FR 502 and continue about another 7 miles to the parking area near the Childs Power Plant. The last hundred yards or so down into the campground is very rough. You may need to park up top and walk in.

From the north end of the campground look for a sign marked "River Crossing for Hot Springs, I mile." Follow this trail north, across a wooden bridge at the power plant and along the river until it heads inland up a hill for a short jog to a two-lane, dirt jeep road marked "Hot Springs Road." Follow this road until you see a trail down to the river on your left marked with stone pilings. The hot springs are across the river, visible from the jeep road. Look for palm trees across the river and a stone wall along the riverbank. Depending on the river level, it may be necessary to ford the river twice, first to an island and then to the springs.

Important Note: These directions keep you on public land. Any attempt to cross fences puts you in real danger of entering private property and getting shot. When the Verde River level is high after heavy rains or spring runoff, be sure to check at the ranger station before attempting to cross the river.

Source maps: *Coconino National Forest*, USGS *Verde Hot Springs*. GPS: N 34.357 W 111.710

Camilla Van Sickle and Bill Pennington, owners of El Dorado, and indefatigable travelers who contributed greatly to this book.

Sheep Bridge Hot Spring: The thick bullrushes surrounding the tub provide a nice screen for the tub and some shade during the hot summer months.

504   SHEEP BRIDGE HOT SPRING

● **Southeast of Prescott**

Cement tub on a ledge above the Verde River, surrounded on three sides by a dense growth of bulrushes. Elevation 1,400 feet. Open all year; be aware of flooded roads.

Natural mineral water flows out of a spring at 99° and is piped to a masonry pool close to the river. Other natural pools may be found, depending on water level, below the tub. The apparent local custom is clothing optional.

There are no services available on the premises. A level camping area is seventy-five yards upstream. It is fifty miles to all other services in Black Canyon City.

Directions: It is possible to reach this spring via a very difficult 4WD (high clearance vehicle recommended) route from Carefree. However, the following is the recommended route: From I-17 north of Black Canyon City, take the Bloody Basin off-ramp and drive southeast on FS 269 for 37 miles. This road crosses several streambeds that are usually dry. The first 16 miles to Summit (elevation 4,500 ft.) is a good gravel road. The remaining 21 miles is a poor dirt road, but it is passable by a high-clearance 2WD vehicle. From a parking area at the bridge, walk 75 yards upstream to the soaking tubs. An alternate, perhaps easier route goes from Carefree through Seven Springs

To locate the campground, drive .3 miles back up from the bridge and look on the north side of the road for the remains of a building foundation. A steep path (4WD only!) leads 150 yards down to a level camping area by the river. The soaking tub is 75 yards downstream from this area. There is a shady camping area south of the bridge on a flat area near the river.

Source maps: *Mazatzal Wilderness, Tonto National Forest,* USGS quads, *Brooklyn Park, Bloody Basin, Chalk Mountain.*

505   EL DORADO HOT SPRING

■   PO Box 10   623 393-0750
Tonopah, AZ 85354
HotSpring@El-Dorado.com

At El Dorado Hot Springs, odorless, tasteless, and crystal clear hot mineral water is creating a verdant desert oasis surrounded by bamboo and distant mountain views. Elevation 1,123 feet. Open 365 days a year. In summer, misting nozzles, shade cloths, and cooled spring water make for refreshing soaking even in the hottest weather.

Natural mineral water is pumped from an enormous subterranean spring. The 112° water flows to more than a dozen outdoor pools, some with moveable shade cloths. Four private areas (seven pools total) can be rented hourly. Semi-private soaking can be by the hour or for the day. Some spring water is cooled in a 5,000 gallon tank; soakers use it to adjust the tub and mineral water shower temperatures. With a ph of 8.3, the waters act like a natural conditioner. After warming the tropical fish pond, the runoff irrigates a wide variety of plants that are creating the oasis. No chemicals are necessary in the single tanks. Soakers can fill water jugs at a special tap to take home or use in their RV. Common areas are free of alcohol, tobacco, and pets. One toilet, the whole tenting area, and two soaking pools are handicap accessible. Free dump station.

Massage by appointment. Tent space, fire rings, washer/dryer, and soda machines. A cozy rental cabin heated by hot spring water is now open. All services, including a motel and full service campground, are one-quarter of a mile away in Tonopah. Meals from world-famous Alice's Restaurant can be delivered to soakers poolside.

Free phone for email and local calls. Visa and MasterCard accepted. Hiking, mountain biking, four-wheeling, petroglyph and wildlife viewing, old gold mines, rock climbing, and more available on 900,000 acres of BLM land beginning 2.5 miles away. Email or phone ahead for additional information.

Directions to El Dorado: Take exit 94 off the I-10 between Phoenix and Quartzsite and go south on 411th Ave. Turn right on Indian School Rd. (Texaco Star Mart on the corner) and go west .1 mile. El Dorado is on the left (south) side of the road at number 41225, surrounded by ever-growing bamboo.

Photos on pages 98-99 are courtesy of El Dorado Hot Spring

Choose your temperature!

One of the original tubs–notice the crystal clear water.

You can shower from the top down and from the bottom up.

Age makes no difference when you want a great soak.

"A Million Miles from Monday..." Prepare to be cordially greeted by the very hospitable people at *El Dorado Hot Spring* and to enjoy the desert vistas during the day and the brilliant stars at night. The goal here is to keep the hot spring and surroundings naturally rustic while providing the basic amenities.

An old hand water pump provides a warm shower and a retractable sun shade allows you to count the stars at night.

The newest pool to be added.

Tonopah (which means "hot water under the bush" in the local Native American language) is rich in mineral bath history and once boasted five hot spring emporia; the ruins of two of these spas border El Dorado.

506   BUCKHORN MINERAL WELLS

NUBP–Baths are closed.

507   SAN CARLOS WARM SPRINGS

● **East of Globe**

A series of pools in the slow-flowing San Carlos River on the San Carlos Apache Reservation. Located in a tree-covered canyon with an abundance of wildlife. A permit is an absolute requirement. Elevation 3,500 feet. Open all year; pools may be under water during high runoff.

Natural mineral water bubbles up from several spots in the bottom of the river at temperatures between 85-95°. Warm spots can be found both upstream and downstream, but most are above the ford in the river. You can also follow the trail of green algae to where the warm spots are. Clothing optional would be all right during low use times, or head upstream for more private areas, but suits seem to be mandatory on weekends and holidays.

There are three campgrounds on the reservation (make arrangements at the Recreation Department). Gas is available one mile west of the Recreation and Wildlife Department along US 70. The business center on the Reservation has a market. All other services are 20 miles away in Globe.

Directions: From Globe, take AZ 70 and go 20 miles east to the San Carlos Recreation and Wildlife Department, where you must stop and buy a permit. From the headquarters, continue east 4 miles to Hwy 8. Turn left (north) and continue 15 miles. Turn left on an unmarked gravel road (Indian Hwy 3). At four-way intersection turn left onto Road 1500 (marked with small sign by the fence) for 3.5 miles to where the road ends at the river. It is possible during low water for 4WD vehicles to cross the river and explore the other side.

508   WATSON WASH HOT WELL

● **Northwest of the town of Thatcher**

Stone tub with foot bath surrounded by willows in a primitive setting. Elevation 3,000 feet. Open all year, subject to flash floods.

Natural mineral water flows out of a well casing at 102° and directly into a volunteer-built stone tub large enough for six or eight people. The overflow creates a foot bath that should be used to remove the surrounding sand before getting into the tub. The apparent custom is to drain the tub if there's no one soaking when you leave. It takes less than fifteen minutes to refill. Since this area is also used as a party spot, be prepared to pack out more trash than you packed in. Clothing optional is the local custom only in the evening or during the week. Defer to the preference of those soaking first.

There are no services available on the premises. The surrounding BLM land allows for fourteen days of free camping. Undeveloped picnic sites are along the road. It is four miles to a store, cafe, service station and other services. Steps lead into the tub, which is handicap accessible with assistance.

Directions: From US 70 at the west end of Thatcher, go north on Reay Ln. 3.2 miles to the "Y" intersection, which is Safford-Bryce Rd. Turn left and drive .25 miles to the first wash across the road. Turn right and drive up the unimproved wash bottom .5 miles to the hot tub, going left at the first "Y" and right at the second. Most portions of the road are rough gravel, with some areas of hard-packed earth and a few sandy spots, all of which are passable in a standard passenger vehicle, except during or just after heavy rains.

509   THATCHER HOT WELL

As of 1997 the city capped off the flow of hot water. It is now NUBP (not useable by the public).

510   ESSENCE OF TRANQUILITY

■ 6074 S. Lebanon Loop   520 428-9312
    Safford, AZ 85546   877 895-6810

El Dorado Hot Spring

This spiritually uplifting retreat is surrounded with mesquite, eucalyptus, desert willow, salt cedar, tamarack, and palm trees. Elevation 2,990 feet. Open all year. Tubs are rented by the hour or for day use; call for open hours.

Natural 108° mineral water flows out of a 1,632-foot artesian well into one communal (clothing required) and five private (clothing optional) stone and concrete tubs with a continual flow-through system requiring no chemicals. Temperatures range from 98-106°. No bathing in tubs, a shower is available. Facilities are handicap accessible with assistance.

Primitive and tepee campsites are available by reservation. Camping fees include unlimited use of the mineral springs communal kitchen/recreation room. Massage, reflexology, herbal sweat wrap, and ear coning available by appointment only. No food is provided on the premises; however, there is a convenience store within one and one-half miles. It is five miles to Safford.

No RVs, no credit cards, no alcohol, no glass, no open nudity. Minimal noise. Prefer no children or dogs.

Directions: Starting in Safford at the intersection of US 70 and US 191, go south 6 miles on US 191. Turn right at Lebanon Rd. and follow road .5 miles to a 90-degree curve onto Lebanon Loop. Continue .6 miles further. Establishment is on the right.

From I-10 go north on US 191 approximately 25 miles to mile marker 115. Turn left on Cactus Rd. Approximately .5 miles west, turn right (north) on Lebanon Loop. The establishment is .25 miles on the left. Park in front. Call for days, hours, appointments, and reservations.

Justine Hill

511   KACHINA MINERAL SPRINGS SPA

■ Route 2, Box 987   520 428-7212
    Safford, AZ 85546

Therapy-oriented bathhouse, recently remodeled, located in the suburbs south of Safford. Elevation 3,000 feet. Open all year.

Natural mineral water flows out of an artesian well at 108° and is piped into private-room soaking tubs where water temperature measures around 104-106°. There are six large, tiled, sunken tubs. They are drained, cleaned, and refilled after each customer so that no chemical treatment is necessary. An addition to the old bathhouse has two large soaking pools, a hot one at 104°, and a cold one, large enough for eight to ten people. No bathing suits are needed in the private tubs.

Facilities also include an exercise room, sweat wraps, massage, and reflexology. A free hot-pool soak comes with each therapy service. No credit cards are accepted. Phone for rates and reservations.

Directions: From the intersection of US 70 and US 191 in Safford, go 6 miles south on US 191, then turn right on Cactus Rd. for .25 miles.

El Dorado Hot Spring

Photos by El Dorado Hot Spring

512 A ROPER LAKE STATE PARK
Route 2, Box 712   520 428-6760
■ **Safford, AZ 85546**

A small, neatly constructed outdoor soaking pool in a popular state park surrounded by rolling desert hills. Elevation 3,100 feet. Day-use fee. Open all year, 6 AM to 10 PM.

Geothermal mineral water flows from an artesian well at 99° directly into a stone and cement pool large enough for six to eight good friends. The water flows through continuously, so no chemical treatment is needed. There is a fifteen-minute limit when other people are waiting. Bathing suits are required. Access to the tub is ramped, with stairs and a handrail leading into the tub.

Facilities at the state park include camping and RV spaces, rest rooms, changing rooms, day-use picnic ramadas, a swimming beach, two stocked lakes for fishing, a boat ramp, and nature trails. A mini-mart and gas are available four miles north and all other services are approximately six miles away in Safford.

Directions: From Safford, drive south on US 191 for 6 miles, turn left (east) at the sign for Roper Lake State Park, and continue .5 miles to the park entrance.

512 B DANKWORTH PONDS

● **Located in Roper Lake State Park**

A shallow, warm, sandy-bottom ditch which has been widened to allow for soaking. Day-use fee.

Warm artesian water continually bubbles up out of the ground and flows through the ditch and out into the bullrushes. The one-foot deep warm ditch is ideal for children. Bathing suits are required.

There are nearby shaded picnic tables, barbeque grills, rest rooms, and trash containers.

Directions: From Safford continue 3 miles south of the Roper Lake State Park turnoff, watch for "State Park Picnic Area" sign on the east side of the road, just past mile marker 113. Turn left (east) for .1 mile.

Lynn Foss

Marjorie Young

513   HOT WELL DUNES

●   **Southeast of Safford**

Two fenced-in soaking pools and one shallow pond surrounded by hundreds of acres of Bureau of Land Management (BLM) desert sand dunes open to, and popular with, off-road vehicles. Elevation 3,450 feet. Open all year, subject to flash floods.

Geothermal mineral water flows out of an artesian well at the rate of 200 gallons per minute and a temperature of 106° into two fenced soaking tubs. Overflow from the tubs spills into an adjoining shallow sand-bottom pool that provides soaking at a lower water temperature. Bathing suits are required.

A few developed tent or RV camp sites, fire grills, trash can, and vault toilets are available on the premises. Two weeks of camping are permitted on the level ground in this desert area, except where indicated right near the tubs. You will need to bring all your own supplies, including water. It is thirty-two miles to all services in Safford.

Directions: There are several access roads to the area but only the following one is recommended for standard passenger vehicles. From Safford, follow US 70 east for 7 miles to the Agricultural Inspection Station for vehicles entering from New Mexico. At .3 miles east of the station, turn right (south) onto an unmarked gravel road (Haekel Rd.). When road forks at 1.5 miles, take left fork. Continue south for 25 miles and turn left at the sign for Hot Well Dunes.

514   BUENA VISTA HOT WELLS

■   **East of Safford, North of San Jose**

Soaking areas in the bottom of an irrigation canal are shared with the fish, and the people fishing and farming in this rural agricultural area. Elevation 3,000 feet. Open all year.

Hot mineral water flows through open pipeways at temperatures between 130-150° and drops into an irrigation canal. There are no pools per se, and warm areas are found by walking up and down the canal area to a comfortable spot. Since the bottom of the canal is sandy, it is possible to scoop out a soaking pool. Bathing suits are a good idea as there seem to be a fair number of people around.

There are no services at the site. All services can be found about ten miles back in Safford.

Directions: From Safford, drive 7 miles east on US 70 and turn left onto San Jose Rd. After 2 miles, the road splits. Take Buena Vista Rd. to the left about .8 miles and make another left onto a dirt road. This road crosses the irrigation ditch, and there is parking to your right. There is also pullout parking right before you cross the ditch, and a path leads down into the canal, probably the easiest way to get into the water.

515 POTTER'S AZTEC BATHS BED AND BREAKFAST

● PO Box 8443   520 865-4847
Clifton, AZ 85533

A flood in 1996 washed out the hot well on the property of Potter's Aztec Baths, so at press time the hot tubs are not usable, but the bed and breakfast is still operational with plans to dig a new well.

Justine Hill

Primitive seeps along the San Francisco River on the Potter property have been used for years by volunteers who build simple rock and mud pools that get washed out and rebuilt every year. They are located a quarter-mile south of the B&B where the three branches of the San Francisco converge. The pools collect the slow seeping hot water which mixes with cold river water. Move the rocks around to adjust the pool temperature.

Note: Potter Ranch management doesn't mind if the public uses these pools, but please call ahead to let them know you are coming, and for directions. Also, please stay on the trail to protect the eroding, twenty-five foot high riverbank.

516 GILLARD HOT SPRINGS

● **Near the town of Clifton**

Remote hot springs along the Gila River in the Black Hills area of southeastern Arizona. Located at the end of a six-mile drive on unpaved roads and a one-mile walk through a sandy wash. Elevation 3,500 feet. Open all year, subject to road washouts due to heavy rain.

Natural mineral water seeps from underground at over 183° along the northeast bank of the Gila River. Following each year's high water and spring runoff, the primitive rock and mud pools must be redug. Water temperature is controlled by mixing in cold river water. Due to the slow rate of flow, it may take some patience to achieve the proper soaking temperature. Clothing optional.

There are no facilities on the premises, but there is plenty of BLM land where camping is permitted. There are also areas for car camping along Old Safford Rd. near the Gila River. North of the bridge, a road heads down to the river where you can park under the trees. From here it is three miles to the hot springs by the river. Fifty feet downstream from the hot springs is a deep swimming hole. Oozy river mud makes natural mudbaths.

Directions: Drive 35 miles northeast of Safford, AZ on US 70 and US 191 to Three Way (where Hwys 191, 75, and 78 meet). Or, from US 70 in Lordsburg, NM, drive 55 miles northwest through Duncan to the Apache ranger station at Three Way. From Three Way, continue north toward Clifton on US 191 for 5.5 miles. When the divided highway ends, make an immediate left (west) on Black Hills Back Country Byway (also called Old Safford Rd.). Drive 3.5 miles to a primitive dirt road on the right with a sign to Gillard Hot Springs. Turn right onto this unmaintained road for 1 mile to a three-way intersection. Follow the middle fork for .3 miles and park on the right adjacent to the wash on your left. Walk down the wash until you come to a closed gate. Use the pedestrian access and continue down the wash to the Gila River. The seeps are on the northeast bank near the end of the wash. Look for hot steam rising.

Note: There may be washouts and detours due to flooding. The rough and sandy road can be maneuvered by passenger vehicles with a knowledgeable desert driver. A 4WD is recommended.

Source map: USGS *Apache-Sitgreaves National Forests* (springs not shown).

Justine Hill

The rough, difficult roads and the distance to get to the springs almost guarantees you a private soaking spot at *Gillard Hot Springs* (left) or Eagle *Creek.*

Justine Hill

517   EAGLE CREEK HOT SPRING

● **Near the town of Morenci**

Hot water seeps up from the ground in several spots high on a ridge above Eagle Creek in the remote high desert of Eastern Arizona. Reached via a two-mile hike with river crossings and steep scrambles up a rocky bluff. Elevation 4,000 feet. Open all year, subject to river flooding.

Hot 116° water seeps out of the ground and flows through a shallow gully where it cools substantially until it pours over a precipice as a trickling cold waterfall. A soaking pool could be built at the source, which is currently a watering spot for cattle and wildlife. (The entire Eagle Creek canyon is private Phelps Dodge property. Officially visitors should sign in at the P.D. security desk before entering Eagle Creek.) Clothing is optional.

There are no facilities at this remote location except level areas for pack-in camping and car camping on nearby BLM land. Bring plenty of water or a filter for Eagle Creek water.

Directions: (See directions for #516 as far as Clifton.) From Clifton, follow US 191 to Morenci. Turn right at the first traffic light in Morenci and go 1.5 miles to a "Y" at Mine Rd. Stay on US 191 another 3 miles to a small cemetery on your right. Opposite the cemetery is Eagle Creek Rd. (unmarked), a wide gravel road with yellow highway markers. Follow this road for 5.3 miles to a power plant at the creek. Unless you have a 4WD, park here. You will cross the river back and forth 5-6 times to reach Hot Springs Canyon, on your right.

Hike about 1 mile south, past the farmhouse, along the dirt road adjacent to Eagle Creek and look for Hot Springs Canyon on your right. Or, with a 4WD, cross the river by the power plant and immediately cross again. With a high-clearance 4WD, depending on water level,

you may be able to do the river crossings and park opposite the mouth to Hot Springs Canyon (the first large canyon on your right.) Due to flooding, river patterns and crossings may change seasonally. Best landmarks are the canyon walls. When the river level is low, all crossing can be done on foot. Just before the entrance to Hot Springs Canyon, Eagle Creek opens up into a large 5-foot deep swimming hole.

Hike into the canyon approximately 500 feet. On the right is a 35-foot, warm, trickling waterfall. Scramble up the hill to the left of the falls, approximately 80 feet to the top of the ridge. From here look down to the northwest. The dark green areas have the seeps. If you make a sharp left as you start to climb and look uphill you will find a small warm-water cave.

Source map: USGS *Copperplate Gulch.*
GPS: N 33.046 W 109.440

518   MULESHOE RANCH
RR 1, Box 1542   520 586-7072
■ **Willcox, AZ 85643**

Owned and managed by The Nature Conservancy, this area in the Sonoran Desert region includes nature trails, a visitors center, and overnight casitas with access to a hot springs soak. Open all year.

The natural hot mineral water fills two livestock tanks and are only available to those people staying at the ranch. Bathing suits required.

Accommodations include a mix of original and renovated historic buildings dating from the late 1800s. Each unit is fully equipped, containing bath, kitchen, furnishings and linens. Bring your own food.

Be sure to check in at the Visitors Center for information about the numerous trails, where to park, and safety conditions. Horse corrals available for rent. Credit cards accepted.

Directions: From Tucson take I-10 east to Willcox exit 340. (Pick up any needed supplies here.) Go south and turn right at the first right turn, Bisbee Ave. Follow Bisbee past the high school to Airport Rd. Turn right on Airport Rd. It will take you west over I-10 and become a dirt road. After driving about 15 miles, take the right fork at junction right past mailboxes, and continue approximately 14 miles. The ranch is at the end of this road. Take a sharp left at the entrance sign. This brings you across Hot Springs wash and up to the headquarters. After heavy rains a 4WD vehicle may be necessary.

NORTHERN CALIFORNIA

This map was designed to be used with a standard highway map.

MAP SYMBOLS

- ● Natural locations with minor improvements
- ■ Commercial mineral water establishments
- □ Tap water resorts and rental locations

- ∿ Paved highway
- - - Unpaved road
- ⋯ Hiking trail

601 A GLEN HOT SPRINGS

● **Near the town of Cedarville**

Undeveloped cluster of hot springs on a barren slope along the east side of Upper Alkali Lake. Elevation 4,600 feet. The natural mineral water that flows out of several springs into a ditch at 180° is much too hot to soak in. As of this writing there are no pools to get into.

Source map: *USGS Cedarville.*
GPS: N 41.38945 W 120.06213

601 B LEONARD'S HOT SPRING

● **Near the town of Cedarville**

Abandoned and deteriorated old resort on a barren slope along the east side of Middle Alkali Lake. Elevation 4,500 feet. Natural mineral water flows out of the ground from several springs at a temperature of 150°. Like Glen Hot Springs, it is way too hot to soak in and there currently are no pools to get into.

Source map: *USGS Cedarville.*
GPS: N 41.3557 W 120.0514

Surprise Valley can be reached by plane as well as by car. Each room has its own private pool where hot water flows in over your very own waterfall. Crystal clear skies and stargazing included.

602 SURPRISE VALLEY HOT SPRINGS
PO Box 458   877 warmh2o
■ Cedarville, CA 96104   530 279-2040
www.svhotsprings.com/warmh20@hdo.net

Destination get a way set in a picturesque valley bordered by the majestic Warner Mountains. Elevation 4,600 feet. Open all year.

Private hot tubs on the deck of each room are filled with natural mineral water coming out of an artesian well at a temperature of 208°. The water cascades into the pools over your very own waterfall. The hot water is cooled with water from a cold artesian well to make the tubs a comfortable 104°. Since the tubs operate on a flow-through basis, minimal amounts of chlorine are used only for cleaning when the tubs are drained and refilled. Pipes using the hot water run under the cement decks to keep them warm in the winter. And, using a system created by the first member of the Rose family to own the property (they are now in the fourth generation), the place is geothermally heated.

Accommodations offered include the deluxe villa (with a complete kitchen) that can sleep at least four. The standard villa has a refrigerator and microwave and sleeps two. Catch and release fishing can be done in the pond right on the property. Nearby are opportunities for hiking, biking, fishing, horseback riding and golf. Massage by appointment only.

Soak-and-fly packages include a car for your use waiting at the airport, and a half-hour massage for the pilot or one of his lucky guests.

Call for day-use availability of the pools.

Location: Five miles east on Highway 299 from the town of Cedarville. Four miles from the Nevada border and 3 hours from Reno, Nevada; Redding, California; and Medford, Oregon.

Photos by Phil Wilcox

603 A EAGLEVILLE HOT SPRING

● **South of the town of Cedarville**

Shallow, primitive soaking pool and tub with a commanding view of Surprise Valley and surrounding mountains. Elevation 4,600 feet. Open all year.

Natural mineral water flows out of two PVC pipes in the road embankment at 111°. One pipe goes to a volunteer-built rock and sand soaking pool, and the other goes to an adjacent five-foot redwood tub. The pools are not visible from the road, so the apparent local custom is clothing optional. Local custom also expects new arrivals to await the departure of those already there.

There are no services available on the premises. It is seven miles to Eagleville and twenty-three miles to Cedarville.

Directions: From Cedarville, on Modoc County Road 1 (Surprise Valley Rd.), drive south 15 miles to Eagleville. From the post office, drive 7.7 miles. You will pass two houses on your left with a stone fence. Drive 1 miles further to a dirt drive on the east side which goes down about .1 miles to a parking lot. Walk 135 yards north to the pool and tub. If you come to an abandoned cement house .1 mile further on the east side of the street, you've gone too far. However, this is where Wild Mint Hot Spring is. (See 603 B)

GPS: N 41.1237 W 120.0327

603 B WILD MINT HOT SPRING

● **South of the town of Cedarville**

A delightful soak can be had in this cement tub adjacent to an abandoned cement house, offering wonderful views of the surrounding mountains. Named after the abundance of wild mint growing in the vicinity. Elevation 4,600 feet. Open all year.

Natural mineral water is piped through six small PVC pipes bringing 108° water from the source into the four-foot by eight-foot by three-foot deep cement pool. A small drain near the bottom of the tub must be plugged with a towel or like device to allow the tub to fill to the top. A wooden deck and two wooden chairs are the only amenities on the place. Custom seems to be clothing optional, but the tub can be seen from the road.

Services can be found seven miles away in Eagleville or twenty-three miles away in Cedarville.

Directions: See directions to Eagleville Hot Spring (603 A).

GPS; N 41.12494 W. 120.03340

604   STEWART MINERAL SPRINGS
■   4617 Stewart Springs Rd.   530 938 2222
Weed, CA 96094
www.starhawk.com

A well-kept rustic retreat available to individuals or groups for special events or seminars. Located on a mountain stream in a green canyon northwest of Mt. Shasta. Elevation 3,900 feet. Open all year (closed December 18-28) on a reservation basis only.

Natural mineral water is pumped from a well at 40° and is propane heated. There are thirteen individual bathtubs and larger tubs in private rooms. Water temperature is controlled, as desired, by mixing cold and hot mineral water. Tubs are drained and refilled after each use, so no chemical treatment of the water is necessary. Bathing suits are required in public areas.

Facilities include rooms, restaurant (for groups of ten or more), camping spaces, and tepees. Massage is available by appointment. A sweat lodge is available for groups. Plans are to have an outdoor soaking tub open by spring of 2001. Credit cards accepted. It is seven miles to a store, service station, and public bus. Pickup at the bus depot and at the Weed airport can be arranged.

Directions: Take the Edgewood exit on I-5 north of Weed. Turn north on the west side of I-5 and take the first left onto Stewart Springs Rd. Drive 4 miles to the resort at the end of the road.

The usual custom is to soak in the tub, experience the sauna, and take a dip in this cold mountain spring. This is repeated four times—once for each compass direction.

Phil Wilcox

605   HEALING WATERS
■   196 Hot Springs Rd.   530 337-6602
Big Bend, CA 96011

Once again in the process of renovation. The loan is in place and the permits are being applied for. Call for a progress report. Located fifty miles northeast of Redding on the tree-shaded south bank of the Pit River. Elevation 2,000 feet.

Jayson Loam

Hopefully one day soon the magical pools at *Healing Waters* will be reopened to the public.

Photos by Phil Wilcox

606 A   HUNT HOT SPRINGS

● **Near the town of Big Bend**

Delightful rock-and-cement soaking tub and several creekside rock pools situated on Kosh Creek close to where it joins the Pit River. Located in a beautiful river valley near Mount Shasta. Elevation 2,000 feet. Open all year; road may not be passable during wet weather.

Natural mineral water flows out of several hillside seeps at 104° and cools on its way through several pools down to Kosh Creek. There are two rock and cement pools large enough for four. It is a good idea to bring a bucket for the cold creek water to help regulate the pool temperatures. A varying number of volunteer-built rock pools along the river seem to get the most use as temperature-wise they are easier to regulate. Clothing is optional.

There are no services available on the premises, but there is plenty of wide open space where camping is not restricted. A general store, service station, cafe, and ranger station are approximately two miles away in Big Bend.

Directions: From Big Bend store, proceed across Pit River Bridge. About .8 miles, FS 37N02 goes off to the right. Continue straight (FS11) another 100 yards and take the first dirt road to the left. Go right at the fork. From this point the road is quite rough for the 1 mile down to the end (just past the Wright Historical Cemetery on your left). Low clearance vehicles may have a problem.

A wonderful few days could be spent in the area around Big Bend visiting the natural springs on the river near *Healing Waters*, and hiking into *Hunt Hot Springs* and *Kosh Hot Springs*.

606 B   KOSH CREEK HOT SPRINGS

● **Near the town of Big Bend**

Charming volunteer-built rock pool for two on a steep hillside in a beautiful river valley near Mt. Shasta. Situated along Kosh Creek near its intersection with the Pit River. Elevation 2,000 feet. Open all year; road may not be passable in wet weather.

Natural mineral water flows out of a rocky cliff above the creek at a perfect 104° and flows directly into the pool below. Clothing is optional.

There are no services available on the premises, but there is plenty of wide open space where camping is not restricted. A general store, service station, cafe and ranger station are approximately two miles away in Big Bend.

Directions: (See Hunt Hot Springs 606A). Climb the steep, well-used trail immediately behind Hunt to the other side of the hill and back down to Kosh Creek. The tub will be visible as you descend.

The dirt road off of the paved road has deteriorated badly making it very rough even for 4 WD. Then, at the historic Indian Cemetery, the large culvert has washed out leaving a very steep ditch. Since this section is private property it is doubtful if or when it will be repaired. Consider hiking in.

Several hot source springs are used to feed the swimming pool at *Drakesbad Guest Ranch* which is located in beautiful Lassen Volcanic National Park.

607 DRAKESBAD GUEST RANCH
c/o California Guest Services, Inc.
2150 Main St. #5 916 529-1512
■ Red Bluff, CA 96080

A rustic mountain ranch/resort, by reservations only, with a mineral-water swimming pool, plus horses and guides for riding and hiking. Registered guests only. Located in a superb mountain meadow within the boundaries of Lassen Volcanic National Park. Elevation 5,700 feet. Open first part of June to first part of October.

Natural mineral water flows out of two springs at temperatures between 140-150° and is piped to the pool. The swimming pool is maintained at 95° during the day and 105° at night by mixing the two hot water flows. Minimal amounts of chlorine are added to control algae growth. The lodge is handicap accessible. Bathing suits are required.

Facilities include lodge, rooms, cabins, bungalows, and dining room. Saddle horses and guides are available by the hour. Visa and MasterCard are accepted. Telephone for reservations.

Directions: From CA 36 in the town of Chester, take Warner Valley Rd. northwest 17 miles to the resort, which is at the end of the road. The last 3 miles are a dirt/gravel road.

608 TERMINAL GEYSER HOT SPRINGS

According to information received from the United States Department of the Interior, National Park Service regulations prohibit soaking in the hot springs. And I quote, "The reason for this prohibition is that 'bathers,' both through manipulation of water flow to form pools and by the very act of soaking in the pools, disrupt the natural biologic and geologic processes which the National Park Service is mandated to protect. Persons in hot pools observed by Park Rangers will be issued a violation notice and will be subject to either a fine or a court appearance, depending on the individual circumstances."

609 WOODY'S FEATHER RIVER HOT SPRINGS
● Twain, CA 95984

As of press time (January 2001) the resort itself is closed. There is a sign both at the resort and down by the pools telling you to enjoy the springs, take good care of them, and please leave a donation if you can. Reports are that the place is kept very clean, so someone must be taking care of it.

Natural mineral water flows directly into the cement, sandy-bottom pool where temperatures vary from 90-100°. The apparent local custom is clothing optional.

Directions: On CA 70, go 4 miles west from the Quincy-Greenville "Y" at the junction of Hwy 89 and Hwy 70. Located at mile post 28.

Woody was the owner of the springs. She believed that soaking should be free to all—a tradition still in effect—although donations are accepted to help keep the tubs cared for, especially with the resort closed.

610   SIERRA HOT SPRINGS

■   PO Box 366   530 994-3773
     Sierraville, CA 96126

A 600-acre resort surrounded by secluded forests, meadows, and streams has been restored and expanded by a nonprofit intentional community. Visitor use of the facilities is welcome. While this is a membership facility, non-resident fees are minimal. Elevation 5,000 feet. Open all year.

Natural mineral water flows out of several springs on a wooded slope at temperatures up to 112° into several terraced pools and waterfalls which range in temperature from 98-110°. The Medicine Bath (at 100°) is a natural sandy-bottom rock pool on the edge of a large alpine meadow. The Temple Dome, built at the end of the swimming pool houses a hot pool kept at 105°. There are also cold tile and rock plunges and a large outdoor warm water pool with a large sun deck. Private tubs are to be found at the Phoenix Baths. No chemicals are needed in any of the pools. Clothing is optional in all pool areas.

Historic hotel, private lodge rooms, dormitory, and camping spaces are available. Call ahead for massage and other healing treatments. A restaurant and facilities for cooking your own food are also on the premises. It is two miles to all other services in Sierraville. No pets, alcohol, drugs, soap or bathing is permitted. They also operate the Globe Hotel in town—a stay there will get you a pass to soak. Major credit cards accepted. Phone for reservations.

Directions: From the junction of CA 89 and CA 49 in Sierraville, take CA 49 east for 1.1 miles and follow CA 49 north to Lemon Canyon Rd., which runs along the north edge of the airport; then turn right on Campbell Hot Springs Rd., which runs along the east edge of the airport, and continue into the foothills to the lodge office.

The small airport is within walking distance of the springs.

Top and middle photos by Chris Andrews
Bottom photo by El Dorado Hot Spring

Photos by Phil Wilcox

611 SONOMA MISSION INN & SPA

PO Box 1447   707 938-9000

■ Sonoma, CA 95476

www.smi@smispa.com

Luxuriously restored resort providing multiple beauty and health packages for your benefit and enjoyment in a lovely, romantic setting. Elevation 100 feet. Open all year.

Mineral water flows out of the source at 135° and is piped to a large swimming pool kept at 82°, a watsu pool at 98°, a spa pool at 92°, and an outdoor whirlpool kept at 104°. All pools are lightly treated with bromine and refilled daily. Mineral water showers are also available in the spa. All pools are handicap accessible.

Beautifully appointed guest rooms, conference facilities, a gourmet four-star restaurant, a cafe/market, coed exercise and spa facilities, and an eighteen-hole golf course are available on the premises. In addition, over forty different spa treatments are offered. Major credit cards accepted. Call for rates, reservations, directions, and details.

612 MORTON WARM SPRINGS RESORT

■ 1651 Warm Springs Rd.   707 855-5511

Kenwood, CA 95452

www.mortonwarmspring.com

A summertime neighborhood recreation facility in the middle of Jack London's famed Valley of the Moon. Elevation 100 feet. Open May to October; closed Mondays.

From a natural artesian spring located one-hundred feet below Sonoma Creek, mineral-rich natural mineral water (pure enough to drink) at 88-94° fills a diving pool, a three-foot to five-foot deep family pool, and a four-foot deep baby pool. All pools are treated with chlorine Bathing suits are required.

The Wappo campground has barbecue grills and picnic seating at each site, with access to water source. Sites in the back meadow have electricity. A secluded creekside grove of trees in the back meadow is ideal for weddings and other events. Catering can be arranged for groups of over fifty. They welcome special events such as company picnics. Massage, Ayurvedic spa treatments, and yoga in the meadow are offered. Softball, volleyball, horseshoes, bocce ball and basketball are available, as are swimming lessons. Credit cards accepted.

Marjorie Young

Photos by Phil Wilcox

613 WHITE SULPHUR SPRINGS RESORT
3100 White Sulphur Springs Rd.
■ St. Helena, CA 94574   707 963-8588

A simple historic spa-retreat nestled in its own tranquil wooded canyon in the heart of the Napa Valley. Elevation 400 feet. Open all year.

Several sulphur mineral springs flow naturally in and out of an outdoor rock-lined soaking pool. The water is not chemically treated and is naturally warm at about 85-87°. Also available is a large outdoor jet tub with treated spring water at about 103° and a swimming pool at ambient temperature. All pools and grounds are for the use of overnight guests, and spa guests are encouraged to build a day around their treatments. Call about the availability of day use. Bathing suits are required.

Three types of lodging are offered: a row of small one-room Creekside Cottages and two small inns with fourteen rooms each. The Inn has private bathrooms and the Carriage House has men's and women's shared bathrooms down the hall. All of the rooms are very small and simple without phones, televisions or refrigerators.

Guests have access to phones and a refrigerator, microwave, fireplace, and hot beverages in a Hospitality Lounge. Rooms are sleeping rooms (quiet time after 10 PM) with amenities found outdoors, including lounge chairs, hammocks, shaded picnic tables, lawns, redwood grove, pools, and a connection with nature. Spa service is also available offering Swedish massage, herbal facials, and body wraps. Private outdoor massage for two can be enjoyed under the trees by a babbling brook (weather permitting).

Reservations can be taken only within thirty days of the requested date. All reservations are prepaid and non-refundable. Visa, MasterCard are accepted. Call for directions.

This lower photo is of the natural hot mineral pool which requires no chemical treatment.

CALISTOGA SPAS

Calistoga Chamber of Commerce
1458 Lincoln, Ste. 9 Calistoga, CA 94515
707 942-6333   www.calistogafun.com

All of the following locations are in or near the charming town of Calistoga, adjacent to the Napa Valley wine country. These facilities are open all year and stores, restaurants, etc., are available in the town.

Each of the locations has its own hot wells which are used to supply the water to the soaking and swimming pools. (In order to offer a complete listing of available services, locations offering only spa services are included.) Chlorination of the pools is a state regulation. Soaking tubs in bathhouses are drained and filled after each use so no chemical treatment is necessary. Unless otherwise noted, resorts with pool facilities are available for day use except during peak times and holidays. Bathing suits are required in all public areas. Major credit cards accepted.

614 A   CALISTOGA OASIS SPA
■   1300 Washington St.   707 942-2122

Spa facility offering mud and mineral baths, facials, and massages with private spaces for couples and individuals. Limited selection of spa and bath products. Located on the grounds of Roman Spa. (See complete listing under Roman Spa.)

614 B   CALISTOGA SPA HOT SPRINGS
■   1006 Washington St.   707 942-6269

Resort motel with separate men's and women's bath areas. Offers volcanic ash mud baths, mineral baths, steam baths, blanket wraps, and massage.

Resort has four naturally heated mineral baths: outdoor soaking pool, 100°; outdoor swimming pool, 83°; outdoor wading pool, 90°; and a covered hydropool, 105°. Area surrounding pools has places to lounge and a refreshment stand. Indoor men's and women's bathhouses each contain individual tubs, two mud baths, and three steambaths.

All rooms are equipped for light housekeeping. Aerobic classes, workout rooms, and a conference room are available on the premises.

614 C   CALISTOGA VILLAGE INN AND SPA
■   1880 Lincoln Ave   707 942-0991

Offers a wide range of affordable lodging, some with Roman tub or whirlpool in room. Spa offers traditional mud bath, therapeutic massage, salt scrubs, facials, and reflexology.

Spa has an outdoor swimming pool at 80-85°, wading pool at 90-95°, and enclosed hydropool at 100-105°. Indoor men's and women's bathhouses, each containing two hydrotherapy tubs, two mud baths, two steam cabinets, and a sauna.

Facilities include forty-one rooms, conference meeting rooms, and an on-site restaurant serving all meals.

614 D   CARLIN COUNTRY COTTAGES
■   1623 Lake St.   707 942-9102

Fifteen cottages, seven with a two-person, in-room spa, are decorated with an Irish and Shaker country theme. Pools for registered guests only.

MIneral water outdoor pool is maintained at 90-95° in winter and 85° in summer. Outdoor hydropool is 104°. Cottage pools are controllable to 104°.

Continental breakfast served buffet style; can be taken to the poolside or to your room. Late afternoon refreshments are also provided.

614 E   COMFORT INN
■   1865 Lincoln Ave.   707 942-9400
                      Spa number   707 942-4636

Fifty-four beautifully decorated rooms. Complete spa facilities offered across the street at Calistoga Village Inn and Spa (see above).

Large geothermal outdoor swimming pool is maintained at 85-90°; one whirlpool is 104°. Sauna and steamroom are also available.

Complimentary continental breakfast included with room. Facilities include a meeting room and non-smoking and handicap rooms.

614 F ■ DR. WILKINSON'S HOT SPRINGS
1507 Lincoln Ave.   707 942-6257

One of the original locations (since 1946) offering massage, mud baths, blanket wraps and skin care.

Two outdoor mineral pools are 82° and 92°; one tropical-foliage indoor mineral pool is 104°. Indoor men's and women's bathhouses each contain four individual tubs, two mud baths, and a steambath.

Forty-two rooms, contemporary or Victorian style lodgings, some with kitchenettes. Massage and facial salon.

614 G ■ EUROSPA AND INN
1202 Pine St.   707 942-6829

Luxurious full-service spa surrounded by poolside gardens with a view of mountains and vineyards.

Outdoor unheated mineral water pool and heated whirlpool are 103-105°. Three gas-heated, tap water hydropools allow customers to control temperatures.

Thirteen nicely decorated rooms available. Massage and facials.

614 H ■ GOLDEN HAVEN HOT SPRINGS SPA AND RESORT
1713 Lake St   707 942-6793

One of only two spas in town offering coed mud and mineral baths as well as massage. Spa open to the public,, you need not be a guest at the resort.

Enclosed mineral water swimming pool is 80°; covered hydropool is 102°. Handicap accessibility dependent on services used.

Rooms, some with private sauna or hydropool, some with kitchenettes, are available.

614 I ■ HIDEAWAY COTTAGES
1412 Fairway   707 942-4108

Seventeen cottages for adults only. Spa facilities at Dr. Wilkinson's (see listing).

Outdoor swimming pool is 82° and hydropool is 104°. Reserved for registered guests; no day use.

Various accommodations include some non-smoking rooms some with kitchens. A conference room for up to twenty-five people is also available.

614 J ■ INDIAN SPRINGS
1712 Lincoln Ave.   707 942-4913

California's oldest continuously operating pool and spa offering mud baths, soaking tubs, steam room, massage, and facials. Three active geysers on the premises supply the hot mineral water.

Outdoor, Olympic-size swimming pool is 90-102°, depending on the season. Men's and women's bathhouses, each containing five one-person mud or mineral water soaking tubs and a steam room. Only this spa uses pure volcanic ash, no additives. Pool is handicap accessible.

Comfortable bungalows have recently been restored. Clay tennis court, shuffleboard, bicycle surreys, croquet, and rose gardens are available on the premises.

614 K ■ LAVENDER HILL SPA
1015 Foothill Blvd.   707 942-4495

A garden spa for couples offers two private bathhouses and a full range of mud and seaweed baths, herbal wraps, aromatherapy, facials, massage, and reflexology. You can also make an appointment to create a personalized perfume just for you. Included is a choice of herbal essentials to enhance the soak.

No lodging facilities.

614 L ■ LINCOLN AVENUE SPA
1339 Lincoln Ave.   707 942-5296

Mud wraps, herbal and sea mud wraps, massage, facial, acupressure face lifts.

No lodging facilities.

614 M MOUNT VIEW SPA (AT THE MOUNT VIEW HOTEL)

■ 1457 Lincoln Ave.   707 942-5789

Eurospa offering Fango mud baths for two, massage, facials and body wraps. Private rooms designed for couples.

Outdoor pool and mineral water hot tub.

Elegantly decorated rooms and a wonderful restaurant.

614 N NANCE'S HOT SPRINGS

■ 1614 Lincoln Ave.   707 942-6211

One of Calistoga's original spas offering mud baths, mineral baths, blanket wraps, and massage.

Indoor mineral pool is 103°. Indoor men's and women's bathhouses contain four individual tubs (up to 110°), three mud baths, and two steambaths in each section.

Quality lodging features kitchens and rooms for the handicapped. Gliders for rent at the adjoining airport.

614 O ROMAN SPA

■ 1300 Washington St.   707 942-4441

This three-diamond property has natural mineral pools and well-appointed rooms set amidst an exquisite garden setting of arbors, fountains, and flower-filled courtyards. Calistoga Oasis Spa is on the premises. This full service spa offers massage, reflexology, coed mud baths, mineral baths, herbal wraps, and facials. Four mud tubs are 101°, and two single and two double whirlpools allow customers to control temperatures.

Outdoor swimming pool is 92-95°, the outdoor hydrotherapy whirlpool is 104°, and the indoor hydrotherapy whirlpool is 100°. There are segregated men's and women's saunas.

Attractive lodgings with each room having TV, air conditioning, and a refrigerator. Suites are available, as are rooms with large roman tubs piped with untreated mineral water. Most rooms are non-smoking, some have kitchens, and two rooms are handicap accessible.

614 P SILVER ROSE INN HOT SPRINGS AND SPA

■ 351 Rosedale Rd.   707 942-9581

A three-star rating ranks this romantic, upscale resort as one of the best. All the intimacy of a bed and breakfast inn. Hot mineral water supplies all the showers. Spa area offers four massage rooms for couples or a massage in your room. Full range of body and facial treatments, mud and herbal soaks, bodywraps, and hydrotherm massage are also available. Facilities for registered guests only.

Two large outside pools are 80-90°, and two outdoor whirlpools are 102°. Two hydrotherapy tubs can accommodate couples or singles. Many facilities are handicap accessible.

Twenty guest rooms are each decorated around a theme. Many rooms offer fireplaces, two-person whirlpool tubs, and private balconies. Breakfast can be enjoyed in the dining area, outside on the terrace, or delivered to your room. Entire inn is non-smoking. Afternoon hospitality hour and a "California" style breakfast is included.

Courtesy of Silver Rose Inn

Courtesy of the Roman Spa

615 HARBIN HOT SPRINGS
PO Box 782   707 987-2477
■ Middletown, CA 95461

Surrounded by 1,100 acres of secluded forest, meadows, and streams, this historic resort is constantly being enlarged by a nonprofit residential community in the spirit of preserving the springs as a place to come for rest and renewal. Located in a rugged foothill canyon south of Clear Lake. Elevation 1,500 feet. Open all year.

Two natural hot mineral water springs (one sulphur, one iron) flow out of the earth at 120°, and the water is piped to an enclosed cement pool that has an average temperature of 110-115°, and an adjoining cement pool, fed by the overflow, that has an average temperature of 95-98°. The heart pool, cold plunge, and swimming pool are filled with pure cold water from the same springs that feed the drinking supply. The temperature of the heart pool is maintained at 95-98°. The temperatures of the cold plunge and the swimming pool depend on the weather. All pools operate on a frequent cleaning and flow-through basis combining sand filters, peroxide and ozone injections, and ultra-violet sterilizers. Clothing is optional everywhere within the grounds except in the front office, in the kitchen and dining room, and on the main roads where public access is allowed. Limited handicap accessibility.

Facilities include day use of pools, camping, dorm rooms, several conference buildings for the many retreats and workshops offered, one general store, a book store, a cafe by the pools, an espresso bar, and a vegetarian restaurant with a wonderful view where freshly prepared, mostly organic meals (breakfast and dinner) are served.

Rooms are beautifully and comfortably decorated, and small cottages are just perfect for a romantic getaway. Movies and daily yoga programs are available. A wide range of massage techniques are offered in the separate massage building. For a special summer treat, indulge yourself in the Harbin Clay Works and create a therapeutic body mask for yourself. State accredited training in massage and Watsu is available on the premises. Visa and MasterCard are accepted. It is four miles to a service station in Middletown. Phone for rates, reservations, and directions.

Courtesy of Harbin Hot Springs

Unwinding from city stress at *Harbin* can mean anything from silent soaks and massages to a hike on their extensive grounds and decorating your body with clay. For a complete weekend, rent one of their charming cottages and stay overnight.

Erana

Marjorie Young

616　WILBUR HOT SPRINGS

■　3375 Wilbur Springs Rd.　916 473-2306
Williams, CA 95987

A self-styled "Health Sanctuary" twenty-two miles from the nearest town, with an abundance of hot mineral water. The large soaking pools, sundecks, and restored turn-of-the-century hotel are located in the foothills of the western Sacramento Valley. Elevation 1,350 feet. Open all year.

Natural mineral water flows out of several springs at 140°, through a series of three large concrete tubs measuring about twenty-feet long by five-feet wide and about two feet deep under an A-frame structure, and into an outdoor swimming pool. Soaking pool temperatures are approximately 107° down to about 103°, with the swimming pool kept warm in the winter and cool in the summer. The water is not chemically treated. Bathing suits are optional in pool areas, required elsewhere.

Massage, nineteen private rooms, a private apartment, a dormitory, and communal kitchen (bring your own food) and a group recreation room are available on the premises. Two-hundred-forty acres offer good mountain biking and hiking areas. Various types of massage are offered. Visa and MasterCard are accepted. It is twenty-two miles to a restaurant, store, and service station.

Note: Please, no drop-in visitors. Phone first for reservations and confirmation of services or uses.

Directions: From I-5 in Williams, go west on CA 20 to the intersection with CA 16. A few yards west of the intersection, take a gravel road heading north and west for approximately 5 miles and follow signs to the springs.

To really take advantage of the atmosphere of the turn-of-the-century hotel, bring your own food and be prepared to stay for at least a weekend. Hike on the grounds, swim in the pool, or soak in the hot tubs which are located under the rooftop pictured below.

Photos courtesy of Wilbur Hot Springs

617   VICHY HOT SPRINGS RESORT AND INN

2605 Vichy Springs Rd.   707 462-9515
FAX 707 462-9516

■   **Ukiah, CA 95842**
www.vichysprings.com
vichy@vichysprings.com

The only Vichy baths in North America. Historic, beautifully restored resort in the Ukiah Valley foothills of Mendocino County. Famous for its warm and naturally carbonated mineral water. Guests are invited to explore the 700-acre ranch where wildlife abounds. Elevation 800 feet. Open all year.

Naturally carbonated mineral water flows out of the million-year-old springs at 90° and through redwood pipes to ten enclosed, two-person concrete soaking tubs from the 1860s. Tubs are drained and filled after each use, so no chemical treatment is necessary. One large, communal soaking tub in which the water is treated with ozone is heated to 104°. The Olympic-size swimming pool contains ozone-treated mineral water maintained at approximately 80° during the summer. All tubs and pools are available to the public for day use and to registered guests at any time. Pools, public area and two cottages are ADA handicapped accessible.

Facilities include a tree-shaded, five-acre central lawn ringed by country style cottages and rooms, overnight parking for self-contained RVs, a tree-ringed pond, a running stream, and a thirty-minute hike to a lovely waterfall. Massage, facials, and bed and breakfast are available by reservation on the premises. Credit cards accepted. It is five miles to a campground and four miles to Ukiah.

Phone, fax, or email for brochure, rates, reservations, and directions.

Built in 1854, this cottage is the oldest structure in all of Mendocino County. *Vichy* has hosted such famous persons as Mark Twain, Jack London, Ulysses Grant, and Teddy Roosevelt. This historical landmark provides fun and relaxation.

This beautiful wisteria-laden Monet bridge leads to the soaking tubs (pictured on right) which were originally built in the 1860s.

● **East of the town of Upper Lake**

Natural hot pools adjacent to a creek-fed stream with a cold swimming hole for a quick plunge. Located in a remote, beautiful rock canyon in Mendocino National Forest. Elevation 2,400 feet. Open all year; roads impassable during wet weather.

Natural mineral water flows out of the ground at approximately 106° into three volunteer-built pools. The first pool uses sandbags and rock to keep the cold creek water out and accommodates six to eight persons. The second pool (built with rock and cement) and located about three feet above the creek-fed swimming hole is just right for two and is drainable. The third pool located at the west end of the swimming hole and built of sand-bags and rocks will accommodate ten to twelve people. Depending on air temperature, water varies between 98-104°.

There are no services on the premises, although overnight camping is not prohibited. It is approximately four miles to Bear Creek Campground (uphill from springs and left at "T"). All other services are twenty miles away in Upper Lake.

Directions: From Hwy 20 in Upper Lake proceed north on Main St. Turn right at Second St. and take first left onto Middle Creek Rd. Reset odometer. Pass ranger station on left at .5 miles. Right turn at 1 mile on Pitney Lane. Pass red barn on right at 1.5 miles, left turn at horse corral at 1.9 miles onto 16N30, a paved road. Pavement ends shortly (at 2.5 miles). At 9.9 miles road becomes 16N01; bear left at fork toward Deer Valley, (don't take 16N01A which forks off to the right). At 12.6 miles turn right on 17N11 to French Ridge. Stay on "main" road at questionable forks. At 18.1 miles cross small creek/seep. At 18.4 miles turn left on 17N04. Park at 19.1 miles at the end of the road in a wide gravel area at the confluence of two creeks and walk .25 miles downstream to the springs.

Note: As the springs are on private property, please make a special effort to keep the area clean.

Source map: *Mendocino National Forest.*
GPS: N 39.1743 W 122.4930

Phil Wilcox

Crabtree is one of the more beautiful series of wilderness pools in California. The surrounding terrain is somewhat fragile so please be careful with vehicles and any other activities so that your presence does not impact the environment.

Debbie Johnson

Courtesy of Saratoga Springs

This crystal clear soaking pool is filled with cold mineral water boosted by propane to make it a perfect temperature for you.

Phil Wilcox

619 SARATOGA SPRINGS RETREAT
10234 Saratoga Springs Rd. 800 655-7153
■ **Upper Lake, CA 95485**

Beautiful conference center and lodge situated on 260 acres in a private valley covered with old oaks and black walnut trees in an area of plateaus, hills, and mountains. Elevation 1,400 feet. Open all year by reservation only.

Twelve cold mineral wells supply water to the resort, the swimming pool maintained at ambient temperatures, and the eight-feet by seventeen-feet by four-feet hot pool where the water is boosted by propane heat. The hot tub is treated minimally with bromine and chlorine is used in the pool. Bathing suits are optional, depending on those present. A new building is handicap accessible.

Lodge, cabins, rooms, areas for camping, meeting rooms, fully equipped kitchen (you cook, or they do by prior arrangement), and sweat lodge are all available on the premises. The 2,000 square foot Heart Lodge is available for conferences, workshops, and seminars. All other services are in Upper Lake. Credit cards accepted.

Location: Four miles north of Upper Lake or 21 miles east of Ukiah on Hwy 20.

620 ORR HOT SPRINGS
13201 Orr Springs Rd. 707 462-6277
■ **Ukiah, CA 95482**

A small, tranquil resort nestled in the rolling hills of the Mendocino Coastal Range. Located on a wooded creek under Douglas fir and madrones, thirty-one miles inland from Mendocino. Elevation 800 feet. Open all year by reservations only.

Natural mineral water flows out of several springs at 100° and is piped to a swimming pool, an indoor soaking pool, and four bathtubs in private rooms. The swimming pool averages 70°. The indoor tub and outdoor soaking pool are housed in a bathhouse built in 1858. Some of the water is heated to 105° and pumped to an enclosed redwood tub that overflows into an adjoining shallow outdoor soaking pool famed for stargazing. All pools operate on a flow-through basis, so no chemical treatment is added. Clothing is optional in all bathing areas. Handicap (wheelchair) accessible areas being added.

Facilities include a fully equipped kitchen, rooms, hostel-style accommodations, small cottages with kitchens, tent spaces along the creek, car camping, one dry sauna and a steam room. Massage is available by reservation. No pets are allowed, and there is a strict policy regarding the child-to-adult ratio. Visa and MasterCard are accepted. The entire facility can be rented. It is thirteen miles of steep and winding roads to all other services in Ukiah.

Directions: From Route 101 in Ukiah, take the North State St. exit, drive .25 miles north to Orr Springs Rd., turn west, and drive 13 miles to the resort.

GPS N 39.1349 W 123.2202

621   SWEETWATER SPA AND INN

955 Ukiah St.   707 937-4140
❏   Mendocino, CA 95460

A peaceful and elegant combination of soothing redwood hot tubs, steaming saunas, fine woodwork, and stained glass. Elevation near sea level. Open all year.

Pools are for rent to the public and use gas-heated tap water treated with bromine. One private enclosure with a sauna can be rented by the hour. The water temperature is maintained at 104°. One communal hydropool is available at a day-rate charge. The water temperature is maintained at 104°, and a sauna is included.

Special features: Sweetwater has a variety of unique lodging options, including ocean view units, cottages, and romantic water tower rooms. One private suite can be rented by the hour and also by the night, and a sauna is included. One deluxe Oriental room with spa, ocean view, fireplace, and private sun deck offers privacy and romance. All room rentals include use of tubs. Bathing suits are optional everywhere except in the front office. Professional massage offering a wide range of body work is available on the premises. Visa and MasterCard are accepted.

Note: The management has access to several other wonderful housing options in the area. Phone for rates, reservations, and directions.

622   FINNISH COUNTRY SAUNA & TUBS

5th and J St.   707 822-2228
❏   Arcata, CA 95521

A charming pond surrounded by grass-roofed Finnish style saunas, private outdoor hot tubs, and a European-style coffeehouse in a small Northern California coastal town. Elevation 50 feet. Open every day except Christmas and Thanksgiving.

Tubs are for rent to the public and use gas-heated tap water treated with bromine. There are six private wood hot tubs (two teak and four eucalyptus) rented by the half-hour and maintained at 104°. The conical tubs have benches all the way around and jets at three different levels. Clothing is optional in private spaces.

Facilities include two private sauna cabins and Cafe Mokka, a coffeehouse serving espresso and juices with live folk music on the weekends. No credit cards are accepted. Phone for rates, reservations, and directions.

Located on a quarter acre, complete with pond, island, and outdoor seating area.

Marjorie Young

CENTRAL CALIFORNIA

739
738
737
740
736 A-C
742
741 A-B
San Francisco
Oakland
743
735
744 I-580
745
734
732 A-D
733
Santa Cruz
CA 152
731
Monterey
G 16
730
729
728
727

San Jose

Stockton

CA 16
CA 88
701
702 A-C
I 80
CA 99
CA 49
CA 108
US 395
703
CA 120
704
705
Bridgeport

Merced
CA 120
Mono Lake
CA 120
Hot
Creek
Area 706 A-1
707
NEVADA
708
709
710 A-B
711
712 A-B
Bishop
CA 168
CA 168
CA 140
CA 41

Fresno
CA 180
CA 198
713
715
US 395
US 136
714
716
717
CA 155
CA 41
726 A-C
CA 46
CA 178
CA 178
718A-B
San Luis Obispo
725
724
CA 99
719
Bakersfield
CA 58
CA 166
CA 154
722 A-B
CA 33
723
721
720
Santa Barbara
CA 126
Ventura

Pacific Ocean

CA 1
US 101
I 5

This map was designed to be used with a standard highway map.

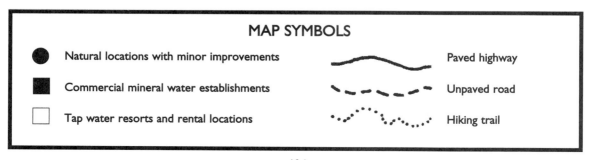

MAP SYMBOLS

●	Natural locations with minor improvements		～	Paved highway
■	Commercial mineral water establishments		- - -	Unpaved road
□	Tap water resorts and rental locations		⋯⋯	Hiking trail

701   GROVER HOT SPRINGS
Box 188   530 694-2248
Markleeville, CA 96120

Swimming pool and soaking pool next to a major state campground and picnic area, located in a wooded mountain valley. Elevation 6,000 feet. Open all year.

Natural mineral water flows out of several springs at 147° and into a holding pond from which it is piped to the pool area. The soaking pool, using natural mineral water treated with bromine, is maintained at approximately 103°. The swimming pool, using domestic water treated with chlorine, is maintained at 70-80°. Domestic water is used to cool down the hot mineral water. Admission is on a first-come, first-served basis, and the official capacity limit of fifty persons in the hot pool and twenty-five in the cold pool is reached early every day during the summer. Bathing suits are required. For handicap accessibility there is a ramp to the pool, although there is not a ramp into the pool. Bathrooms and parking spaces are provided.

Campground spaces are available by prior reservation, as with all other California state parks. Cross-country skiers are encouraged to camp in the picnic area during the winter and to ski in to use the soaking pool. The road is also plowed during the winter making for easy access. It is four miles to the nearest restaurant, motel, and service station in Markleeville.

Location: On Alpine County Road E4, 4.5 miles west of Markleeville. Follow the signs.

Photos by Mark Gillespie

In summer, as big as this hot soaking pool is, it fills up very quickly. In winter, skiing or driving in lets you soak almost by yourself.

Three wonderful hot springs with beautiful mountain views are to be found along the banks of the East Fork of the Carson River in Toiyabe National Forest. The springs are accessible during the rafting season, approximately May through July, depending on water flow. Elevation 5,000 feet.

There are no services available at any of the hot spring sites. While the apparent local custom at the pools is clothing optional, please be respectful of those people already there. These springs are not shown on any Forest Service or USGS map but are well known to raft trip guides.

Word has it that a brand new tub has just been built, possibly in this area. Any one soaked in it yet?

702 A   RIVERSIDE HOT SPRING

● **Near the town of Markleeville**

Approximately eight miles downstream from where you put into the water three small pools are visible from the river on your right (east). Natural mineral water flows into the upper pool at approximately 92° and then continues flowing into the lower pools. The lower tub has been lined with a tarp by some volunteers. During high water these pools are often underwater and need to be rebuilt annually.

Camping is possible near the springs.

Note: It is possible to access this spring by car from Gardnerville, however, according to all reports, it is at the end of "seven of the most miserable miles a 4 WD can handle." It also takes you across a working ranch; during the months of April to November they really do not want you on the property. During the other months you must stay out of the fields and travel only on the road. The field hands will chase you out of the area, although they often can be bought with a six pack, but don't count on it. An extremely steep trail requiring the 4 WD vehicle puts you down at the river's edge where there is a campground and outhouse on BLM land. The pool is located directly across the river and in plain sight. During low water time in the summer you can walk or drive very carefully across the river. The spring is totally inaccessible during spring runoff except by raft.

Photos by Marjorie Young

While you can navigate this river yourself if you are an experienced kayaker, for a real treat, one-day and two-day raft trips (Class 2 rapids) are available through commercial outfitters.

702 B   RIVER RUN HOT SPRINGS

● **Near the town of Markleeville**

Natural mineral water emerges from several springs on the hillside at 110° or hotter and cools as it flows toward the river. The temperature of the water drops to approximately 100° by the time it reaches the large shallow pool near an eight-foot cliff at the river's edge. The small upper pools are quite hot and should be approached with caution. When the river water is low, it is possible to stand in your boat under the water coming off the cliffs.

There is a large open area available for camping, but there are no facilities except an outhouse near the springs.

Jayson Loam

Depending on the river level and the amount of water flow you could just shower in your raft, or for a more relaxing soak, walk up to the large pool on the top which overlooks the river.

Marjorie Young

702 C   HOT SHOWERBATH

● **Near the town of Markleeville**

One mile downstream from River Run Hot Springs, a small pullout is visible on the left (west). Follow the warm ooze about 500 yards up into the canyon, where natural mineral water flows out of a spring at 110° and cools to approximately 98° before dropping over a twenty-foot bank into a warm, squishy-bottomed pool.

Marjorie Young

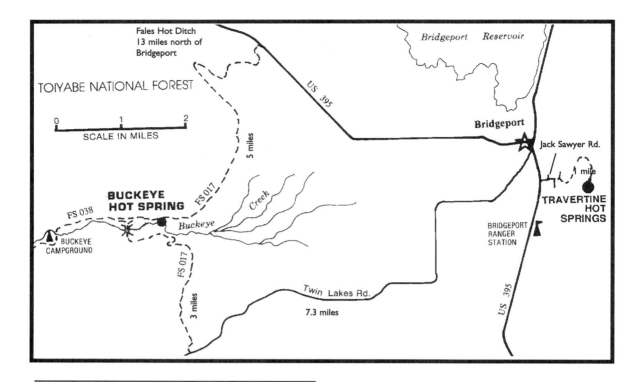

703   FALES HOT DITCH

● **North of the town of Bridgeport**

A primitive pool on Hot Springs Creek in the sage-brush foothills of the Eastern Sierra. Elevation 7,200 feet. Open all year.

Natural mineral water emerges at 140° from a spring on the property of an old resort, now closed, and flows down Hot Springs Creek, gradually cooling as it goes. Volunteers have dammed the creek to form a thigh-deep, rock and sand pool, ten-feet by twelve-feet and four-feet deep on the east side of the highway .3 miles past the old resort (which is on the west side of the highway). Although the soaking pool is twenty feet below the highway and out of sight of passing vehicles, it is advisable to wear a bathing suit or have it close at hand.

There are no services on the premises. It is seven miles to a Forest Service campground and thirteen miles to all other services in Bridgeport.

GPS: N 38.2103 W 119.2402

Directions: From Bridgeport, drive north on US 395 for 13 miles to a boarded-up, fenced, brown wooden structure that used to be Fales Hot Springs Resort (on the west side of US 395). The gated property just north of the old resort is private and posted "no trespassing." However, from the old resort, drive .3 miles north and park along the shoulder of US 395 on the east side of the road. The pullout is right before mile marker 90. The creek and soaking pool are 20 feet below the highway (not visible until you park and look over the small cliff).

GPS: N 38.35253 W 119.40484

Marjorie Young

Along with these soaking pools by the river, there is a small cave (to the left under the overhang) where the water drips off the roof forming a soaking area.

704   BUCKEYE HOT SPRING
(see map on page 128)
● **Near the town of Bridgeport**

Delightful hot spring in a superb natural setting on the north bank of Buckeye Creek in Toiyabe National Forest. One of the best. Elevation 6,900 feet. Open all year; not accessible by road in winter.

Natural mineral water flows out of the ground at 135°, runs over a large cliff built up by mineral deposits, and drops into the creek. Volunteers have built loosely constructed rock pools along the edge of the creek below the hot waterfall. The pool temperature is controlled by admitting more or less cold water from the creek.

There is another small outflow of hot geothermal water on the bluff near the parking area. Volunteers have dug a shallow soaking pool that maintains a temperature of approximately 100°. It is near the foot of a tree located in the upstream direction from the parking area. The apparent local custom at both pools is clothing optional.

Three hundred yards upstream from the parking area are several acres of unmarked open space on which overnight parking is not prohibited. It is one mile to a Forest Service campground and nine miles to a restaurant, motel, store, and service station in Bridgeport.

There are no services on the premises. There is a parking turnout on the south side of the road on the bluff above the springs.

Directions: (This is the easier route.) At the north end of Bridgeport, take Twin Lakes Rd. west for 7.3 miles to Doc & Al's Resort. Turn right (north) onto FS 017, a two-lane, graded, washboard road, for 3 miles to the second bridge over the creek, where the road intersects with FS 038 toward Buckeye Campground to the left. Branch off to the right for a few hundred yards up a short hill on the north branch of FS 017 to a large flat parking clearing on a big knoll. The upper pool is a few steps away (slightly downhill and to the right) under a tree, at the crest of the knoll overlooking Buckeye Creek. Several unofficial paths lead down the slope to the pools located along the creek at the foot of a large mound covered over by the mineral deposits.

Source maps: *Toiyabe National Forest*, USGS *Matterhorn Peak*.

GPS: N 38.23973 W 119.32613

Photos by Henry Young

I can never resist a soak at *Buckeye*, the first natural hot spring that I ever went to, and still one of my favorites.

Travertine Hot Springs is named after the mineral which has built up here to form this tufa mound. The area around the pools is carefully maintained so please stay on the trails to help conserve the fragile vegetation.

705   TRAVERTINE HOT SPRINGS
(see map on page 128)
● Southeast of the town of Bridgeport

An unusual group of volunteer-built soaking pools on large travertine ridges with commanding views of the High Sierra. Located two miles from the center of Bridgeport. Elevation 6,700 feet. Open all year.

The flow of natural mineral water (130-160°) out of several geothermal fissures can be interrupted or shifted to a new outlet by underground movement resulting from local earthquakes. The scalding water is channeled to a series of volunteer-built soaking pools in which the individual pool temperatures are controlled by temporarily diverting the hot water inflow as needed. The upper pool is handicap accessible with assistance. The apparent local custom is clothing optional.

At the upper ten-feet by five-feet by two-foot pool, scalding water bubbles up from under large rocks and is directed through a stepped channel with a "bear claw" configuration at pool's edge. The source can be capped to control pool temperature. There is a plug for draining and cleaning the pool, which is done fastidiously by volunteers. Overflow goes into a small adjoining foot bath for rinsing off before entering the pool. Since you can drive right up to this pool it is handicap accessible with assistance.

Three lower rock-and-cement pools, one-hundred yards below, are at the foot of a large granite boulder where water seeps up through the rock and gently trickles into the pools at 100°. A primitive 80° rock and mud pool nearby is fed by a separate underground source.

There are no services and overnight camping is not permitted. Port-a-potties have been installed. Other primitive amenities include a large deck around the pools covered with old carpets for sunbathing, a wooden bench,

and "butt cans." There is no trash collection, so please pack it out. All other services are available in Bridgeport.

Directions: From the ranger station .5 miles south of Bridgeport, drive north on Hwy 395 for .2 miles. Turn right on Jack Sawyer Rd., the first paved road on your right. At .4 miles the paved road makes a 90-degree turn to the right. Do not bear right. Continue straight ahead on the unpaved, ungraded road for approximately 1 mile to the pools. On the way you will pass a sign on your left to Bridgeport Barrow Pit; continue straight to the forest service sign on your left. Across from this on the right is a turnoff to a flat camping area. If you continue straight, the second turnoff just ahead on the right leads to the lower pools. Or continue uphill to where the road curves around to the right to reach the upper cement pool.

GPS: N 38.24548 W 119.20539

Volunteers have done an amazing job of keeping this area clean and the pools sparkling. Thank you!

Photos by Marjorie Young

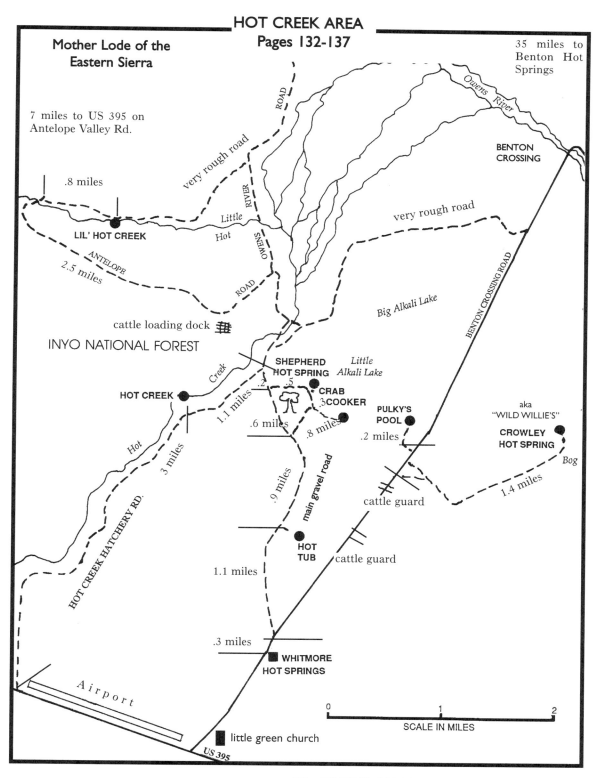

Mother Lode of the
Eastern Sierra

35 miles to
Benton Hot
Springs

7 miles to US 395 on
Antelope Valley Rd.

ROAD

very rough road

**BENTON
CROSSING**

Little

RIVER

Hot

OWENS

.8 miles

LIL' HOT CREEK

ANTELOPE

ROAD

2.5 miles

very rough road

Owens River

BENTON CROSSING ROAD

cattle loading dock

Big Alkali Lake

INYO NATIONAL FOREST

Creek

*Little
Alkali Lake*

**SHEPHERD
HOT SPRING**

HOT CREEK

.5

.2

1.1 miles

**CRAB
COOKER**

.3

**PULKY'S
POOL**

aka
"WILD WILLIE'S"

.6 miles

.8 miles

.2 miles

**CROWLEY
HOT SPRING**

Hot

3 miles

Bog

.9 miles

main gravel road

1.4 miles

cattle guard

HOT CREEK HATCHERY RD.

**HOT
TUB**

cattle guard

1.1 miles

.3 miles

**WHITMORE
HOT SPRINGS**

A i r p o r t

0   1   2

SCALE IN MILES

little green church

US 395

Photos by Phil Wilcox

706 A   HOT CREEK

(see map on page 131)

● **East of the town of Mammoth Lakes**

Primarily a geologic observation and interpretive site with some limited use by bathers. Open daylight hours only.

Natural mineral water with a slight sulfur smell emerges from many fissures as steam or boiling water, and several danger areas have been fenced off for safety. Substantial amounts of boiling, geothermal water also flow up from the bottom of the creek. A bend in the creek provides a natural eddy in which the mixing of hot and cold water stays within a range of 50° to 110°. Those who venture into this confluence experience vivid thermal skin effects, but they must be careful to avoid the geothermal vents because of the danger of scalding. The trail from the main pool goes upstream 400-500 feet where cold water is diverted around other hot spots in the river. Bathing suits are required.

In the past, night use of this location has resulted in many injuries and some fatalities, so the area may be used only from sunrise to sunset. Citations are issued by the Forest Service to anyone found there after sunset or before sunrise. During the winter, when snow blocks the access road, skiers and hikers may still enter the area during daylight hours.

Facilities include men's and women's changing rooms, pit toilets, and an asphalt parking area with a paved, fenced pathway down to the creek, making the area handicap accessible with assistance. Overnight parking is prohibited. It is ten miles to all services in the town of Mammoth Lakes.

Directions: From US 395, 3 miles south of the Mammoth Lakes turnoff, turn east on Hot Creek Hatchery Rd./Airport. At .8 miles, turn right at the sign to "Hot Creek Geothermal Area." From this sign, it is 3 miles to the parking area for Hot Creek. Only the first 1.2 miles are paved. Or, from Benton Crossing Rd., take 3S50, the main gravel road, for 2.8 miles. Turn left for .3 miles to the Hot Creek gate and another .8 mile to the parking area.

Source maps: *Inyo National Forest*, USGs *Mt. Morrison*.

GPS: N 37.66049 W 118.82834

Bill Franks

Phil Wilcox

706 B   LIL' HOT CREEK

(see map on page 131)

● **East of the town of Mammoth Lakes**

A very hot flowing creek fed by a 180° geothermal spring. The name Lil' Hot Creek has been given to a large, squishy-bottom soaking pool located just below where the flow from several cold springs cools the hot stream to approximately 107°. The thigh-deep cement and rock pool has tiered seats so you can soak at different depths. Pool temperature can be controlled by opening or capping a four-inch plastic pipe that brings the water in from the nearby creek. There's a plug for draining and cleaning the pool. Spillover goes through a tiny channel back to the creek. As you leave, please shut the inflow of hot water so the next ones in will not be scalded—water can get up to 120-125°.

Plenty of level ground, as well as hideaway spots among the pine trees in the nearby national forest, are available where overnight parking is not prohibited. The apparent local custom is clothing optional.

Directions: There are four routes, depending on your starting point.

1. (This is the best.) From the main gravel road (3S50, Benton Crossing Rd.), drive a total of 3.3 miles to the sign for Owens River Rd. (This is .7 miles past the turnoff to Shepherd.) You'll pass a cattle loading dock on the left just before Owens River Rd. Turn left for .7 miles to Little Antelope Rd. Turn left onto Antelope Rd. for 2.5 miles across a flat open area. At 2.5 miles, at the beginning of the pine forest, is a cattle guard. Make a sharp right just past the cattle guard and follow this very rough, ungraded dirt road for .8 miles to the springs on your right.

Hot water from the tub is recycled back into the hot stream. Water temperature varies greatly, often up to 120 degrees, so be careful!

Whenever the road forks, keep bearing right, following the fence until you come to a flat open area for parking. You'll see steam rising from the creek to your right as you follow the fence. At the parking area, look for a small wooden portion in the wire fence and a cattle-proof entrance. Go through the gate and over log planks across the creek to reach the hot soaking pool.

2. Take Hot Creek Hatchery Rd. from US 395 for 3 miles to the Hot Creek asphalt parking area. Continue past the parking area for another 1.1 miles to a fork in the unpaved road. Do not bear right, but continue straight ahead for another .1 mile to where the road ends at a wide gravel road. This is 3S50, the main gravel road. Turn left, and on your left you'll see the cattle loading dock mentioned above. Follow directions above.

3. A very beautiful but much longer drive begins at US 395. At the turnoff to Mammoth Lake, instead of heading west toward the lakes, turn east and follow the sign to Little Antelope Valley (not Chalk Hills). At 6.3 miles you will be at the cattle guard at the edge of the pine forest. Turn left onto the ungraded dirt road and follow the fence as described above to reach the soaking pool.

4. For those with 4WD vehicles, or at least with good clearance, continue past the turnoff to Antelope Rd. another 1.3 miles and turn left. Follow the washboard road 2 miles to the springs, which are now on the left.

GPS: N 37.89027 W 118.84259

Phil Wilcox

Steve Heerema

When last visited, there was no water flowing into the pool. I'm sure the cow was disappointed.

706 C SHEPHERD HOT SPRING
(see map on page 131)

● **East of the town of Mammoth Lakes**

Natural mineral water flows out of a spring and through a plastic pipe to a twenty by twenty-four inch deep rock and cement tub. There are benches in the pool, which is large enough for three or four people. Pool temperature is controlled by diverting the hot water flow from the nearby source pool which can often be as hot as 130°. The white plastic inflow pipe has a ball valve to control the flow and if allowed to run the temperature in the pool can be very, very hot–be careful. There is a plug for draining the pool, capped with a tennis ball. However, local volunteers prefer emptying the pool with a bucket before scrubbing. A scrub brush is on site.

There are no facilities except a primitive campfire ring. A posted sign prohibits overnight parking. The apparent local custom is clothing optional.

Directions: From Benton Crossing Rd., turn north on 3S50 (the main gravel road) .3 miles past the Whitmore public swimming pool. Drive 2.6 miles to a dirt road on your right. Follow this across an open bog for .5 miles to the pool on your left.

From Crab Cooker, follow the dirt road back the way you came in for .5 miles to a four-way, dirt-road intersection. To reach Shepherd, turn right at this intersection and go .2 miles to the small clearing where the pool is located.

GPS: N 37.40014 W 118.48213

706 D CRAB COOKER
(see map on page 131)

● **East of the town of Mammoth Lakes**

Natural mineral water flows out of a spring at over 120° and through a pipe to a rock-and-cement soaking pool. The pool temperature can be controlled by turning off a valve in the pipe inside the pool when the desired soaking temperature is reached. (Please turn off this valve when leaving so as not to scald the next soakers.) Do not tamper with the pipes in the nearby well, as special plumbing equipment is required to fix them.

There are no facilities on the premises. The apparent local custom is clothing optional.

Directions: Follow the main gravel road for 2 miles from Benton Crossing Rd. (.9 miles past the turnoff to Hot Tub). Watch for a lone juniper tree on the right side of the road. The road to Crab Cooker is on the right just before this tree. Two separate roads appear to head off to the right, but they merge after a short oval and continue as a rocky, one-lane dirt road for .1 mile to a large white mound of rocks. Follow the road around the left side of these rocks for another .2 miles to a four-way dirt-road intersection. Continue straight for another .5 miles across cow pastures to where the road ends at a flat open area where you will see the pool.

Note: As of this writing, there was no water flowing from the source into the pool.

GPS: N 37.66292 W 118.80845

706 E   DAVE'S WARM TUB

● **East of the town of Mammoth Lakes**
    As of 1995, there was no longer a tub here and the existing water is only 80° in a shallow seep.

Phil Wilcox

706 F   PULKY'S POOL

(see map on page 131)

● **East of the town of Mammoth Lakes**
    Natural mineral water flows out of a spring at 131° and through a PVC pipe to a free-form, rock and cement pool up on the plateau, offering views of the Sierra. This pool, with a temperature of about 107° features a very clear water and a drain to facilitate easy cleaning. The hot water pipe has a gate valve and a second pipe admits cold water allowing for temperature control.
    Primitive facilities include a small carpeted deck for undressing and sunbathing, and a cement bench. The area is posted for day use only; no overnight parking is permitted. The apparent local custom is clothing optional.
    Directions: From US 395, drive 2 miles past Whitmore Pool over one cattle guard to the second cattle guard. The turnoff to Crowley, 706-G, is just past the second cattle guard on the right (south). For Pulky's, continue on Benton Crossing Rd. for another .2 miles to an unpaved road on the left (north). Follow this road as it curves around a large alkali field for .4 miles to a flat parking area and park by fence. The pool is up on the plateau. Caution: Do not attempt to drive to the plateau, stay on the road; even 4WD vehicles have become stuck in the soft ground.
    GPS: N 37.961 W 118.472

706 G   CROWLEY HOT SPRING
(ALSO KNOWN AS WILD WILLIE'S)
(see map on page 131)
● **East of the town of Mammoth Lakes**
    Natural mineral water flows out of a spring and down a small creek channel at 110°, then into a cement and rock pool large enough for thirty people. Surface cooling keeps the pool temperature about 104° most of the year.
    Fifty feet away, at the foot of a large rock outcropping, is a mud-bottom pool at approximately 100°. Natural mineral water flows from a separate source near the rock into this knee-deep pool. The pool is large enough for a half-dozen people. Clothing optional.
    There are no facilities on the premises, but overnight parking is not prohibited in the large parking area.
    Directions: From Benton Crossing Rd., drive 2 miles past Whitmore Pool. Immediately past the second cattle guard, two rough dirt roads cut off to the right. Take either one (they join up) and drive 1.1 miles to a large rock. Follow the road to the right side of the rock and take an immediate left at the fork. Drive .3 miles to a large level parking area bordered by logs. Do not attempt to drive any farther. To reach the pools, follow the walkway from the end of the parking area for approximately 250 yards to where it joins a trail from the opposite direction and a path leading down a small hill to the left. The primitive pool is under some trees near the big rock ahead on your left; the pool with the deck is ahead on the right.
    Caution: Do not attempt to drive across the bog to the pool area. Even 4WDs have been trapped. A new wooden walkway has been constructed from the parking lot to the pools—please use it!
    GPS: N 37.3955 W 118.4627

706 H HOT TUB

(see map on page 131)

● **East of the town of Mammoth Lakes**

Natural mineral water flows out of a spring at 110° and through a black PVC pipe to a three-foot deep rock and cement pool. The pool temperature is controlled by diverting the hot water inflow whenever the desired soaking temperature has been reached. There is a plug for draining, and the pool is kept clean by a group of local volunteers. The thigh-deep pool can hold about six people comfortably.

There are no facilities, but there is plenty of level area surrounding the pool, and overnight parking is not prohibited. Campers, please be considerate of others. Park away from the tubs, and keep the noise level down. The apparent local custom is clothing optional.

Directions: From Benton Crossing Rd., drive 1.1 miles on 3S50 (the main gravel road) to the second one-lane dirt road on the right. Turn right and go for .1 mile to a clearing, then bear left for another .1 mile to the pool.

GPS: N 37.3884 W 118.4850

706 I WHITMORE HOT SPRINGS
(see map on page 131)
904 Benton Crossing Rd.   760 935-4222
■ **Mammoth Lakes, CA 93546**

Large, conventional public swimming pool jointly operated by Mono County and the town of Mammoth Lakes on land leased from the Los Angeles Department of Water and Power. Open during the day, Monday through Saturday, approximately mid-June to Labor Day.

Natural mineral water is pumped from a well, propane boosted, and piped to the swimming pool where it is treated with chlorine. Depending on air temperature and wind conditions, the pool water temperature averages 82°. An adjoining shallow wading pool averages 92°. Bathing suits are required. Bathrooms, showers, and slide-gate entrance are handicap accessible.

A small access fee includes showers (campers take note) and a barbeque area. A full aquatic schedule is available on the premises. Parking is permitted only during hours of operation. No credit cards are accepted.

Photos by Phil Wilcox

Justine Hill

Facilities include snacks and beverages. A gas pump is located across the street. There are now camping spaces on the premises. It is four miles to a campground/RV park and store in the town of Benton, and fifteen miles to a motel, restaurant, and casino north on US 6 at the state line.

Directions: From Bishop, take US 6 north for 36 miles to the tiny town of Benton. Turn west on CA 120 and drive 4 miles until you see the old green and white house on the north side of the street. Or, from US 395 in Lee Vining (Tioga Pass from Yosemite), take CA 120 east for 46 miles to Benton Hot Springs. If you are coming from the series of natural springs outside Mammoth, take Benton Crossing Rd. south of the Mammoth Airport for 36 miles to where it ends at CA 120. Take 120 east for 3 miles to Benton Hot Springs.

707 THE OLD HOUSE AT BENTON HOT SPRINGS

■

55045 Hwy 120   760 933-2507
Benton, CA 93512

A group of redwood tubs were cut from an old redwood pipeline that used to go to the generating plant. The tubs are on the property of an historic 1860s house now selling arts, crafts, antiques, and collectibles. The tubs are located in an oasis-type setting under cottonwood, Russian olive, tamarisk, and locust trees in high desert and sagebrush-type country along the eastern border of California near the Nevada state line, with views of Montgomery and Boundary Peaks (highest points in Nevada). Elevation: 5,500 feet. Pools are rented by the hour, and reservations are suggested. Open all year.

Natural, soft, silky mineral water flows out of a spring at 135° and supplies water to the entire town of Benton Hot Springs. A cooling/evaporation tank at The Old House provides the only cool water in town. There is no chemical treatment of the water in the tubs. The four tubs, located under the trees, are drained and scrubbed with bleach after each use. Each tub has a hot and cold faucet to adjust water temperature. The five-foot diameter tubs are about three feet deep, have seats inside, and are large enough for four to six people. Bathing suits are optional in the tubs, which are separated by hedges. Owners request that nudity be discreet and only at the tubs.

Steve Heerema

The small wooden hut in the background provides a private place to change and to keep your clothes.

Photos by Steve Heerema

708   RED'S MEADOW HOT SPRINGS

● **In Red's Meadow Campground near Devil's Postpile National Monument**

Tin-roof shed with six cement shower-over bath tubs in six small private rooms, on the edge of a mountain meadow campground. Elevation 7,000 feet. Open approximately Memorial Day to September 20.

Natural mineral water flows out of the ground at 100°, into a storage tank, and then by pipe into the bathhouse. Depending on the use, water temperature out of the shower heads will vary from 90-100°. No charge is made for the use of the tubs, which are available on a first-come, first-served basis.

In summer, all water from the spring is diverted into the bathhouse. During the winter, the cement hot water storage tank is used for soaking and can only be reached by snowmobiles and cross-country skiers.

A Forest Service campground, open during the summer, adjoins the hot springs. It is four miles to a cafe, general store, rustic cabins, and pack station at Red's Meadow Resort, and twelve miles to an RV park and other services in Mammoth Lakes.

Directions: From the town of Mammoth Lakes, take CA 203 west to the end, then follow signs through Minaret Pass to Devil's Postpile National Monument and to Red's Meadow Campground. Note: During the day in summer, private vehicles are prohibited beyond Minaret Pass. A frequent shuttle bus service originates at Mammoth Mountain Inn.

Source map: *Inyo National Forest*; USGS *Devil's Postpile*.

709   IVA BELL (FISH CREEK HOT SPRINGS)

● **South of Devil's Postpile National Monument**

A delightful cluster of volunteer-built soaking pools, some with spectacular views of the wilderness. Elevation 7,200 feet. Open all year.

This location adjoins the Iva Bell camp area which includes numerous camping sites separated by meadows and stands of pines. The two main soaking pools are not visible from the main camping area but are to be found fifty yards east, up and behind an obvious bare rock ledge.

The most popular pool has a nice sandy bottom and is nestled on the back side of this ledge, where a 106° trickle flows out of a fissure slowly enough to maintain a 101° pool temperature in the summertime. A 100° squishy-bottom pool may be reached by following a path thirty yards across a meadow.

From the first pool, another path leads due east for fifty yards to a cozy campsite. From this site, a steep one-hundred-yard path leads up to four more pools, ranging in temperature from 101° to 110°.

The twelve-mile hike (one way) from the road end at Red's Meadow involves an elevation change of 1,000 feet. Detailed directions to such a remote location are beyond the scope of this book. We recommend *Sierra North*, published by Wilderness Press; also consult with the Mammoth Ranger District of Inyo National Forest, 760 873-2408.

Source map: *USGS Devil's Postpile.*

710 A MONO HOT SPRINGS

(Summer) 7200 Hwy 168   559 325 1710
Mono Hot Springs, CA 93642
(Winter) PO Box 215
Lake Shore, CA 93634
Northeast of Fresno
www.monohotsprings.com

A vacation resort offering fishing, hiking, and camping in addition to mineral baths with access across the river to several natural springs. Located on the south fork of the San Joaquin River near Edison Lake, Florence Lake, and Bear Dam in the Sierra National Forest. Elevation 6,500 feet. Open May to October.

Natural mineral water flows from a spring at 107° and is piped to a bathhouse containing four two-person soaking tubs in private rooms. Tubs have geothermal water only, measuring 100-105°. Tubs are drained and refilled after each use, so no chemical treatment of the water is necessary. An outdoor hydrojet pool is maintained at 103-105° and is treated with chlorine. Bathing suits are required except in private rooms. Facilities are available on a day-use basis, as well as to registered guests, and are handicap accessible with assistance.

On the south side of the river directly across from the resort is a series of springs and soaking pools that are open all year, but only to cross-country skiers and snowmobilers in winter. Water from one spring feeds into a holding tank. From there it is piped across the river to the resort. Nearby is a cement soaking tub called "The Coffin" due to its size and shape. Above the riverbank are several cement soaking tubs that remain from an historic bathhouse. A rock and mud pool is near the cement tubs and another primitive pool, called "The Rock," is next to a large boulder ten feet up the hill from the cement tubs. Pool temperatures are approximately 101°. Bathing suits are advisable in the daytime.

Facilities include a restaurant, store, service station, and cabins. A forest service campground is on the edge of the property. Massage is available on the premises. Visa and MasterCard are accepted.

Directions to the resort: From the city of Fresno on CA 99, go 80 miles northeast on CA 168 to the ranger station at the northeast side of Huntington Lake. Inquire here about road conditions before attempting to drive in. The one-lane road is very narrow and winding. Allow at least one hour for this 15-mile stretch.

At 15 miles, you come to the High Sierra Ranger Station. Stop here for info and campfire permits, needed even for cooking in your van. One mile past this station the road forks. Bear left to Mono Hot Springs. At 1 mile, you will cross a small bridge. Continue downhill to a second green bridge. Mono is less than .25 miles past the bridge on your left.

To reach the soaking pools on the south side of the river, use the wooden bridge that starts at the forest service campground. "The Rock" is up a small hill to your left, the cement pools a few feet ahead uphill from the river.

The cement pools are the remains of an old bathhouse located across the river from the resort. The pool below is located right next to the building where you can book a relaxing massage sure to feel good after a day of hiking and fishing.

Photos by Phil Wilcox

710 B   LITTLE EDEN

● **Northeast of Fresno**

A primitive, squishy-bottom, thigh-deep pool surrounded by grass and large enough for a dozen people,
with a gorgeous view of the surrounding mountains and a
real feeling that you are out in nature. Elevation 6,500
feet. Open all year; accessible only to cross-country skiers
and snowmobilers in the winter.

Natural mineral water bubbles up through the sandy
pool bottom at around 100°. Because of its large size,
pool temperatures measure only in the nineties. The
apparent local custom is clothing optional.

There are no facilities on the premises. Services are
less than a mile away at Mono Hot Springs Resort.

Directions: Follow directions given for Mono Hot
Springs to the High Sierra ranger station. 2.1 miles past
the station, and 1.1 miles down the left fork at the "Y" is
a steel bridge. Park at turnout on right just before bridge
or on left just past the bridge. A steep, unofficial trail to
the pool begins on the left (north), approximately 50 feet
before the bridge, and goes around a large rock outcrop-
ping, through some marshy spots, and down to the pool
at the base of the rocks.

GPS: N 37.1929 W 119.0106

Phil Wilcox

● Southeast of Florence Lake

A combination hot spring and mudbath in a grassy High Sierra meadow, 9.5 miles from the road's end at Florence Lake. Elevation 7,600 feet. Open all year.

Natural mineral water oozes up through the squishy bottom of a large pool, maintaining a temperature of approximately 102°, and then flows into a nearby small, warm lake. The apparent custom is clothing optional.

There are no services at this location except nearby backpacker campgrounds. It is ten miles to a store, service station, etc.

The eleven-mile trail from the road's end has an elevation gain of 500 feet and requires fording the South Fork of the San Joaquin River. In the summer it is possible to avoid five miles of walking by riding the Sierra Queen ferry across the lake. From this part of the John Muir Trail it is only a hike of five miles down the Florence Lake Trail to reach the springs.

We recommend *Sierra South*, published by Wilderness Press, for detailed directions, or consult the Pine Ridge Ranger District at 559 855-5360.

Nearby is Muir Trail Ranch, which offers rustic log cabin comfort to organized groups on a bring-your-own-food basis. Ranch guests enjoy private rock-and-tile mineral water pools. From the end of the road at Florence Lake, the hiking distance is eleven miles. But summer guests can ride the Sierra Queen ferryboat across the lake and then ride ranch horses or hike the remaining five miles. For information, write the owner, Adeline Smith, Box 176, Lakeshore, CA 93634 from mid-June to October, or Box 269, Ahwanee, CA 93601 in other months.

Source map: USGS *Blackcap Mountain.*

The top pool is the public pool found one and one-half miles above Blayney Meadows. The bottom two beautifully designed pools are available to guests at the Muir Trail Ranch.

All photos by Bill Ralph

712 A KEOUGH HOT SPRINGS
■   800 Keough Hot Spring Rd. 760 872-4670
        Bishop, CA 93514

The Sierra foothills is home to this historical site where the pool was built in 1919. Elevation 4,200 feet. Open all year.

Natural mineral water flows out of the ground at 128° and into the enclosed 100-foot by 40-foot swimming pool (87-95°) and the 24-foot by 40-foot wading pool (100°), using flow-through mineral water so that only minimal chlorine needs to be added. Full-time lifeguard on duty. Bathing suits are required.

An RV campground and snack bar are available on the premises. There are several campgrounds nearby. No credit cards are accepted. It is seven miles to the nearest restaurant, motel, service station, and store. Call for schedule and rates.

Directions: Go 7 miles south of Bishop on US 395, then follow signs west from US 395.

Photos by Phil Wilcox

712 B KEOUGH HOT DITCH

●   **Near Keough Hot Springs**

Runoff from Keough Hot Springs cools as it flows through a series of volunteer-built rock pools in a treeless foothill gully. Elevation 4,100 feet. Open all year.

Natural mineral water flows out of the ground at 128° on the property of Keough Hot Springs, then meanders northeast over BLM land for about a mile before joining with a cold water surface stream. Volunteer-built rock dams create several primitive soaking pools and swimming holes on both sides of the road, each one cooler than the preceding one upstream. The apparent local custom is clothing optional.

No services are available on the premises. The land is posted for day-use only, no overnight parking, but reports are that parking for one night is not a problem as long as you leave nothing but tire tracks. Please do not bring any glass objects to the area, since broken glass is the biggest problem at Keough. It is one mile to an RV park and eight miles to a restaurant, store, and service station in Bishop.

Directions: Seven miles south of Bishop on US 395, turn west on Keough Hot Springs Rd. at approximately .6 miles. At the only intersection with a paved road (old US 395), turn north 200 yards to where a cold stream crosses the road. (Note: There is an abundance of level parking space on the north side of the cold stream, but the stream must be forded with care.) Walk an additional 50 yards north to Keough Ditch. Either stream may be followed to where they join, forming a series of warm swimming pools.

GPS: N 37.1534 W 118.2244

This is only one of the soaking areas available to you at *Keough Hot Ditch.*

713   SALINE VALLEY HOT SPRINGS

● ### Northeast of the town of Olancha

A sometimes crowded, spring-fed oasis located on a barren slope of BLM land in a remote desert valley that was recently annexed to Death Valley National Park. Elevation 1,500 feet. Open all year, but access roads may become impassable at any time of the year due to heavy rainstorms or snow.

Natural mineral water flows out of the two main source springs at 107°. Volunteers have installed pipes to carry this water to a variety of cement and rock soaking pools. By mutual agreement, no one bathes in the source pools. A third (upper) source spring flows into a natural, squishy-bottom pool that maintains an average temperature of 102°. All pools have valves and drains for controlling water flow and cleaning, except the natural upper warm spring. Most of the pools and facilities are handicap accessible with assistance. The area is currently designated as clothing optional by the Park Service.

Vault toilets have been installed by the Park Service. There is level space on which overnight parking is permitted, with a limit of up to thirty days per calendar year for the entire park. It is more than fifty-five miles, mostly unpaved, to a store or service station in Big Pine, and more than eight-five to Olancha. Everyone hauls out their own trash, as well as ashes from campfires, which are permitted in the existing firepans.

Temperatures regularly soar over the 110° mark in the summer, so this desert location with very little natural shade is preferred in the fall and spring. It becomes very crowded on major holidays and three-day weekends. The peace and quiet of the desert can best be enjoyed during the week.

Phil Wilcox

Directions: The southern route via Olancha is shown on the map. The unpaved portion of the Saline Valley Road is county maintained. An alternate route starts just north of Big Pine on US 395. Drive northeast on CA 168 for 2.5 miles and turn right (southeast) on Death Valley Road. Drive approximately 15 miles and turn right on Waucoba-Saline Rd. Drive 32 miles south to a triangular intersection on the left (east) side of the road. Turn left (east) for 7 miles to the first group of springs. From US 395 it is at least a 3-hour drive via either route. All roads in are quite rough and a high clearance vehicle is recommended. The 2.2-mile road from the lower springs to the far upper springs is particularly rough. Either entrance route may be temporarily washed out by infrequent but severe flash floods, or blocked by snow. Inquire about road conditions before making the trip.

There is now a full-time caretaker to assist with emergencies. For current information on road conditions, contact the Death Valley Ranger at 760-786-2331.

Source maps: So. CA Auto Club *Death Valley*, USGS *Waucoba Wash and New York Butte.*

GPS (lower springs): N 36.80576 W 117.77340

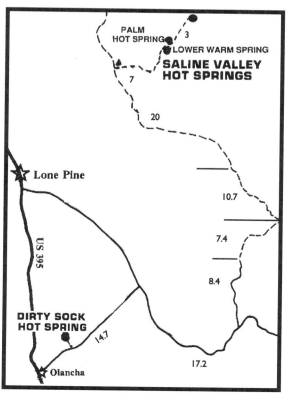

Miners from the now extinct silver mine of Cerro Gordo used to come down out of the surrounding hills to bathe here.

714   DIRTY SOCK HOT SPRING

● **Near the town of Olancha**

Large, shallow pool in an open desert area. Elevation 3,600 feet. Open all year.

Natural mineral water flows up through a large vertical pipe into the bottom of a circular, cement-edged pool at 90° and flows out at various lower temperatures, depending on wind and air temperature. Several sets of step lead down to the somewhat slippery pool bottom. The apparent local custom is clothing optional.

No services are available on the premises, and there are no remaining buildings. There are many acres of unmarked level space on which overnight parking is not prohibited. It is five miles to the nearest restaurant, motel, service station, and store.

Directions: From the intersection of US 395 and CA 190, go five miles northeast on CA 190. There are no signs on the highway, so look for a narrow, paved road on the northwest side and follow it 300 yards to the spring.

GPS: N 36.1975 W 117.5690

715   KERN HOT SPRING

● **On the upper Kern River**

A small concrete soaking pool offering a truly spectacular view in return for a very strenuous three-day hike from the nearest road. Elevation 6,900 feet. Open all year.

Natural water flows out of the ground at 115° directly into a shallow soaking pool built at the edge of the Kern River. Water temperature is controlled by adding buckets of cold river water as needed. Bathing suit policy is determined by the mutual consent of those present.

There are no services available except a backpacker campground 100 yards away. The spring is 31.5 miles west of Whitney Portal and 37 miles east of Crescent Meadow. Situated in the mile-deep canyon of the upper Kern River, this spring has magnificent views in all directions. Detailed directions to such a remote location are beyond the scope of this book. We recommend that you purchase *Sierra South*, published by Wilderness Press, and also consult the Tule Ranger District of the Sequoia National Forest, 32588 Highway 190, Springville, CA 93265. 209 539-2607.

Source map: USGS *Kern Peak*.
GPS: N 36.2868 W 118.2428

Justine Hill

Courtesy of California Hot Springs

716   JORDAN HOT SPRING

● **Northwest of the town of Little Lake**

Hot water flows meet with cold creek water on Ninemile Creek in the southernmost part of the Golden Trout Wilderness. Elevation 6,500 feet. Open all year.

Natural mineral water flows out of a spring at approximately 120° down to the river where it may be mixed with cold creek water to form casual pools. Permanent pools are not permitted.

It is six miles to the nearest paved road at Sequoia National Forest Road 21S03, reached via County Road J41 from south of Little Lake on US 395. The trail has an elevation change of 2,500 feet. Detailed directions to such a remote location are beyond the scope of this book. We recommend that you purchase *Exploring the Southern Sierra, East Side*, published by Wilderness Press, and also consult with the Mt. Whitney Ranger District of Inyo National Forest, Lone Pine, CA 93545. 760 873-2408.

GPS: N 36.1375 W 118.1810

Gateway to the Giant Sequoia National Monument.

717   CALIFORNIA HOT SPRINGS
42177 Hot Springs Dr.   661 548-6582
■   California Hot Springs, CA 93207

Historic resort that has been restored and expanded to offer family fun. Located in rolling foothills at the edge of Sequoia National Forest. Elevation 3,100 feet. Open all year except Thanksgiving and the week before Christmas.

Odorless natural mineral water flows out of several artesian wells at a temperature of 125° and is piped to the pool area where there are two large, tiled hydrojet spas maintained at 100° and 104°. A flow-through system eliminates the need for chemical treatment of the water. There is one large swimming pool containing filtered and chlorinated spring water that is maintained at 85° in the summer and 94° in the winter. Handicap access is at west end of pool. Bathing suits are required.

The restored main building houses the office, delicatessen, ice cream parlor, pizza stand, gift shop, and dressing room facilities. With advance notice, meals can be arranged for groups. Massage is available on the premises by appointment only. Full-hookup RV spaces are adjacent to the resort area. Credit cards accepted. It is two miles to a motel, store, and gas station.

Directions: From CA 99 between Fresno and Bakersfield, take the J22 exit at Earlimart and go east 38 miles to the resort.

718 A   REMINGTON HOT SPRINGS
(see map on page 147)
● **Near the town of Lake Isabella**

A delightful, two-person cement tub, an adjoining river-level tub and a one-person tub higher up on a hillside in an unspoiled, primitive, riverside setting of rocks and trees. Located in the Kern River Canyon down a steep trail from old Highway 178. Elevation 2,500 feet. Open all year, except during high water in the river.

Natural mineral water at 104° emerges from the ground at 3.5 gallons per minute. This flow comes directly up through the bottom of a volunteer-built, cement, two-person tub and provides a form of hydrojet action, maintaining the pool temperature at 105°. There is a second, larger tub adjacent to the first and further out into the river. An enlarged and deeper riverside tub, with steps leading to the river is filled by a pipe and drained by pulling the plugs so it can be cleaned. A new cement and rock pool is filled with the overflow from the first pool along with a valve-controlled pipe and is around 98°. Twenty yards uphill is a drainable, one-person rock an cement pool that is fed by a smaller flow of 96° water, and has a valve for draining. The apparent local custom is clothing optional. However, don't be surprised by clothed people floating down river in rafts, inner tubes, or canoes.

There are no services available on the premises. It is six miles to a motel, restaurant, and service station and two miles to a Forest Service campground.

Directions: From Bodfish (by Lake Isabella) drive west on Kern Canyon Rd. (old CA 178, now CA 214) to Hobo Forest Service Campground. Continue west 1.5 miles to a large turnout on the right with a telephone pole in the middle. (This is the second turnout with a telephone pole.) Flat areas for camping can be found near the parking areas. From the parking area, two trails head

The ecosystem in this area is very fragile. Do not attempt to bring vehicles down to the river and please walk on already defined trails to help preserve the vegetation which in turn prevents erosion.

down toward the river, 300 yards below. A steep, narrow dirt trail on the left leads to a flat area along the river where camping is permitted. To reach the tubs, hike down the very steep trail to the right to the rock foundation of an old building. Do not attempt to bring a vehicle down this road as it is often muddy and vehicles can get stuck. Also, it is very destructive to the hillside area. Just before this foundation on your left is a footpath with some natural rock steps leading down toward the river. Under a tree on your left, a spur path leads to the shallow rock and cement pool. Follow the main path to the cement pools by the river. This is not a good area for children, please be careful. (Consider going to Miracle Hot Springs with the kids.) Help keep this special place beautiful by packing out all trash.

GPS: N 35.3454 W 118.3312

Many beautiful stones and jewelry are embedded in the cement around the pools.

Photos by Phil Wilcox

Photos by Phil Wilcox

718 B   MIRACLE HOT SPRINGS

(see map)

● **Near the town of Lake Isabella**

Surrounded by trees and bordered by the beautiful Kern River, five steaming concrete and rock pools have been reconstructed by Friends of the Hot Springs (the associate organization of Miracle Hot Springs Preserve, an incorporated, non-profit organization). The use of the pools is free although there is a charge for parking. The money collected is used to continue rebuilding and maintaining Miracle. Staff is present twenty-four hours a day. Pools are closed between 10 PM and 6 AM; open Saturday and Sunday until midnight. Elevation 2,500 feet.

Natural mineral water bubbles to the surface at 120° and cools to approximately 104° as it flows into five pools, each one successively cooler. The wind from the river keeps the air temperature in the 80s even when it is much hotter away from the pools. Snow melt keeps the river quite cool even in the summer. One pool, now under construction, will be clothing optional during the day. De facto, it is clothing optional after dark.

Store at entrance carries hot and cold beverages, snacks, basic supplies, books and local information. Toilets (handicap accessible) and picnic area are available. Inquire about group rates, frequent-use discount passes, special seminars.

Directions: Take Highway 178 from Bakersfield or Ridgecrest. Four miles west of the town of Lake Isabella turn right on Borel Rd. right. Turn right again at Old Kern Canyon Rd. Approximately two miles down the road is the bridge over Clear Creek. Immediately turn right and then left and look for the sign.

The attempt to keep *Miracle Hot Springs* nice and natural must be succeeding because many avid hot springs goers have described this place as the most beautiful and the cleanest spring they have visited.

Miracle Hot Springs Preserve is operating to preserve and protect the endangered hot springs and the fragile ecosystem in this area. Please join them in this effort. They can be reached at Miracle Hot Springs Preserve, PO Box 782, Lake Isabella, CA 93240-9459. 760 379-4407.

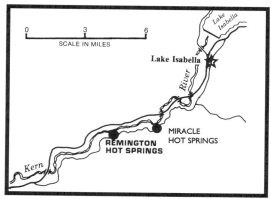

Phil Wilcox

Mark Stover

719   PYRAMID HOT SPRING

● **At the lower end of Kern River Canyon**

A delightful but hard to find, natural pool beneath a giant boulder at the edge of the Kern River. Open all year but not accessible during the high water of spring runoff. Elevation 1,900 feet.

Natural mineral water flows out of the ground at 109°, under a giant boulder, and into a sandy-bottom soaking pool large enough for two people, where it maintains a temperature of 103°. The apparent local custom is clothing optional, but the site is visible to vehicles on CA 178.

There are no services available at the location. It is one and one-third miles east to a Forest Service day-use campground (Live Oak) and fifteen miles to all other services in Bakersfield.

Directions: From Bakersfield, go east on CA 178 to the beginning of the Kern River Canyon. Continue 2.5 miles east beyond dam and power plant to a paved turnout on the left with a 6-foot high pyramid-shaped boulder at its east end. Look across the river slightly westward to locate a large, cube-shaped boulder on the opposite bank. The pool is under that boulder. To reach it, follow the trail from the east end of the turnout to the large downstream boulder where you can hop across the river. Then follow a faint unmarked path upstream to the pool. Stay next to the river and beware of poison oak.

GPS: N 35.2864 W 118.4511

720   SESPE HOT SPRINGS

(see map)

● **Near the Sespe Condor Sanctuary**

A remote, pristine hot spring located in the rugged, desert mountains of a designated wilderness area. Elevation 2,800 feet. Open all year, subject to flash flooding and Forest Service closures.

Natural mineral water flows out of the side of a mountain at 185°, cooling as it flows through a series of shallow, volunteer-built, river-rock soaking pools. The apparent local custom is clothing optional.

There are no services on the premises. Access is via a steep nine-mile hiking trail from Mutau Flat or via a seventeen-mile hiking trail from Lion Campground. Horses and mules are also allowed on the trails. A Forest Service permit is required to enter the area at any time. Be sure to inquire at the Los Padres National Forest office about fire season closures, flood warnings, and the adequacy of your preparations for packing in and packing out.

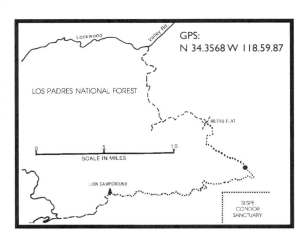

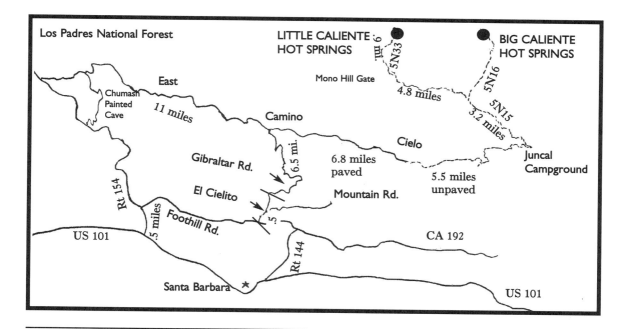

721 THE HOURGLASS

213 W. Cota   805 963-1436
☐   Santa Barbara, CA 93101

Private spa and rental facility located on a creekside residential street near downtown Santa Barbara. Open evenings, Thursday through Sunday.

Three private indoor rooms with pools and eight private outdoor enclosures with pools are for rent to the public. Gas-heated tap water treated with chlorine is maintained at 104°.

A private sauna, a juice bar, and massage are available on the premises. Visa and MasterCard are accepted. Phone for rates, reservations, and directions.

---

722 A LITTLE CALIENTE HOT SPRINGS

(see map)

●   **Near the city of Santa Barbara**

Two small volunteer-built pools in a rocky canyon at the end of a wooded, winding, unpaved Forest Service road. Elevation 1,600 feet. Open all year, subject to fire season and rain/mud closures.

Natural mineral water flows out of a spring at 105° and through a pipe into the upper six-foot by six-foot by eighteen-foot rock and cement soaking pool. From here it spills over into the lower slimy-bottom rock and mud pool where the temperature cools a degree or two. The pipe in the upper pool can be detached to stop the inflow

and control water temperature. Remains of a volunteer-built wooden sunning deck and red wooden benches along the lower pool have collapsed due to erosion. The apparent local custom is clothing optional.

No services are available on the premises. It is one mile to a pack-in campground, six miles to a primitive National Forest campground, and twenty-seven miles to all other services.

Directions: See the directions to Big Caliente. At Juncal Campground, turn left on 5N15 for 3.2 miles where the road forks. Bear left for 4.8 miles where the road forks again. Bear right and drive another .9 miles to the parking area. At the upper end of the parking area, use the makeshift wooden steps to cross the creek and continue walking 100 yards to the spring. The brush becomes gradually greener as you get closer to the springs. Before heading to Little Caliente, it is advisable to check with the ranger station for information on road conditions and where to park. At times several of the gates are locked, (which may require more hiking), but generally the gates are open and you can drive to the spring.

Source map: *Los Padres National Forest.*
GPS: N 34.5405 W 119.6196

> Important Note: According to the sign at the springs all parked vehicles must display a Forest Adventure Pass which is available in town at places like Big 5 Sporting Goods, Mountain Air Sports, Far West Gun and Supply, and Dodge City Gun and Supplies. Be sure to get yours before you take the drive up there!

722 B   BIG CALIENTE HOT SPRINGS
(see map)

- **Near the city of Santa Barbara**

A concrete pool provides a soak at this hot spring located in a sparsely wooded canyon reached via ten miles of very windy, rocky gravel road. Elevation 1,500 feet. Open all year, subject to fire closure and road conditions during rainy season. Check with Los Padres National Forest Ranger Station.

Natural mineral water flows out of a bluff at 115°, then through a faucet-controlled pipe to a six-foot by ten-foot concrete pool. Water temperature in the pool can be controlled by diverting the inflow hose or shutting off the faucet. Please close the valve and divert the hose out of the pool when leaving, to prevent scalding others. When the valve is open, hot water showers into the pool. Continual flow-through keeps the water clean. A galvanized pipe ladder leads into the pool, and concrete decks and benches are on two sides. The apparent custom is clothing optional by mutual consent, although it is advisable to keep bathing suits handy in case the rangers check. Since you can drive right up to the pool, it is handicap accessible with assistance.

A second primitive soaking pool is at creek level below the source spring. From the far end of the parking area, a marked trail leads off toward Big Caliente Debris Dam. Across the creek, water seeps down the mountain from a source spring under a cottonwood tree to the primitive 105° pool at creek level, which fills up with silt and mud and needs to be dredged periodically. This pool can be reached by rock-hopping where a pipe is visible underwater, approximately 100 yards from the trailhead.

Facilities include nearby changing rooms, clean pit toilets across the level parking area, and a picnic table under the trees. A trail from the changing rooms leads down to the cold creek, which has small waterfalls and several small sunning beaches. Several primitive Forest Service campgrounds are within three miles, and it is twenty-five miles to all other services in Santa Barbara.

Directions: Coming from the south on Hwy 101 in Santa Barbara, take Milpas St. exit (Rte. 144). Follow Rte. 144 east through city residential streets, and a five-point roundabout, for a total of 6.3 miles, to the end at Rte. 192. Turn left on Rte. 192 (Stanwood Dr.) for 1.2 miles to El Cielito Rd. At .3 miles, El Cielito crosses Mountain Dr. Continue straight uphill on El Cielito .5 miles to Gibraltar Rd. Turn right and follow Gibraltar for approximately 6.5 miles to the end at East Camino Cielo. Turn right on very windy East Camino Cielo which is paved for the first 6.8 miles, then unsurfaced for the next 5.5 miles. At Juncal Campground, turn left on 5N15 for 3.2 miles where the road forks. Take the right fork (5N16) 2.5 miles to the spring. (The left fork goes to Little Caliente.)

Coming from the north on Hwy 101, take Rte. 154 exit, heading east for .5 miles to Rte. 192 (called Foothill Rd.). At 4.7 miles is a reservoir (Foothill has changed to Mountain Dr. and again to Mission Ridge). At .4 miles past the reservoir, Rte. 192 makes a sharp left at a fire station and becomes Stanwood Dr. Follow Stanwood to El Cielito Rd. and continue as described above.

Source map: *Los Padres National Forest.*
GPS: N 34.5392 W 119.5646

Little Caliente (above) and *Big Caliente* (below) are the only natural hot springs accessible to the public in the Santa Barbara area.

Photos by Chris Andrews

723   LAS CRUCES HOT SPRINGS

(see map)

● Near Gaviota State Park

Two primitive, mud-bottom pools on a tree-shaded slope a few miles from the ocean. Elevation 500 feet. Open all year for day-use only.

Natural mineral water emerges at 96° directly into a shallow, knee-deep rock and mud soaking pool with relatively clear water, large enough for six to eight people. The overflow forms a waterfall over the earthen retaining wall into the larger lower pool, which averages 80° and has a slimy bottom. The water is murky. Clothing is optional with the mutual consent of those present.

There are no services available on the premises and overnight parking is prohibited in the parking area at the trailhead where a day-use self-parking fee is charged. Rangers check frequently and cite vehicles without valid parking receipts. It is three miles to a campground with RV hookups and six miles to all other services.

Directions: On Hwy 101 approximately 35 miles north of Santa Barbara is Gaviota State Beach with its landmark railroad bridge. From here it is 3 miles to the turnoff for CA 1, west toward Lompoc. Directly across from this turnoff is the small road paralleling the highway and heading south to the parking area for Las Cruces. After Gaviota State Beach you will pass a rest area and go through a tunnel. It is 1 mile past the tunnel to the turnoff.

From the parking area, follow the steep dirt 4WD trail to where it forks at a white sign saying "no horses past this point." Bear right on a narrow trail approximately .75 miles from the parking area to the pools.

Oscar Voss

Marjorie Young

Avila Hot Springs has been in the hot water business since 1907, continually updating what is offered to the public to keep up with the times.

724   AVILA VALLEY HOT SPRINGS SPA AND RV PARK

250 Avila Beach Drive   805 595-2359
■ San Luis Obispo, CA 93405

RV resort with natural hot mineral water located in a foothill hollow at a freeway exit. Elevation 40 feet. Open all year.

Natural mineral water flows out of an artesian well at 130° and is piped to the outdoor twenty-foot square soaking pool (104-107°) which is drained and filled daily and requires no chemicals. The fifty-foot by one-hundred-foot outdoor swimming pool (86°) is filled with tap water and treated with chlorine and now has two small water slides. Bathing suits are required.

Massage, pizza kitchen and grill, arcade, RV hook-ups, lawn tent spaces, and a small store are located on the premises. All spa treatments include unlimited use of the pools. Major credit cards are accepted. It is one mile to all services in San Luis Obispo.

Directions: From San Luis Obispo, drive south 8 miles on US 101, take the Avila Beach Dr. exit (not San Luis Bay Dr.), and go north 1 block to the resort entrance.

Photos courtesy of Sycamore Mineral Springs

725　SYCAMORE MINERAL SPRINGS

1215 Avila Beach Dr.　　805 595-7302
800 234-5831

■　San Luis Obispo, CA 93401
www.sycamoresprings.com

Delightful resort offering secluded redwood hot tubs out under the oaks and a private redwood mineral spa on the balcony of every hotel room. Located on a wooded rural hillside two miles from the ocean. Elevation 40 feet. Open all year, twenty-four hours per day.

Natural mineral water is pumped from a well at 110° and piped to the tubs on the hillside and on the hotel balconies. Each tub has a hot mineral water faucet and a cold tap water faucet. Each tub also has its own jet pump, filter, and automatic chlorinator. The swimming pool is filled with tap water treated with chlorine. The" oasis," a natural-looking rock spa that will hold thirty people, is located next to the pool. Bathing suits are required except in the hillside hot tub. Some pools and areas are handicap accessible.

Facilities include a restaurant, hotel rooms and suites with hot tubs on the balcony (complete with a full breakfast), new deluxe suites with spas and fireplaces, a one-bedroom cottage with its own hot tub in a private enclosure, dressing rooms, meeting space, and a gift shop. Building continues on several new buildings which will provide more luxurious accommodations. Several varieties of massage and facials are available. A half-hour soak in one of the outdoor tubs is included in each appointment. On request, directions to a nearby clothing-optional state beach will be provided. Major credit cards accepted. Phone for rates and reservations.

Directions: From US 101 8 miles south of San Luis Obispo, take the Avila Beach exit, then go 1 mile west on Avila Beach Dr. and watch for the resort sign on the south side of the road.

Photos by Marjorie Young

726 A   FRANKLIN LAKES HOT SPRINGS

● **Near the town of Paso Robles**

Soaking tub, swimming area, and fishing hole in the rolling hills outside Paso Robles. Be prepared to see many species of waterfowl, muskrat, beaver and even huge turtles. Open all year, sunrise to dusk. Small fee.

A thousand-foot-deep well produces 98° water at over 700 gallons per minute. At this printing, new soaking tubs are under construction, but there is a temporary pool for soaking where the water is piped into the soaking pool and then spills into a large (five acres) stocked fishing lake. The water is high in sulfur and has some sodium bicarbonate.

Picnic tables and toilets are provided and there are plans to build changing rooms and showers. Bathing suits are required. Alcohol is prohibited.

Directions: From 101 southbound at Paso Robles take the 16th St. exit and turn left on Riverside Dr. Go .8 miles to 13th St. and turn left. 13th St. becomes Creston Rd. Continue 4.5 miles on Creston Rd. to the hot springs.

From 101 northbound at Paso Robles take the Spring St. exit and go right on Niblick Ave. Go 1.8 miles to Creston Rd. and turn right. Continue 2.3 miles to the hot springs.

GPS: N 35.58993 W 120.64258

The soaking pond on the left, complete with sunshade, is temporary until the more permanent pools are finished. The water from the pond flows over into the five-acre lake where you can fish and swim.

The Inn was a fashionable favorite among sports heroes, millionaires, political bigwigs and Hollywood movie stars in its heyday. Today it is being restored to its former glory. The Inn is set in a tranquil setting of lush gardens and oak trees.

726 B   PASO ROBLES INN

■

1103 Spring St.	805 238-2660
Paso Robles, CA 93446	800 676-1713
www.pasoroblesinn.com	

Originally built in 1864 and featuring a hot mineral springs bathhouse. The Inn, now a member of the National Trust Historic Hotels of America, has been completely refurbished. Located on the main street in Paso Robles. Open all year.

A newly redrilled geothermal well supplies the hot mineral water to the Inn's hot springs wing which features a mix of personal therapy spas and larger, family jet tubs. The pools themselves sit on the balconies which can be closed off with canvas curtains for a private soak. There are fireplaces in each room. There is also a large swimming pool and hot tub. Most of the rooms overlook the beautiful garden court. There is an indoor dining room, as well as one outdoors and a coffee shop.

Future plans include eighteen new spa rooms, the restoration of the hundred-year-old Grand Ballroom, a full-service health spa and salon with indoor/outdoor mineral water plunge bath, and a state-of-the-art conference center and meeting space. Phone for status of construction.

Beautiful Garden Setting

726 C PASO ROBLES HOT SPRINGS AND SPA
■
3725 Buena Vista Dr.   805 238-4600
Paso Robles, CA 93446
www.pasohotsprings.com

Located amidst North County's rolling hills and beautiful wine country with both indoor patio spas and outdoor pools. Elevation 100 feet. Open all year.

An artesian well with a very mild mineral and sulphur content fills all of the tubs. The spa pavillion offers five patio spas which are cleaned and refilled daily, filtered every three minutes, and require only minimal chemical treatment. Three outdoor, private tubs set into the hillside and named after varieties of your favorite wine, offer views of the rolling hills and magnificent oaks. The water in all the tubs is kept at 104° with the ability to add additional hot or cold water. The indoor premises are handicap equipped, the tubs with assistance.

Facials and massage include a half-hour soak. The lakeside setting offers a wonderful site for weddings and special events for up to 350 guests. Plans are to develop this into a large destination resort, complete with equestrian center.

Location: Conveniently situated off Hwy 46 East on Buena Vista Dr.

Photos by Marjorie Young

You have a choice at this beautiful new spa. You can choose an indoor soak and be pampered at the spa pavillion, or you can choose to soak out under the oaks and enjoy nature.

Esalen is in the process of building new decks and pools. Until they are finished, use is restricted to those people registered at the Institute.

---

727   ESALEN INSTITUTE
Workshop, Room Reservations
831 667-3000

■   Big Sur, CA 93920
www.esalen.org

Primarily an educational/experiential center rather than a hot spring resort. Located on CA 1, 45 miles south of Monterey. Elevation 100 feet. Open all year.

Esalen specializes in residential programs that focus on education, philosophy, and the physical and behavioral sciences. Access to the grounds is by reservation only for those wishing to take workshops or rent an available cabin. The hot springs are also open by reservation for up to thirty-two people each weekday morning from 1 AM to 3:30 AM at a charge. To make a bath reservation, please call 831 667-3047. (This procedure will resume after the tubs destroyed during El Nino are rebuilt–hopefully by the summer of 2001. Call for status.)

Natural mineral water flows out of the ground at 120° and into a bathhouse built on a cliff face, fifty feet above a rocky ocean beach. During El Nino, many of the baths were destroyed. Currently the temporary baths are limited to registered guests only. Handicap access is limited; make arrangements in advance.

Facilities include housing and a dining room for registered guests. It is eleven miles to a restaurant, store, and service station. Massage is available on the premises. Visa, MasterCard, and American Express are accepted for registered guests.

728   BUDDHIST MEDITATION CENTER

Overnight Reservations   415 865-1899
Day Reservations   408 659-2229

■   Carmel Valley, CA 93924

Primarily a Buddhist Monastery with accommodations available to the public from early May to early September. Located in wooded mountains southeast of Monterey. Elevation 1,500 feet.

Please, no drop-in visitors. Prior reservations are required. Guests are expected to respect the spirit of a monastic community.

Natural mineral water flows out of the ground at 140° into two large, enclosed soaking pools that average 110° and two outdoor pools at 106°. The water, which is not chemically treated, cools as it flows into nearby streambed soaking areas. The outdoor swimming pool is approximately 75°. There are also steambaths in the separate men's and women's bathhouses. Bathing suits are required in the swimming pool only.

Rooms and meals are included as part of confirmed overnight reservation arrangements. The use of meditation facilities is also included. No credit cards are accepted. It is ninety minutes to a store, cafe, and service station. The road is steep and dangerous, requiring good brakes and low gears.

Susan Harris

729   PARAISO HOT SPRINGS

831 678-2882

■   Soledad, CA 93960

A quiet resort for adults, with several acres of tree-shaded grass areas, located on the west slopes of the Salinas Valley. Elevation 1,200 feet. Open all year.

Natural mineral water flows out of the ground at 115° and is piped to three pools: an indoor soaking pool with temperatures ranging from 104-106°, an outdoor soaking pool with temperatures between 100-102°, and an outdoor swimming pool with a temperature of 80°. The swimming pool is treated with chlorine. Bathing suits are required. No cut-offs permitted.

Cottages, RV spaces, overnight camping, a snack bar, and a cocktail lounge are available on the premises. Credit cards accepted. It is eight miles to a restaurant and service station.

Directions: From US 101, exit on Arroyo Seco Rd., 1 mile south of Soledad. Go 1 mile west to stop sign, then go straight onto Paraiso Springs Rd. Continue uphill for 6 miles to resort at end of road.

730   SYKES HOT SPRING

(see map)

●   Near the village of Big Sur

Remote, undeveloped hot spring on the Big Sur River in the Ventana Wilderness portion of the Los Padres National Forest. Elevation 1,110 feet. May be submerged during high water in the river.

Natural mineral water flows out of the ground at 100° from under a fallen tree and into a volunteer-built shallow soaking pool. There is also a riverside pool large enough for abour five people. This location involves a ten-mile hike on the Pine Ridge Trail, and a Wilderness Permit must be obtained from the Forest Service. The spring is near one of the most popular hiking routes, so the distance is no assurance of quiet or privacy during the summer months.

The Forest Service issues a trail map to those holding Wilderness Permits, and on request, will mark the hot-spring location on that map. Check your preparations, including water supply, with the ranger.

Source maps for trails: USGS *Ventana Cones, Partington Ridge* (springs not shown).

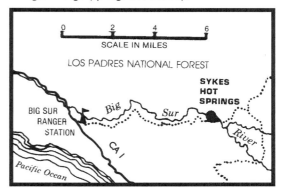

Courtesy of Mercey Hot Springs

731 MERCEY HOT SPRINGS
■ 62964 Little Panoche Rd. 209 826-3388
Firebaugh, CA 93622
www.merceyhotsprings.com

One hundred sixty acres of rolling hills in California's central valley is home to the only hot spring resort in this area. Spring and Fall are choice times to visit when you can spend warm days in the swimming pool and cool evenings in one of the hot tubs. Altitude 1,200 feet. Open all year.

Natural hot mineral water comes out of a spring at temperatures of 119° and fills a swimming pool kept at a low of 75° in the winter and 94° in the summer. A clothing-optional community hot tub is maintained at 106°. Currently, there are two private indoor tubs and one outdoor soaking tub. (More tubs are planned in the near future.) Chlorine is only used in the swimming pool and bathing suits are required. New tubs will be handicap accessible.

Cabins with and without kitchens and fireplaces are available for rent. The hotel is being refurbished and is expected to open in late fall of 2001. There are also camping spaces and full RV hookups although electricity is provided only when the resort generator is running. Day-use entitles you to the use of the picnic areas, swimming pool, and public hot tub. Groups of ten or more get a ten percent discount. Gas and camping supplies can be bought thirty-five miles away in Los Banos. (A small store is expected to be open by spring of 2001.)

Directions: From the North—go south on I-5 for 24 miles past the I-5/Hwy 152 interchange. (Do not take the Mercey Hot Springs Rd. exit!) At the Shields Ave./Little Panoche Rd. exit (J1), go right (west) for 13 miles.

From the South—go north on I-5 for 70 miles past Coalinga to the Shields Ave./Little Panoche Rd. exit (J1). You must go past the Panoche Rd. exit 11 miles to reach the Little Panoche Rd. exit. Take a left and drive west for 13 miles.

732 A HEARTWOOD SPA
□ 3150A Mission Dr. 831 462-2192
Santa Cruz, CA 95065
www.heartwood-spa.com

A clothing-optional, tree-shaded hot tub rental establishment located on a quiet suburban side street with a beautiful garden filled with blooming plants and shade trees.

A wooden hot tub, cold tub, sauna, and communal sunning areas are available for a day-rate charge. One private redwood tub with a water temperature of 105° can be rented by the hour. All pools use gas-heated tap water treated with chlorine. The private tub area is wheelchair accessible. Bathing suits are optional everywhere except at the front desk.

Massage is available on the premises. The entire facility may be reserved for private parties before and after regular business hours. No credit cards are accepted. Gift certificates available. Phone for rates, reservations, and directions. (Community area open on Sunday evenings for women only.)

Jayson Loam

Marjorie Young

732 B   KIVA RETREAT

☐   702 Water St.   831 429-1142
          Santa Cruz, CA 95060

Trees, grass, and flowers lend a parklike setting to this unusual, clothing-optional, hot-pool rental establishment. Located near the city center.

A single day rate gives entry to the communal grass area, two large hot tubs, a cold-tub plunge, and a large sauna. Adjoining indoor dressing and social rooms are also available. Pools use gas-heated tap water and are treated with chlorine and ozone. Two private enclosures, rented by the hour, have water maintained at 102°. Bathing suits are optional everywhere except in the front entry.

Massage is available on the premises. Major credit cards are accepted. Phone for rates, reservations, and directions.

732 C   TEA HOUSE SPA

☐   112 Elm St.   831 458-9355
          Santa Cruz, CA 95060

Beautiful hot pool and sauna rooms overlooking a Japanese bamboo garden, located in the heart of downtown Santa Cruz and available for rent by the hour.

Four private-space suites, consisting of a shower, changing area, and tub use bromine-treated tap water. The fiberglass pools offer a view of the garden and a sliding glass door can be opened. Two of the suites also offer saunas. Water temperatures are maintained at 104°. Many of the tubs are handicap accessible. Herbal tea and large towels are provided.

Massage is available on the premises. Credit cards accepted. Phone for rates and reservations.

Photo courtesy of Well Within

Marjorie Young

732 D   WELL WITHIN

☐

417 Cedar St.   831 458-WELL

Santa Cruz, CA 95060

New, beautifully appointed hot pool establishment with Japanese gardens and waterfalls visible from the individual rooms. Located in downtown Santa Cruz and available for rent by the hour.

Four private indoor tubs and two outdoor tubs are maintained at approximately 102°. Two of the indoor tubs and both outdoor tubs have saunas. The outdoor tubs can accommodate up to six people each and the gate between the two tubs can be opened to hold up to fourteen people. The tubs are treated with bromine. The entire facility is handicap accessible and one of the outdoor tubs is equipped with special railings.

A shower and changing area are found in each room. Towels and herbal tea are included. Massage and skin care services are available by appointment. Visa and MasterCard are accepted. Phone for rates, reservations, and directions.

733   GILROY YAMATO HOT SPRINGS

■

Phone: 415 434-2180

Fax: 415 333-3550

www.gilroyhotspringsresort.com

Two indoor bathhouses, an outdoor soaking pool and a few cabins are all that remain of a 242-acre resort first built in the late 1860s. Located in the oak-studded foothills adjacent to Henry Coe State Park, the facility offers lovely areas for hiking, picnicking, and just relaxing and enjoying the beautiful natural surroundings and wildlife. Designated a state historical landmark. Open by reservation only (do not go without one as you will be turned away).

Hot mineral water comes out of a spring at temperatures ranging from 100-105° and is piped directly into the large tiled soaking tubs in the separate men's and women's bathhouses (no suits allowed). The spring also feeds the outdoor cement pool where large rocks are used as seats. All pools operate on a flow-through basis and require no chemicals.

Dressing areas in each bathhouse with places to rest. Picnic tables are also available. The current owners are in the process of some major renovations and hope to reopen the resort. Suggested items to bring with you: bathtowel, lunch, drinks, empty container for spring water (up to two gallons per person), bathrobe, sandals, slippers, camera, bathing suit for outdoor tub. No children under three are allowed.

Phone or fax for reservations and directions.

**734   GRAND CENTRAL SAUNA AND
HOT TUB CO.**
☐   376 Saratoga Ave.   408 247-8827
San Jose, CA 95129

One of a chain of urban locations established by Grand Central, the pioneer in the room rent-a-tub business.

Twenty-one private indoor tubs are heated to 102-104° and treated with chlorine. The individual rooms each have a sauna and dressing room. Towels and soap are provided.

No credit cards or reservations are accepted. Phone for hours, rates, and directions.

735   WATERCOURSE WAY
☐   165 Channing Ave.   650 462-2000
Palo Alto, CA 94301
www.watercoursway.com

The beautiful oriental decor creates a comfortable and interesting environment, offering a variety of enjoyable rooms and experiences.

Pools for rent to the public use gas-heated tap water treated with chlorine. Nine individually decorated private rooms each have a different combination of hot pool, cold pool, sauna, and steambath. Water temperature in the pools is approximately 103°. To accommodate larger groups, two rooms can be joined.

Facials, spa treatments, and massage (specializing in hot-stone massage) are available on the premises. Visa and MasterCard are accepted. Phone for rates, reservations, and directions.

736 A   THE HOT TUBS
☐   2200 Van Ness Ave.   415 441-TUBS
San Francisco, CA 94109

One of the few stress-reduction establishments offering tile tubs and decks in a chrome and glass urban environment. Located on a main street just west of downtown.

Pools in twenty private rooms are for rent to the public. Gas-heated tap water treated with chlorine is maintained at 104°. A sauna, music, and rest area are included. Towels and soap are provided.

Massage and a juice bar are available on the premises. No credit cards are accepted. Phone for rates, reservations, and directions.

736 B   FAMILY SAUNA SHOP
2308 Clement St.   415 221-2208
☐   San Francisco, CA 94121

One of the pioneer stress-reduction centers in San Francisco. Located in the Richmond district.

Two private rooms with pools for rent to the public use gas-heated tap water treated with chlorine. Water temperature is 104°.

Four private saunas are available for rent. Massage and facials are available on the premises. Visa and MasterCard are accepted. Phone for rates, reservations, and directions.

**736 C   GRAND CENTRAL SAUNA AND
HOT TUB CO.**
15 Fell St.   415 431-1370
☐   San Francisco, CA 94102

The first of a chain of urban locations established by Grand Central, a pioneer in the private room rent-a-tub business.

Pools in twenty-six private rooms, each with a sauna, are for rent to the public. The pools use gas-heated tap water treated with chlorine and are maintained between 102-104°. Towels and soap are provided.

Tanning booths are available on the premises. Credit cards are not accepted. Reservations are not accepted. Phone for rates and directions.

The brochure for *The Hot Tubs* welcomes you to "The Home of the 60-Minute Vacation." and "A Total Relaxation Experience." Sounds great!

737 F. JOSEPH SMITH'S MASSAGE THERAPY

158 Almonte   415 383-8260

☐ Mill Valley, CA 94941

www.josephsmithmassage.com

A Marin county healing center with two five-foot deep hot tubs nestled under redwood trees, located in a country setting.

Two private enclosures with chlorine-treated water and temperatures of approximately 104° are rented to the public. One of the tubs is available for communal use during the day. A sauna is also for rent. Bathing suits are optional in the tub and sauna areas.

The prayer garden is open for relaxation and meditation. The crystal room also provides a space to meditate. Massage and advanced body therapy classes are available on the premises, as are chiropractic and acupuncture services. Massage classes and workshop space are available. Phone for rates, reservations, and directions.

738 SHIBUI GARDENS

19 Tamalpais Ave.   415 457-0283

☐ San Anselmo, CA 94960

An inviting blend of Marin County natural redwood hot tubs and lush landscaping. Located on a suburban side street.

Three privately enclosed hot tubs using bromine-treated, gas-heated tap water are for rent by the hour. Water temperatures are 101°. Enclosures are also equipped with cold showers. Bathing suits are optional inside the pool and sauna spaces.

A private indoor sauna is for rent on the premises. Massage is available. Phone for rates, reservations, and directions.

739 FROGS

School Street Plaza   415 453-7647

☐ Fairfax, CA 94930

One of the first rent-a-tub facilities in the San Francisco Bay area. Located in a Marin County suburb and kept in pristine condition.

There are two outdoor hot tubs in private enclosures, plus a large communal hot tub and a cold plunge. There are two saunas, one completely redone in cedar, (and kept at the hottest temperatures in the Bay area) and a completely renovated clothing-optional sundeck.

Voted "Best of Marin" for massage therapy, with therapists available until midnight. Walk-ins encouraged. Phone for rates, reservations, and directions.

740 ALBANY SAUNA AND HOT TUBS

1002 Solano Ave.   510 525-6262

☐ Albany, CA 94706

www.albanysauna.com

Established in 1934 as one of the earliest rent-a-tub establishments in the Bay Area, it has since been extensively remodeled. Located two blocks west of San Pablo Ave.

Three outdoor, privately enclosed pools for rent to the public use gas-heated tap water treated with chlorine and cleaned with a diatomaceous earth filtering system. Water temperature is maintained at approximately 105°. There are railings throughout the facility.

Four private rock-steam saunas, individually controlled for temperature with an outside air source for comfortable breathing, are available for rent. Swedish-Esalen massage, and hair and skin care products are available on the premises. Major credit cards are accepted. Phone for rates, reservations, and directions.

Courtesy of Albany Sauna

741 A THE HOT TUBS

1915 University Ave.   510 843-4343
☐ Berkeley, CA 94704

One of two urban locations in Berkeley and San Francisco.

Fourteen private rooms with pools use gas-heated tap water treated with chlorine. Water temperature varies between 102-104°. A sauna is included.

Towels and soap are provided. A juice bar is available on the premises. No credit cards or checks. Reservations are not accepted. Phone for rates and directions.

741 B THE BERKELEY SAUNA

1947 Milvia St.   510 845-2341
☐ Berkeley, CA 94704

A stress-reduction establishment located a few yards north of University Ave.

Three private rooms with hot tubs, filled with gas-heated tap water. The bromine-treated water is maintained at temperatures from 104-106°.

Three private saunas are also for rent. Massage is available on the premises. Credit cards accepted. Phone for rates, reservations, and directions.

742 A AMERICAN FAMILY SAUNA AND HOT TUB

2367 Pleasant Hill Rd.   925 472-0852
☐ Pleasant Hill, CA 94523

Outdoor rent-a-tub establishment located near intersection of Gregory and Pleasant Hill Rd.

Eleven private outdoor tubs are for rent by the hour. Gas-heated tap water treated with chlorine is maintained at 102-104°. Sauna and massage are available on the premises. Major credit cards accepted. Phone for rates, reservations, and directions.

742 B SUNSHINE SPA

1948 Contra Costa Blvd.   925 685-7822
☐ Pleasant Hill, CA 94523

Funky, fun-loving, rent-a-tub business, that prides itself on its great massages. Located in the Pleasant Hill Plaza, fifteen miles east of Oakland.

Pools using gas-heated tap water treated with bromine are for rent to the public. There are seven private rooms, each with an in-ground hot tub, shower, massage table, and mural. Pool temperatures range from 90-102°. Handicap accessible.

Massage is available on the premises. Major credit cards accepted. Phone for rates, reservations, and directions.

743 PIEDMONT SPRINGS

3939 Piedmont   510 652-9191
☐ Oakland, CA 94611
www.piedmontsprings.com

Urban rent-a-tub establishment situated in downtown Oakland.

Four hot tubs, one in combination with a sauna, were built outdoors in private enclosures, complete with redwood decks, changing areas, and showers. Water temperature is maintained at 102-104° and can be cooled down with hoses. All tubs are chlorine treated.

Massage, facials, salt scrubs, and other skin care treatments are available. Phone for rates, reservations, directions, or a brochure .

744 HOT TROPICS

17389 Hesperion Blvd.   510 278-8827
☐ San Lorenzo, CA 94580

Seniors, families, singles, and couples are welcome at this rent-a-tub establishment just a couple of blocks off Hwy 880.

Fourteen private indoor rooms with tubs heated to 102-105° and treated with chlorine. Seven rooms are also equipped with saunas, futons, showers, and radios. Seven rooms do not have saunas but do have large skylights that roll open when the weather permits. Special minerals are added to the tubs. Handicap accessible.

Available on the premises are eleven state-of-the-art tanning booths.

No credit cards or reservations are accepted. Phone for hours, rates, and directions.

745 PARADISE SPAS

5168 Mowry Ave.   510 793-7727
☐ Fremont, CA 94538
www.paradisetans.aol.com

Suburban rent-a-tub and tanning center located in a shopping center just off Highway 880.

Eight private rooms, including two with special black lighting, come complete with tubs and showers. The water is heated to 102-104° and is chlorine treated. Towels and radios are supplied.

Tanning booths are available. Visa and MasterCard are accepted. Phone for reservations.

SOUTHERN CALIFORNIA

This map was designed to be used with a standard highway map.

MAP SYMBOLS

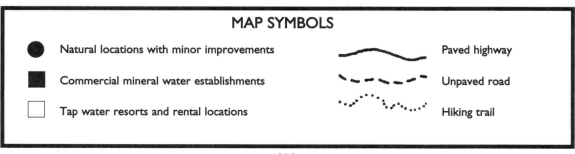

● Natural locations with minor improvements

■ Commercial mineral water establishments

□ Tap water resorts and rental locations

〜 Paved highway

--- Unpaved road

⋯ Hiking trail

801 A FURNACE CREEK INN RESORT

PO Box 1   760 786-2345

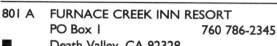 Death Valley, CA 92328

www.furnacecreekresort.com

An historic resort built around a lush oasis on a barren hillside overlooking Death Valley. Elevation, sea level. Open mid-October to mid-May.

Natural mineral water flows out of a spring at 89°, into two outdoor pools, and through a large, palm-shaded arroyo. The swimming pool maintains a temperature of approximately 85°, and the flow-through rate is so great that no chemical treatment of the water is necessary. Bathing suits are required. Pools are for the use of registered guests only.

Facilities include two saunas, lighted tennis courts, rooms, two restaurants, live entertainment, dancing, and a bar. Major credit cards accepted.

801 B FURNACE CREEK RANCH RESORT

PO Box 1   760 786-2345

Death Valley, CA 92328

A family setting, the Furnace Creek Ranch was the home of the original "20-mule team." Located just down the hill from the Furnace Creek Inn in a green oasis setting surrounded by Death Valley National Park. Elevation 214 feet. below sea level. Open all year.

Water from a natural warm spring is piped down from the 89° spring serving the Inn to a swimming pool at the ranch. The rate of flow-through is so great that a temperature of approximately 85° is maintained and no chemical treatment is necessary. The pool is for the enjoyment of registered guest only. Bathing suits are required. Most facilities are handicap accessible; handicap rooms are available.

Other amenities include 224 guest accommodations (all recently refurbished), three restaurants, a saloon, three retail shops, a service station, an eighteen-hole golf course, tennis courts, basketball courts, a children's playground, and horseback riding (October-May). All major credit cards accepted. Contact resort for further information.

Skip Hill

802 A   WARM SPRINGS

● **North of Shoshone,
In Death Valley National Park**

Fig trees, bamboo, mesquite, oleanders, cottonwood trees, tamarisk, and lots of grapevines line the trail to this warm spring located in a rocky canyon near several abandoned buildings and mines. Open all year, weather dependent.

Natural mineral water trickles out of the rocks at the top of a canyon creating a small pool about four-feet wide, six-feet long, and maybe a foot deep. The water temperature is 94°. The cooler water in this very hot climate would be great on one of those baking desert days.

No services on the premises but camping is not prohibited. All services are back in Shoshone.

Directions: One and one-half miles north of Shoshone, turn west on SR 178 heading toward Badwater. Continue 28 miles past Ashford Junction to West Side Rd. Turn west on this good gravel road for 3 miles, then turn left on Butte Valley Road and go 11 miles that gets worse and worse the closer you get to the springs. You will travel through an abandoned talc mlne as you head west through a canyon just before the turnoff to the springs. On the left at the base of the mountains are some large trees and the parking area.

GPS: N 35.57995 W 116.55918

802 B   SHOSHONE INN

Box 67   760 852-4335
■   Shoshone, CA 92384
www.shoshonevillage.com

Older resort located on CA 127 in desert foothills near the southern entrance to Death Valley. Elevation 1,600 feet. Open all year.

Natural mineral water flows out of a spring at 93° with such pressure that no pumps are needed to push it through the pipes to the outdoor swimming pool. The rate of flow-through is so great that a temperature of 92° is maintained and no chemical treatment of the water is necessary. A waterfall at the end of the pool cools the inflow for pool use in the summer. Pool use is available only to registered guests. Bathing suits are required.

Sixteen rooms, recently remodeled to include phones and cable TV, a restaurant, bar, store, and service station. RV hookups and overnight camping spaces are available at the Shoshone RV Park (802 C). Major credit cards are accepted.

Location: Shoshone is 28 miles south of Death Valley Junction and 58 miles north of Baker on CA 127.

802 C   SHOSHONE RV PARK

■ Box 67   760 852-4569

Shoshone, CA 92384

Lush, green, tree-shaded RV park one hundred yards north of the Shoshone Inn on the main street (CA 127) in Shoshone.

The natural mineral water outdoor swimming pool described at left is adjacent to the RV park and is for the use of registered guests of either facility and for local residents. Non-guests may use the pool by paying a day use fee (which is the same as the overnight RV park fee).

Half the hot geothermal well water supplies the RV park's showers, the inn, and the pool; the other half is used for the town water supply. A reverse osmosis process is used to treat all the water

Major credit cards accepted.

Shoshone and Tecopa photos by Justine Hill

803 A   DELIGHT'S HOT SPA

■ Box 368   760 852-4343

Tecopa, CA 92389

One of the original hot spring spas in the arid, alkali desert east of Death Valley, originally established in the early 1940s. For adults only (ages 21-101). Elevation 1,400 feet. Open all year.

Hundreds of warm mineral springs supply water to the entire region. Delight's has four large, three-foot deep, private, coed cement tubs that hold two to three people. Water flows from a 285-foot artesian well into three of the tubs. The fourth is fed by a small spring that comes directly into the spring house, where it measures 106°. Pools are open from 5 AM to 9 PM and are drained and scrubbed nightly. A new radical hydroxil system will ensure chemical-free water. Pools have stairs and bars and are handicap accessible with assistance. No suits allowed in the pools.

Facilities include rustic housekeeping cottages with refrigeration (no TVs, radios, or phones), full hookup RV spaces, showers, and rest rooms. The clubhouse has a stage, pool table, and fireplace and is large enough for banquets and weddings. Plans are to build new pools and add to existing services. Call for status of construction. It is two miles to all other services in Tecopa.

Directions: From CA 127, 5 miles south of Shoshone or 50 Miles north of Baker, drive east on Tecopa Hot Springs Rd. for 3 miles. A red windmill and sign to the spa are on the east side of the street.

803 B TECOPA HOT SPRINGS (OPERATED BY INYO COUNTY PARKS AND RECREATION DEPT.)

PO Box 158   760 852-4264

■   Tecopa, CA 92389

A county-operated RV park, bathhouse and campground located on the Tecopa loop off CA 127. Elevation 1,400 feet. Open all year, seven days a week, twenty-four hours a day; free to park users and the general public.

Natural mineral water flows out of a spring at 108° and is piped to separate men's and women's bathhouses. The women's side has two gravel-bottom, three-foot deep soaking pools maintained at 100° and 105°, plus an enclosed outdoor sunbathing area. The men's tubs are cement. The indoor pool is twelve by twelve and the enclosed outdoor pool is eight-feet by twelve-feet; both pools have steps and grab bars for handicap access. Posted signs require nude bathing. Mixed bathing is not permitted.

A fee is charged for RV hookups and overnight spaces on the premises. There is an air-conditioned community center with library, exercise classes, and social activities. No credit cards are accepted. It is two miles to a store and eight miles to a service station.

The separate men's and women's bathhouses and sunning decks have a long history of no bathing suits allowed. While there has been some attempt to change this custom it has not been successful as of yet.

Justine Hill

803 C TECOPA DESERT POND

●   **Near the town of Tecopa**

A cement-bottom tub with cement steps, located on an open stretch of flat white alkali BLM desert. Elevation 1,400 feet. Open all year.

Natural 98° mineral water flows in through a pipe from an artesian well next to the six-foot by six-foot by two and one-half-foot pool, with overflow running off the far side of the pool in a continual flow-through pattern. During times of low flow there is often a great deal of algae growing and cleaning the pool, which can only be done with buckets and a hose, is left to volunteers,. Clothing is optional.

There are no facilities on the premises. Overnight parking for one night is not prohibited on BLM desert, but not near the pool itself. Partying remains are often evident near the pool. It is one mile to all services in Tecopa.

Directions: Located on the Tecopa loop of CA 127, 5 miles south of Shoshone, 50 miles north of Baker, and 27 miles southwest of Pahrump, NV on CA 178/NV 372. One block south of Delight's Hot Spa on Tecopa Hot Springs Rd. and just north of the county-run Tecopa Hot Springs bathhouse, turn east at the sign saying "Slow, Entering County Park, Co." At .3 miles pass a large duck pond on your left, and the gravel road bears right. Do not bear right, but continue straight ahead on the ungraded, unsurfaced road across the alkali desert. At .2 miles, go to the left of the log barrier and keep driving on the rough road toward the only cluster of green foliage in the area. The tub is at the foot of the small palm tree, a total of .9 miles from Hot Springs Rd. During the rainy season, the road may be impassable.

803 D   TECOPA MUD BATHS

● **Near the town of Tecopa**

Warm, smooth, clay-mud lines the bottom and sides of this undeveloped, natural hot springs less than a mile from the better-known Tecopa Hot Springs Bathhouses. The pool and natural channel are surrounded by three foot high reeds in a starkly beautiful desert setting.

The water emerges from the ground at 118° in at least two points in the upper pool. The water channels through the reeds to an aluminum ladder which allows bathers to climb into 108° water. A few feet downstream temperatures are 104-106°. Cooler water is found in coves downstream where small fish dart in shallow waters.

Local wisdom says the thick, soft, greenish mud is bentonite which helps draw toxins from the body. The deeper pool by the ladder is a good place to wash off before leaving. Although wading rapidly muddies the water, the clay settles back quickly, leaving a clear, see-to-the-bottom entrance for later visitors. The pool near the source is almost always sparkling clear as there is little human use in the shallow, 118° temperature water there. Local tradition seems to be clothing optional. Although water shoes or sandals may seem like a good idea, they stick in the clay and feet slip out. The depths are a few feet at most and the bottom is quite smooth and free of sharp objects. Walking downstream is slippery. An experience that evokes much laughter. Some people prefer to do a combination of dog paddle and propelling themselves on their hands instead of trying to walk.

Except for the ladder and a 4 X 4 support beam, there are no improvements. Restrooms, showers, baths, campground, community center, and pay phone are located a the Inyo County Baths, .9 miles away. A restaurant and laundry are two miles beyond the bathhouses. Dispersed (dry) camping is available on BLM lands outside of town.

Location: The mud bath is .9 miles northeast of the Tecopa Hot Springs Bathhouses on Tecopa Hot Springs Rd. (shown as Furnace Creek Rd. on some maps) or 1.7 miles southeast of the intersection with Hwy 127. Park on the shoulder of the road. A clear but unmarked trail leads off to the right (if coming from the bathhouses; left from highway). On a small rise just to the left of the trail is a sign prohibiting off-road vehicles. It is about 100 yards to the ladder. A small tarp or mat is handy to stand on when drying off as the exit area may be muddy. Be sure to take cool drinking water.

Photos by Betty Prange

Bentonite is a clay formed from decomposing volcanic ash. It absorbs large quantities of water. Spread on the skin, it makes a smooth paste. The surface has some impurities, but a scoop of clay from below the surface is smooth and non-abrasive. It is a traditional healing medium among the Shoshone and Paiute peoples who have used the waters and mud of the ancient Tecopa lakebed for generations.

804   DEEP CREEK HOT SPRINGS

(see map)

●   **Near the town of Hesperia**

Beautiful, remote, year-round springs on the south bank of Deep Creek at the bottom of a spectacular canyon in the San Bernardino National Forest. Elevation 3,000 feet. Open all year.

Natural mineral water flows out of several rock fissures at 108° and directly into volunteer-built, rock and sandbag pools on the edge of Deep Creek. Water temperature in any one pool will depend on the amount of creek water admitted. The local custom is clothing optional.

There are no services, and overnight camping is prohibited in the canyon near the springs. It is seven miles by a year-round trail to an overnight parking area. There is also a steep, two and one-half-mile, slippery trail of decomposed granite down the north side of the canyon from Bowen Ranch, where a fee is charged for admission to the ranch and for overnight parking. From either parking area it is ten miles to all services. Note: The trail from Bowen Ranch ends on the north bank of Deep Creek, which overflows during spring runoff so that it is not safe to ford.

Directions: From I-15, take the Hesperia exit and drive for 8 miles along Main St. to a Y in the road, where Main St. becomes Rock Spring Rd. To reach Deep Creek via Bowen Ranch, continue another 1.1 miles, bear left on Kiowa Rd. for .4 miles, then right on Roundup for 4.2 miles (the last 1.2 miles are unpaved). Turn right (south) on Bowen Ranch Rd., a wide, unpaved, washboard road, and drive 5.5 miles to the ranch. Whenever you come to a fork, bear right to reach the ranch.

Directions to the year-round trail: Follow directions above to Deep Creek Rd. Turn right (south) for 5 miles to the pavement end. Bear left across the open space, heading toward the earthen dam. Park at the southeast end of the earthen dam near the overflow ramp. To reach the trailhead, go up the paved service road next to the overflow. From the top of the service road you can look down to the right and see a bathing beach at the creek and to the left, the trailhead marked with a rusty tin sign. There is short, steep ascent to the trail, which hugs the side of the mountain for 6 miles to the springs.

Source maps: *San Bernardino National Forest*, USGS *Lake Arrowhead*.

GPS: N 117.1767 W 34.3402

Following the fires in the summer of 2000, many alternate routes were suggested for entrance to Deep Creek. According to the latest information from several sources, going through Bowen Ranch is the best and safest way.

Photos by Justine Hill, Chris Andrews, and Melanie Sohler

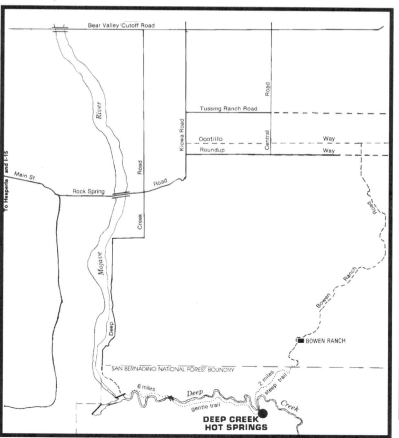

Map labels:

- Bear Valley Cutoff Road
- Tussing Ranch Road
- Kiowa Road
- Central Road
- Ocotillo Way
- Roundup Way
- River
- To Hesperia and I-15
- Main St.
- Rock Spring
- Road
- Creek Road
- Mojave
- Deep
- Bowen Ranch Road
- BOWEN RANCH
- SAN BERNADINO NATIONAL FOREST BOUNDRY
- 6 miles
- gentle trail
- 2 miles steep trail
- Deep Creek
- DEEP CREEK HOT SPRINGS

Miracle Springs Hotel and Spa is one of the newest luxury locations to offer a full array of pampering, along with natural hot mineral water pools.

■ DESERT HOT SPRINGS
RESORTS, MOTELS, AND SPAS

Desert Hot Springs has been called "The Mineral Water Capital of the World," with natural crystal clear, tasteless, odorless, geothermal water throughout the entire town. Over fifty hotels, motels, spas, resorts, swimming pools, RV parks, and mobile home communities have therapeutic hot mineral water facilities. Most facilities are open all year and require reservations.

All of the establishments listed below are in or near the city of Desert Hot Springs, ten miles north of Palm Springs. All of them pump natural mineral water from their own wells and offer at least one chlorine-treated (except where noted) swimming pool and one hydropool. Bathing suits are required at almost all locations. Those places that have indicated that they have handicap access are marked. You may wish to check with other places when you call.

The town of Desert Hot Springs provides all services. Most locations take credit cards, except where noted. For information contact the Chamber of Commerce, 11-711 West Drive, Desert Hot Springs, CA 92240. 760 329-6403. City and zip code for all locations is Desert Hot Springs, CA 92240

805 A   ADOBE INN AND SPA
66365 7th St.   760 329-7292
www.adobespa.com

Outdoor therapy pool and swimming pool. Ten units with kitchens. Airport transportation. Extended day discount.

805 B   AGUA CALIENTE HOTEL AND
MINERAL WATER SPA   760 329-4481
14500 Palm Dr.   800 423-8109

Outdoor mineral water pool. Indoor therapy pool. In-room pools. Some rooms with kitchens. Handicap access. RV spaces.

805 C   AMBASSADOR SPA, A HEALTH HOTEL
12921 Tamar Dr.   760 329-1909
                        800 941-5200

Indoor and outdoor 104° therapy pools, 90° outdoor swimming pool, all with fresh mineral water on a flow-through basis. Also 200-250° dry sauna. Kitchens available.

805 D   BROADVIEW LODGE MOTEL-SPA
12672 Eliseo Rd.   760 329-8006

Indoor therapy pool, outdoor swimming pool, sauna. Rooms with connecting kitchens.

805 E   CARAVAN SPA MOTEL
66810 Fourth St.   760 329-7124

Hot mineral spa, outdoor swimming pool.

805 F   DAVID'S SPA MOTEL
11220 Palm Dr.   760 329-6202

Indoor and outdoor hydropool, swimming pool, steam and dry sauna. Massage. Kosher kitchen.

805 G DESERT HOT SPRINGS HOTEL AND SPA
10805 Palm Dr.   760 329-6000
                                  800 808-7727

805 H DESERT OASIS INN
11330 Palm Dr.   760 251-4560
Outdoor therapy and swimming pool. Seven units with kitchens. Airport transportation. Extended day discount. Handicap access.

805 I DESERT PALMS SPA MOTEL
67485 Hacienda Ave.   760 329-4443
                                  800 468-5984
Six pools on two and one-half acres, enclosed indoor and outdoor spas, sauna. Acu-massage. Handicap access.

805 J DESERT SPRINGS INN
12697 Eliseo Rd.   760 251-1668
A 90° swimming pool, 104° sauna, enclosed sunbathing area. Rooms with kitchens.

805 K DESERT TORTOISE INN
67751 Hacienda Ave.   760 329-9090
                                  800 488-7346
Enclosed hot tub, outdoor swimming pool. No credit cards accepted. Handicap access. Clothing optional. Handicap access.

805 L FLAMINGO MOTEL & SPA
67221 Pierson Blvd.   760 251-1455
Seven mineral pools and swimming pool. Kitchens available. Restaurant on premises. Handicap access.

805 M HACIENDA RIVIERA SPA
67375 Hacienda Ave.   760 329-7010
Day use only. Outdoor swimming pool, enclosed hot pool. Water temperatures vary with the season.

805 N HIGHLANDER LODGE
68187 Club Circle Dr.   760 251-0189
Indoor spa, outdoor pool.

805 O HILLVIEW MOTEL
11740 Mesquite Ave.   760 329-5317
Enclosed hot mineral therapeutic jet pool, large outdoor heated pool.

805 P HOPE SPRINGS
68075 Club Circle Dr.   760 329-4003
www.hopespringsresort.com
Therapy and swimming pool. Ten units, four with kitchens.

805 Q KISMET LODGE
13340 Mountain View   760 329-6451
Swimming pool, hot therapy pool. Handicap access.

805 R LAS PRIMAVERAS RESORT AND SPA
66659 Sixth St.   760 251-1677
104° indoor hot tub, 92° outdoor swimming pool, sauna. State-of-the-art outdoor cooling system cools outdoor temperature fifteen to twenty degrees. Luxury units with jet tubs, kitchens. Handicap access.

805 S LIDO PALMS SPA MOTEL
12801 Tamar Dr.   760 329-6033
Two outdoor pools, large indoor spa, dry sauna. Kitchenettes. Massage.

805 T MA-HA-YAH LODGE & HEALTH SPA
66111 Calle Las Tiendas   760 329-5420
Two indoor hot tubs, 100° and 102° (one has special handicap access), one body-temperature outdoor hot tub, outdoor swimming pool, sauna. Kitchenettes. Sauna, massage, and reflexology. No credit cards accepted.

805 U MINERAL SPRINGS SPA RESORT
11000 Palm Dr.   760 329-6484

Pool, spa, mineral springs waterfall. Rooms with private spas. Bar. Salt rubs. Handicap access.

805 V MIRACLE MANOR RETREAT
12589 Reposo Way   760 329-6641
877 329-6641

Enclosed hot pool, outdoor pool. Therapeutic massage, facials.

805 W MIRACLE SPRINGS RESORT AND CONFERENCE CENTER
10625 Palm Dr.   760 251-6000

Eight outdoor hot spas at different temperatures, including an eighteen-inch deep "champagne" bubbling spa and two dry saunas. Whirlpool bathtubs in separate men's and women's areas. Massage. Restaurant, banquet facilities, approved gaming. Handicap access.

805 X MISSION LAKES COUNTRY CLUB
8484 Clubhouse Blvd.   760 329-6481

Residential country club with eight-unit motel. Swimming pool, spa, and golf course open to public. Handicap access.

805 Y THE MOORS RESORT SPA MOTEL
12637 Reposo Way   760 329-7121

Family oriented. Swimming pool and hot therapy pool are wheelchair accessible.

805 Z NURTURING NEST
11149 Sunset Ave.   760 251-2583

Therapy and swimming pools. Seven units, six with kitchens. Extended day discount.

805 ZZ PYRAMID OF HEALTH SPA
66-653 East Fifth St.   760 329-5652

A 90° swimming pool and 105° mineral water hydrojet pool. Kitchenettes. Handicap access.

805 AA ROYAL PALMS INN
12885 Eliseo Rd.   760 329-7975

Covered outdoor twelve-foot spa. Seven units.

805 BB SAHARA SPA MOTEL
66700 E. Fifth St.   760 329-6666

Indoor spa, indoor swimming pool, sauna, hot waterfall. Handicap access.

805 CC SAM'S FAMILY SPA HOT WATER RESORT
70875 Dillon Rd.   760 329-6457

One of largest, multi-service resorts with all facilities open to the public for day use as well as to registered guests. Large outdoor swimming pool uses chlorinated mineral water. Gazebo-enclosed wading pool and four covered hydropools use flow-through mineral water, requiring no chemical treatment.

Coed sauna, motel rooms, restaurant, RV hookups, overnight spaces, store, laundromat, playground, exercise room. Barbeque area. Handicap accessible with assistance.

805 DD SAN MARCUS INN
66540 San Marcus Rd.   760 329-5304

Indoor therapy pool, outdoor swimming pool, and sauna. Clothing optional.

805 EE SANDPIPER INN & SPA
12800 Foxdale Dr.   760 329-6455

Large swimming pool, therapeutic hot spa, dry and steam sauna.

805 FF SKYLINER SPA
12840 Inaja St.   760 251-0933

Mineral pool with spa; covered citrus patio.

805 GG SPA TOWN HOUSE MOTEL
66540 E. Sixth St.   760 329-6014

Hydrojet therapy pool. Large mineral pool.

805 HH SPA VIEW INN
11076 Ocotillo Ave.   760 329-3455

Therapy and swimming pools. Sauna. Seven units, five with kitchens. Pool and spa services available for day use also. Extended day discount.

805 II   STARDUST SPA MOTEL
66634 Fifth St.   760 329-5443

Hydrojet pool, swimming pool.

805 JJ   SUNSET INN ONSEN RESORT
67585 Hacienda Ave.   760 329-4488
877 966-7367

Pool, two hydrojet spas, dry sauna, wet sauna. Some rooms with kitchens. Massage. Twenty two new rooms with in-room hot mineral tubs.

805 KK   SWISS HEALTH RESORT
66729 Eighth St.   760 329-6912

A 100° indoor mineral pool, 104° hydropool, 80-90° outdoor mineral pool, all flow-through, requiring no chlorine. Various kinds of massage. No children or pets. Handicap access.

805 LL   TAMARIX SPA
66185 Acoma   760 329-6615

Smaller motel with heated mineral pool.

805 MM   TRAVELLERS RETREAT
BED & BREAKFAST
66290 First St.   760 329-0309

Outdoor pool and covered spa. No credit cards.

805 NN   TWO BUNCH PALMS RESORT
AND SPA

A full layout on this resort is found on page 178.

DESERT HOT SPRINGS RV AND MOBILE HOME RESORTS

All locations have as their address Desert Hot Springs, 92240.

806 A   AGUA CALIENTE RV PARK
14500 Palm Dr.   760 329-4481

806 B   ALMAR ACRES MOBILE HOME PARK
70205 Dillon Rd.   760 251-1268

806 C   CATALINA RV SPA
13800 Corkhill Rd.   760 329-4431

Hot mineral swimming pool, therapy pool. Clubhouse with activities. Family oriented.

806 D   CORKHILL RV AND MOBILE
HOME PARK
17989 Corkhill Rd   760 329-5976
800 982-3714

One swimming pool, one hydropool, one soaking pool, and two cold pools, enclosed and covered.

806 E   COUNTRY SQUIRE PARK
66455 Dillon Rd.   760 329-1191

Swimming pool, spa, clubhouse. Family oriented. Overnighters welcome.

806 F   DESERT POOLS PARK
70405 Dillon Rd..   760 329-7346

806 G   DESERT SPRINGS SPA
17325 Johnson Rd.   760 329-1384

Large swimming pool, hydropool, RV park.

806 H   DESERT WILLOWS
65565 Acoma Ave..   760 323-1155

806 I   GOLDEN LANTERN MOBILE VILLAGE
17300 Corkhill Rd.   760 329-6633

One outdoor swimming pool, three enclosed soaking pools. Mobile home spaces, RV hookups, overnight spaces. Used mobile homes for sale. Restaurant, store, and service station next door.

806 J   HEALING WATERS PARK
13131 Langlois Rd.   760 329-5306

One outdoor swimming pool, three therapy pools. Overnighters welcome.

806 K   HIDDEN SPRINGS COUNTRY CLUB
15500 Bubbling Wells Rd. 760 329-9333

806 L   HOGAN'S TRAIL PARK
66036 W. Second St.   760 329-9031

806 M   HOLMES HOT SPRINGS MOBILE PARK
69530 Dillon Rd.   760 329-7934

One outdoor swimming pool, one outdoor soaking pool. RV hookups and overnight spaces.

806 N   MAGIC WATERS MOBILE HOME PARK
17551 Mt. View Rd.   760 329-2600

Outdoor swimming pool and indoor hydropool use hot mineral water. Mobile homes, RV hookups, overnight spaces.

806 O   MOUNTAIN VIEW MOBILE HOME PARK
15525 Mt. View Rd.   760 329-5870

One outdoor swimming pool, one semi-enclosed hydropool. Mobile homes, RV hookups, overnight spaces.

806 P   PALM DRIVE MOBILE ESTATES
15687 Palm Dr.   760 251-2205

806 Q   PALM VIEW ESTATES
64550 Pierson Blvd.   760 251-2207

Swimming pool, spa, clubhouse, playground, BBQ and picnic area.

806 R   PARK WEST MOBILE HOME PARK
64625 Pierson Blvd..   760 329-5841

806 S   SAM'S FAMILY SPA
70875 Dillon Rd.   760 329-6457

See entry 805 CC for full description.

806 T   SANDS RV COUNTRY CLUB
16400 Bubbling Wells   760 251-1030

Swimming pool, two hydropools. Registered guests only. Nine-hole golf course open to the public.

806 U   SKY VALLEY PARKS
74711 Dillon Rd.   760 329-2909

One swimming pool, an outdoor hydropool, an enclosed hydropool on separate patio reserved for adults. Adjoining patio with outdoor swimming pool and outdoor hydropool for family use. Men's and women's saunas. Mobile homes, RV hookups, and overnight spaces.

806 V   SKY VALLEY PARK RV RESORT
74565 Dillon Rd.   760 329-7415

Two outdoor swimming pools, one outdoor hydropool, two enclosed hydropools, one indoor hydropool. Men's and women's saunas. Mobile homes, RV hookups, overnight spaces.

806 W   SPARKLING WATERS PARK
17800 Langlois Rd.   760 329-6551

Mineral water swimming pool, two spas at 100° and 104°. For senior adults. Overnighters welcome.

806 X   TAMARISK MOBILE PARK
18075 Langlois Rd.

Covered swimming pool, hot tub. RV hookups. Overnighters welcome. Visa and MasterCard.

806 Y   TWO SPRINGS RESORT
14200 Indian Ave.   760 251-1102

806 Z   VISTA GRANDE SPA
17625 Langlois Rd.   760 329-5424

Swimming pool, two spas. Senior adults. Overnighters welcome.

806 AA CORKHILL PALMS
17640 Corkhill Rd.

Natural hot mineral water pool and spa. Senior adults.

806 BB DESERT CREST COUNTRY CLUB
69400 Country Club

Swimming pool, spa. Senior adults.

806 CC DESERT VIEW ADULT MOBILE PARK
18555 Roberts Rd.   760 329-7079

Outdoor swimming pool, two indoor hydropools. Mobile homes only.

806 DD JOSHUA MOBILE HOME PARK
18080 Langlois Rd.   760 329-3277

Swimming pool, two enclosed hot pools. Senior adults.

806 EE   LA POSADA PARK
    17555 Corkhill Rd.   760 329-7113

806 FF PALM DRIVE TRAIL PARK
    14881 Palm Dr.   760 329-8341

806 GG   QUAIL HOLLOW MOBILE HOME PARK
    15300 Palm Dr.   760 329-2921

806 HH   RAINBOW SPA, INC.
    17777 Langlois Rd.   760 329-7165
    Mineral water swimming pool, two hydropools at 98-100°
and 100-104°. Senior adults.

806 II   SKY HAVENS MOBILE PARK
    14777 Palm Dr.   760 329-5001

806 JJ WAGNER MOBILE HOME PARK
    18801 Roberts Rd.   760 329-6043
    One   outdoor   swimming   pool,   two   indoor
hydropools, two indoor cold pools. Mobile homes and RV
hookups. No overnighters.

Desert Hot Springs Hotel and Spa describes itself as
"A little of Xanadu, a splash of Shangri-la."

805 NN TWO BUNCH PALMS RESORT AND SPA
67245 Two Bunch Palms Trail
760 472-4334
800 472-4334
■ **Desert Hot Springs, CA 92240**
www.twobunchpalms.com

From their brochure: "Two Bunch Palms reigns supreme as the consummate retro-bohemian spa haven for the new millennium—where the stressed come to naturally decompress." An aquifer provides the resort with both hot (148-152°) and cold mineral water; this was a natural spot for a healing, restful destination resort.

The Grotto, using one of the country's largest free-flowing bodies of natural hot mineral water is regarded by many as the resort's heart and soul. It features two adjoining bodies of hot natural mineral water maintained at slightly different temperatures—each being continuously replenished by free-flowing streams of fresh water requiring only a gentle cleaning with a bromide wash early each morning. The hotpool side of the Grotto is kept at a toasty 104°, while the larger soaking pool side is maintained at a soothing 98°. After passing through the Grotto, the water cascades down through a series of rock-lined brooks and several lakes, nourishing flora and fauna, and ultimately settling into a small marsh thicket where it soaks back down into the earth. The water is virtually odorless and has a wonderful taste. The hot water is used in all of the showers, two watsu treatment pools and the swimming pool, where it is chlorinated. The water from the cooler artesian wells is used for drinking.

Guestrooms, suites, and villas are located in either the spectacular natural hot springs Grotto area offering rustically elegant vintage architecture, or in the dramatically panoramic lake and tennis area where contemporary architecture is surrounded by naturally landscaped gardens and preserved wilderness areas. A full Continental breakfast is included. For the rest of your meals prepare to dine in style. Purchased individually or as a package, you can choose from a large selection of close to forty-five spa treatments and massage modalities.

Courtesy of Two Bunch Palms

The grotto in the top picture features hot mineral spring water in its pool, which is divided into two areas to create two different temperatures. The water is constantly circulated through the pool and is eventually absorbed back into the aquifer after passing through a stream and two lakes. Overlooking the grotto are some of the oldest buildings on the grounds, which are done in rock with Spanish roof tiles.

807 TURTLEBACK MESA B&B
PO Box 8038   760 347-5358
Palm Springs, CA 92263
email: trtlbkmesa@aol.com

Modern spacious adobe located approximately twenty miles east of Palm Springs in the Indio Hills, surrounded by rocky Nature Conservancy land in desert tortoise country. Elevation 1,200 feet. Open all year.

Natural 130° mineral water pumped up from 425 feet underground heats the building through radiant floor coils and flows into a large outdoor swimming pool where it mixes with cold city water. The large outdoor hot tub, which can hold twenty-eight to thirty people, is maintained at 105-110°. No chemicals are added to this mineral water which has the same mineral content as the Ouray Caves in Colorado.

Facilities include two rooms with private toilets and a shared shower. Rooms open directly onto the patio and pool area. Sculptures of turtles from cultures around the world turn this bed-and-breakfast into an ethnic art gallery. All other services, including restaurants, shopping centers and casinos are fifteen to twenty-five minutes away.

Management prefers guests who are comfortable in a clothing optional environment. Facilities are only available to non-smoking registered guests. Call for reservations.

Courtesy of Turtleback Mesa

Courtesy of Palm Springs Resort

809 A BASHFORD'S HOT MINERAL SPA
■ 10590 Hot Mineral Spa Rd. 760 354-1315
Niland, CA 92257

Primarily a winter RV resort for adults, located on a desert slope overlooking the Salton Sea. Elevation 50 feet below sea level. Open October 1 to May 30.

Natural mineral water flows out of an artesian well at 150° and into two cooling tanks from which it is piped to an outdoor swimming pool maintained at 84° and to an outdoor hydropool maintained at 102°. The water in both pools is chlorine-treated. Mineral water is also piped to six outdoor soaking tubs with temperatures from 101-105°. These tubs are drained and refilled after each use so that no chemical treatment is needed. Bathing suits are required.

RV hookups, overnight spaces, and a laundry room are available on the premises, and catfish fishing (no license required) is about one mile away. Credit cards accepted. It is seven miles to a motel, restaurant, and service station.

808 PALM SPRINGS SPA HOTEL
AND CASINO RESORT
■ 100 N. Indian Canyon Dr. 760 325-1461
Palm Springs, CA 92262
www.spa@aguacaliente.org

A major destination resort with an elaborate mineral water spa where you can sample the ancient tradition of the "taking of the water." Located in downtown Palm Springs. Elevation 500 feet. Open all year.

Natural mineral water flows out of historic Indian wells on the property at temperatures of 106°. The spa has separate men's and women's sections, each containing fourteen marble tubs separately controllable with mineral water temperature up to 104°. These tubs are drained and refilled after each use so that no chemical treatment of the water is necessary. Each spa also has vapor-inhalation rooms, a steambath, and a dry sauna. Bathing suits are required in the outdoor pool area, optional in the bathhouse and solarium. Fees to use the spa are discounted for hotel guests.

Services and facilities on the premises include massage, hot stone therapy, beauty shop, rooms (handicap accessible rooms are on the ground floor), restaurant and lounge, pool bar, snacks, airport pickup, and group conference rooms. Also available is an Indian-owned gaming casino, open twenty-four hours. All major credit cards accepted. Pool and spa facilities are available to the public as well as to registered guests.

Directions: Take the Indian Canyon Dr. exit from I-10 and drive south 6.5 miles to the resort.

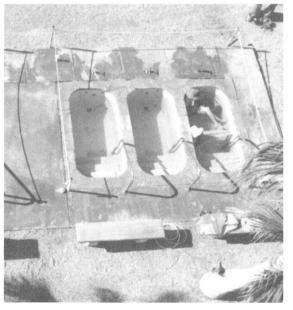

Courtesy of Bashford's Spa

809 C IMPERIAL HOT MINERAL SPA, INC.
10595 Hot Mineral Spa Rd. 760 354-1204
■ **Niland, CA 92257**

The original "Old Spa" location, with the first hot well drilled in this area operates as an RV and mobile home park. Located on a desert slope overlooking the Salton Sea. Elevation fifty feet below sea level. Open all year. Facilities available only to registered guests and tenants.

Natural mineral water flows out of an artesian well at 165° and into a large holding and cooling tank from which it is piped to seven outdoor pools. Five hydropools are maintained at a variety of temperatures from 96-104°. These pools are treated with chlorine. Two mineral-ater Roman tubs are maintained at 96° and 88° and do not require chemicals. Bathing suits are required. Restrooms, showers, and designated full hookup sites are handicap accessible.

RV hookups, overnight camping spaces, and a store are on the premises. No credit cards accepted. It is six miles to a service station on CA 111 across from the border patrol station and seven and one-half miles north to a restaurant and motel in Bombay Beach.

809 B FOUNTAIN OF YOUTH SPA
10249 Coachella Canal Rd.
760 354-1340   800 781-0818
■ **Niland, CA 92257**
www.foyspa.com

The largest of the RV parks in this area, located on a desert slope overlooking the Salton Sea. Elevation sea level. Open all year.

Natural mineral water flows out of an artesian well on the property at 137°, is cooled by heat exchangers, and is piped to two pool areas, one of which is reserved for adults. The two outdoor swimming pools range in temperature from 85-90°. The five outdoor hydropools range in temperature from 100-107°. The water in all pools is chlorine treated. Pools are available to registered campers only. No day use. Bathing suits are required.

The facilities include rental units, a laundromat, store, cafe, RV hookups, overnight camping spaces, recreation rooms, library, exercise and fitness room, and car wash. Winter services include massage, beauty and barber shops. Church services and activity programs are also offered. If no hookup spaces are available, it is possible to dry camp and get on a waiting list. It is two and one-half miles south to a service station across from the border patrol on CA 111 and four and one-half miles north to a motel and restaurant at Bombay Beach.

Directions: From CA 111, 3 miles south of Bombay Beach, drive east on Hot Mineral Spa Rd. for 1.5 miles, then right onto Spa Rd. for 1.1 miles.

809 D LARK SPA
10016 Frink Rd.   760 354-1384
■ **Niland, CA 92257**

Mobile home and RV winter resort located on a desert slope overlooking the Salton Sea. Elevation fifty feet below sea level. Open all year.

Well water, gas-heated and chlorine-treated, is used in an outdoor hydropool maintained at 102°. Bathing suits are required.

Overnight spaces and RV hookups are available on the premises. No credit cards are accepted. It is one mile to a store and service station and four miles to a motel and restaurant.

Directions: From Niland, drive 10.5 miles north to Frink Rd. and turn right (east) for 1 mile. Frink Rd. is 3 miles south of the border patrol station on CA 111.

810　FIVE PALMS WARM WELL OASIS (HIGHLINE NORTH)

● **Near the city of Brawley**

An exotic, true desert oasis surrounded by palm trees and tall bullrushes in the otherwise arid, sparsely vegetated Imperial Valley desert south of the Salton Sea. Elevation 113 feet below sea level. Open all year.

Natural 92° mineral water bubbles up from an artesian well through a three-inch pipe in the middle of a large, clean, sandy-bottom soaking pond that is eighteen inches deep and large enough for a dozen people. In winter, the bullrushes and palms help shade the pool. The custom is clothing optional.

There are no services available except plenty of open BLM desert where overnight parking is permitted with a fourteen-day limit. Caution: choose your parking space carefully; vehicles have been known to get stuck in the soft sand underneath a deceptively firm crust. Parking is not permitted within a 150-foot radius of the springs, and overnight camping is not permitted within approximately a one-half mile radius of the well so that animals will feel safe to come to the water. Please help by cleaning up any party trash. All services are available in Brawley, approximately sixteen and one-half miles away.

Directions: From Brawley, drive 15 miles east on CA 78, crossing the canal. Take the second dirt road right (.5 miles past the canal). Follow the one-lane road for 1.6 miles to five tall palms, the only greenery in the area. The one-lane, graded, unsurfaced road has some soft, sandy spots that can usually be negotiated by normal passenger vehicles.

811　HIGHLINE SOUTH HOT WELL

● **Near the town of Holtville**

Two cement soaking pools and a large pond, fed by an artesian well, located just off the I-8 right-of-way on the east edge of Holtville. Elevation sea level. Open all year; closed midnight to 5 AM.

Natural mineral water flows out of an artesian well at 125° and splashes on the edge of a six-foot by six-foot by three-foot deep cement cistern. Hot water showers in through holes in an overhead swing-arm horizontal pipe, which can be diverted when the desired pool temperature is reached. A smaller, cement, bathtub-size pool is next to the larger tub. There is very little self-cleaning action, and algae growth is rapid. Volunteer snowbirds regularly scrub the pools with bleach, which also removes the algae smell. Because the pools are visible from I-8, bathing suits are recommended. A four-step ladder makes the tub handicap accessible with assistance. A sign reminds campers that "soap is prohibited in spa/pond." The area is posted for day-use only and the sheriff patrols regularly.

Overflow from the tub goes into a large, shallow, sandy-bottom "olde swimming hole" that used to be stocked with fish. Water temperature measures 90°, and fan palms offer a spot of shade.

Facilities include wooden benches, a cement walkway, trash cans, nearby BLM pit toilets, and a fenced-off parking area where overnight parking is prohibited. A primitive BLM campground with a fourteen-day limit is located twenty yards north of the well, across the road. Camping permits are required September to April and a fee is charged. Free overnight camping is available one mile outside the long-term camping area. All services are in Holtville.

Directions: At the east end of Holtville, take the Van Der Linden exit (CA 115) from I-8. Go north and immediately take the first right turn onto a frontage road paralleling I-8. At approximately 1 mile you will cross over the Highline Canal. Just past the canal on the right (south) is a flat, fenced parking area with pit toilets. The pools are just ahead toward I-8

GPS: N 32.45352 W 115.16181.

Top and bottom photos by Justine Hill
Middle photo by Phil Wilcox

Five Palms, pictured above, is a true natural desert oasis for animals and humans. In order to provide a place to soak, the BLM has built concrete pools at Highline. The overflow from the tubs does go into a pond reminiscent of "ye olde swimming hole."

Jayson Loam

812 JACUMBA HOT SPRINGS SPA LODGE AND RESORT
Box 371   935 766-4333
Jacumba, CA 92034
www.jacumbaspa.com

An older motel spa located just off I-8, 80 miles east of San Diego. Elevation 2,800 feet. Open all year.

Natural mineral water with a slight sulfur odor flows out of a spring at 140-150 gallons per minute at a temperature of 101° and is then piped to an indoor hydropool and an outdoor swimming pool. Continuous flow-through maintains a temperature of 97-98° in the hydropool and 85° in the swimming pool, with no chemical treatment of the water required. Hot mineral water showers are in the spa room. The pools are available to the general public for a use fee. Pools are handicap accessible, with assistance. Bathing suits are required.

Facilities include twenty-two poolside rooms, a rustic Alpine restaurant, bar, sauna, tennis and shuffleboard courts, a German "biergarten patio" with Mexican sculpture and pottery, and a lawn area with shade trees. Horseback riding and guided hikes can be arranged. Massage is available on the premises. Major credit cards accepted. It is one block to a store and service station and one-half mile to RV hookups.

Directions: Take the Jacumba exit off I-8 and go 2.5miles to the tiny town of Jacumba. The spa is located on the north side of Old Highway 80, the main street through town.

Courtesy of Agua Caliente

Replacing the old tin quonset hut is a brand new glass pool enclosure.

Courtesy of Warner Springs

813   AGUA CALIENTE COUNTY PARK

For reservations   858 565-3600

■   Located in the Anza Borrego Desert

www.co.san-diego.ca.us/parks

A county-operated, desert campground located in a wildlife refuge area in the Anza Borrego Desert. A wide variety of animals and beautiful spring wildflowers and succulents are native to this area. No pets are permitted at any time! Elevation 1,300 feet. Open September through May.

Natural mineral water flows out of several springs at 96° and is then piped to two pools where it is filtered and chlorinated. The outdoor swimming pool with a water temperature between 90-92° is available for families. The large indoor hydropool is located in a newly built glass pool enclosure. The chlorine-treated mineral water is solar and gas heated to 104°. The hydropool, showers, restrooms, and dressing area (all newly redone) are all handicap accessible. Bathing suits are required. Pool facilities are available to the public for day use, as well as to registered campers. Handicap accessible.

Facilities include RV hookups and overnight camping spaces, hiking trails, picnic and barbeque area, horseshoe pits, shuffleboard, and a children's play area. Credit cards are accepted. It is one-half mile to a small general store, cafe and phone; twenty-five miles to a gas station; and thirty-five miles to a motel. There is a nearby airstrip for small planes.

Directions: Take the Ocotillo exit off I-8, 27 miles east of El Centro and 95 miles east of San Diego. Follow Imperial County Rd. S-2 for 25 miles into the Anza Borego Desert to the sign for Agua Caliente Springs. Bear left .1 mile to the general store and left again for .5 miles to the campground.

814   WARNER SPRINGS RANCH

31652 Hwy. 79   760 782-4200

■   Warner Springs, CA 92086

Private destination resort in rural northeastern San Diego County. Elevation 3,100 feet. Open all year.

Natural mineral water flows out at 130-140° into an Olympic-size swimming pool where it is cooled to 102°. A cool freshwater pool is adjacent to the hot pool. Bathing suits are required. Handicap accessible.

Facilities include cabins, sauna, spa, equestrian center, golf, tennis, a restaurant, and an airport. Massages can be booked ahead. There are no phones or TVs in the rooms. Major credit cards are accepted. Phone for rates, reservations, and directions.

815   THE TUBS

7220 El Cajon Blvd.   619 698-7727

❏   San Diego, CA 92115

San Diego's original rent-a-tub establishment, located on a main suburban street near San Diego State University.

Eleven spa suites for rent to the public use gas-heated tap water that is treated with chlorine and maintained at 102°. Saunas are included in all rooms as are showers, towels, and body shampoo. Each suite is equipped with an AM/FM stereo cassette player. The VIP Suite, large enough for twelve people, has a bathroom, a steambath, a sauna, and includes a VCR and TV.

A juice bar is available on the premises. Credit cards accepted. Phone for rates, reservations, and directions.

Courtesy of Carlsbad Spa

816   CARLSBAD MINERAL WATER SPA
　　　　2802 Carlsbad Blvd.　　　760 434-1887
■　　Carlsbad, CA 92008
　　　　www.carlsbadmineralspa.com

Historic mineral water spa and therapeutic baths located on the site of an 1880s health spa and hotel. The original spa (and entire town) was named for the famous Karlsbad health resort in Bohemia which has a similar mineral water content. Open all year.

Carbonated mineral water from an aquifer 1,700 feet deep is recharged from the Cleveland National Forest, sixty miles east of Carlsbad. No chemicals are necessary as a fresh bath is drawn for each customer. Each room is lavishly decorated using an Egyptian-Roman or Oriental theme.

Services include carbonated mineral water baths, mud or clay facials, total-body clay, aromatherapy, massage, body wraps, and special spa packages.

Phone for rates and reservations.

817 A   LAKE ELSINORE HOT SPRINGS MOTEL
　　　　316 N. Main　　　　　909 674-2581
■　　Lake Elsinore, CA 92330

Older motel and spa located several blocks north of downtown Lake Elsinore. Elevation 1,300 feet. Open all year.

Natural sulphur water flows out of an artesian well at 126° and is piped to three pools and to the bathtubs in all rooms. The outdoor swimming pool is maintained at 104°. All pools are chlorine treated and are available to the public as well as to registered guests. Bathing suits are required.

Facilities include a dry and wet sauna and a recreation room. Rooms and massage are available on the premises. Visa and MasterCard are accepted. It is five blocks to a restaurant, store, and service station and three blocks from the freeway.

817 B   PARADISE HOT SPRINGS MOTEL
　　　　215 W. Graham　　　909 674-3551
■　　Lake Elsinore, CA 92330

An older motel in downtown Lake Elsinore. Elevation 1,300 feet. Open all year.

Natural mineral water flows out of an artesian well at 133° and is piped to two pools and to the bathtubs in every room. The outdoor swimming pool is maintained at 86° and the indoor hydropool at 105°. The water in both pools is chlorine-treated. There is also a dry sauna and outdoor shower. Bathing suits are required.

Rooms are available on the premises. No credit cards are accepted. It is two blocks to a restaurant, store, and service station.

818 GLEN IVY HOT SPRINGS SPA

■

25000 Glen Ivy Road   909 277-3529

Corona, CA 92883   800 454-8772

www.glenivy.com

Large, well-equipped, beautifully landscaped day-use resort and spa located on the dry east side of the Santa Ana mountains seventy miles from Los Angeles. Elevation 1,300 feet. Open all year, except Thanksgiving, Christmas, and New Years. (You must be over sixteen years of age to be admitted).

Natural mineral water from two wells at 90° and 110° is mixed and piped to a wide variety of pools. There are seven sunken hydrojet tubs with temperatures of 104-106°, using continuous flow-through, unchlorinated mineral water. Individual whirlpool baths are are now available. The other pools have automatic filters and chlorinators. An outdoor swimming pool is maintained at 85°, a covered soaking pool at 103°, two outdoor hydropools at 101° and 104°, two outdoor shallow bubble pools at 103° and 100°, a large outdoor floating pool at 90°, and a California red clay-bath pool at 100°. (Guests should bring an old bathing suit to wear in the mud bath as the clay does stain some fabrics.) Bathing suits are required.

Facilities include a new entrance building "Entrada al Paraiso," offering a fine spa boutique, men's and women's locker rooms equipped with hair blowers, a coed dry sauna, and two outdoor cafes. An expanded spa facility offers treatments including Swedish, shiatsu, and aromatherapy massage, eucalyptus wraps, apricot body scrubs, European facials, manicures, pedicures and waxings. Advance reservations for these services are highly recommended. Entrance to the spa facilities and restroom are handicap accessible, but no attendants or lifts for the pools are provided. All major credit cards, ATMs, and personal checks are accepted.

Directions: Eight miles south of Corona on I-15, exit right onto the Temescal Canyon Rd. Go 1 mile south to Glen Ivy Rd., turn right and follow signs to the resort.

The original pool at *Glen Ivy* was a large swimming pool rather than the variety of soaking tubs, such as the ones on the right, they now have.

"Club Mud" is *Glen Ivy's* name for their unique red clay mineral water bath. The pond is filled with fresh mineral water daily and mud mined in the Temescal Valley is added, dissolving in the water to create an all-over mud pack.

819 NEPTUNE'S LAGOONS

2784 W. Ball Rd.   714 761-8325

❑   Anaheim, CA 92804

Modern, suburban pool-rental facility near Disneyland and Knott's Berry Farm. Open Monday to Saturday.

Private-space hot pools using gas-heated tap water are treated with chlorine. There are four indoor fiberglass pools with water temperatures maintained at 101-104°. Three of the rooms have saunas.

Each room has a hydrojet tub with bubble controls, a dimmer for lights, air conditioning, relaxation bed, shower, towels, hair dryer, tape player, and sky light. Each room as an AM/FM cassette player. TV and VCR are available. Handicap accessible.

All major credit and ATM cards are accepted. Phone for rates, reservations, and directions.

820   PUDDINGSTONE HOT TUBS

❏   1777 Camper View Rd.   909 592-2222
    San Dimas, CA 91773

A unique, modern rent-a-tub facility that offers both privacy and a spectacular view. Located in Bonelli County Regional Park overlooking Puddingstone Reservoir, twenty-five miles east of Los Angeles.

Fifteen outdoor pools (twelve private and three deluxe) using chlorine-treated tap water heated by a combination of propane and electricity, are for rent to the public by the hour. The tubs can hold up to six people. The very large unheated community pool has a 360° view with spacious decking, fire pit and barbecue, a food serving area, and a bandstand. It can be reserved for large groups and parties. The smaller tubs offer a beautiful view, tub temperature controls, and a three-sided enclosure for privacy. All facilities are handicap accessible.

A wedding gazebo is available on the premises and intimate picnic-style meals for two can be ordered ahead along with "special occasion" packages with flowers and balloons. You are welcome to bring a picnic basket. An RV park, golf course, picnic area, horse stables, boat rentals, and Raging Waters recreation area are available in the adjoining regional park. Phone for rates, reservations, and directions.

Located off I-10, Fairplex exit.

The deluxe pool is a memorable choice for that special occasion. Other pools, all with magnificent views, are just perfect whether you bring along the kids or it is only you and a friend.

Photos courtesy of Puddingstone Resort

Courtesy of Beverly Hot Spring

821   BEVERLY HOT SPRINGS
308 N. Oxford Ave.   213 734-7000
Los Angeles, CA 90004
www.beverlyhotsprings.com

A modern, Korean-style, indoor spa built over a hot water artesian well a few miles west of downtown Los Angeles. Elevation 300 feet. Open all year.

From a well drilled in the early 1900s, mineral water flows out at a temperature of 105° and is piped to large, tiled, soaking pools equipped with hydrojets in the women's section (first floor) and the men's section (second floor). Each section also has a pool of cooled mineral water. All pools operate on a continuous flow-through basis so that no chemical treatment of the water is necessary and temperatures range from 96-105°. Bathing suits are not required in pool rooms.

Facilities include a dry sauna and a steam sauna in each section, plus a restaurant and beauty salon. Shiatsu massage, cream massage, and body scrubs are available on the premises. Visa and MasterCard are accepted. Phone for rates, reservations, and directions.

822   SPLASH, THE RELAXATION SPA
8054 W. 3rd St.   323 653-4412
Los Angeles, CA 90048
www.splashspa.com

Eighteen beautifully decorated, romantic, very private suites located in an urban location.

All rooms feature a chlorinated hydrojet tub with controls for bubbles, water temperature, and cool-off mists. Also included are dimmer controls for room and tub lights, air conditioning, relaxation bed, and fully equipped dressing room with shower, herbal soaps and towels. Many of the more exotically decorated suites offer additional amenities such as saunas, waterfalls, aquariums, skylights, etc.

Gift certificates, in-suite catering, corporate memberships and overnight stays are available. Group discounts for private parties are also available, as well as help in arranging the party.

Major credit cards are accepted. Phone for rates, reservations, and directions.

Just two of the different rooms you can choose when you soak at Splash.

Courtesy of Splash

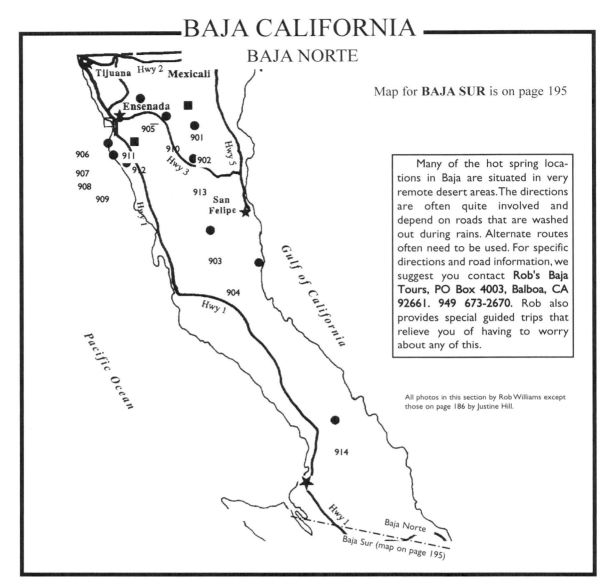

BAJA CALIFORNIA
BAJA NORTE

Map for **BAJA SUR** is on page 195

Tijuana Hwy 2 **Mexicali**

Ensenada

905

901

906 911

907

908 912

909

910

902

Hwy 5

Hwy 3

913 San Felipe

Hwy 1

903

904

Hwy 1

Gulf of California

Pacific Ocean

Many of the hot spring locations in Baja are situated in very remote desert areas. The directions are often quite involved and depend on roads that are washed out during rains. Alternate routes often need to be used. For specific directions and road information, we suggest you contact **Rob's Baja Tours, PO Box 4003, Balboa, CA 92661. 949 673-2670.** Rob also provides special guided trips that relieve you of having to worry about any of this.

All photos in this section by Rob Williams except those on page 186 by Justine Hill.

914

Hwy 1

Baja Norte

Baja Sur (map on page 195)

This map was designed to be used with a standard highway map.

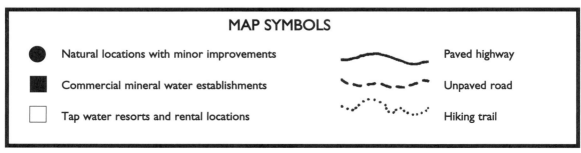

MAP SYMBOLS

● Natural locations with minor improvements

■ Commercial mineral water establishments

□ Tap water resorts and rental locations

⌇ Paved highway

- - - Unpaved road

····· Hiking trail

901 GUADALUPE CANYON HOT SPRINGS

■ **Southwest of Mexicali**

Beautiful mineral water soaking pools, waterfalls, and campsites in a remote palm canyon on the east slope of the Sierra Juarez Mountains. Elevation 1,300 feet. Open all year; summer temperatures often reach 110°. For campground reservations call Rob's Baja Tours at 949 673-2670.

Natural mineral water emerges from several springs at 125° and flows through man-made aqueducts to pools and flush toilets. More than twenty drainable soaking pools, built of rocks and cement, are scattered through palm forests and piles of boulders. Bathing suits are required except at night.

A limited number of campsites at Campo 1, each with its own parking area, palapas, pool, and picnic table, can be rented by the day, week, or month. Reservations require two weeks notice. This Campo has rest rooms and some newer tubs. There is no electricity or telephone. All services are sixty miles away in Mexicali, but there is a restaurant and a small store that sells cold beer and soft drinks. Ancient Indian caves, cascading waterfalls, and thick palm forests are within hiking distance. Other palm canyons may be explored for primitive hot springs, but the use of an experienced guide is recommended.

Directions (via Tecate): From San Diego go East on Hwy 94 approximately 40 miles. Turn south on Tecate Rd. (188) and go 1.3 miles to the border crossing (open 6 AM to midnight). Four blocks past the border, turn left on Mexico Hwy 2. Travel east 41 miles to La Rumorosa (last chance for gas). Just east of La Rumorosa you will begin the winding descent to the desert. At approximately 65 miles (200 yards past the K28 marker) there will be signs for "Cannon De Guadalupe." Turn right onto a graded dirt road. This dirt road has a great number of "washboards" and some bad dips. Ten miles down the road you will see signs for "The Canyon at Rancho Ponderosa." (Ignore any signs that say to turn left. This is an alternate route only in dry weather). At 27 miles, turn right at the sign for the canyon. This last part is 7 miles of good but winding dirt road. The last mile is rough (take it slow). Campo 1 is on the left across the road from a sign which says "BIEN-VENIDOS."

Arturo Loya

Horseback was the best way to enter the Guadalupe Canyon in 1940. Arturo Loya, the owner of the hot springs, first entered the canyon this way while searching for stray cows with his father who was a cattle rancher. "Don" Jose and Arturo soon discover the healing benefits of the mineral water and realized the natural beauty of the palm oasis. They gave up ranching and set up a homestead in the canyon. Arturo built a handful of small hot tubs. The first road which terminated one-half mile from the palm grove and bubbling geothermal waters was built by hand. After forty years the Mexican government finally granted them title to the 1,000-acre canyon. There are now over twenty beautiful hand-made tubs of river rock and cement. Arturo still lives there with his wife Roseanne. The restaurant and store are powered with solar and car batteries, along with propane for the stove. Huge, hundred-pound blocks of ice are brought in by truck to keep the beer and food cold. Arturo still live the ranch lifestyle and at sixty-eight is still going strong. Be prepared to laze around with the chickens and dogs.

The hot summer months often require shade in the afternoons when even the pools are deserted until it cools off.

The pool on the left is a brand new swimming pool. The one above was originally built as a horse trough and is only eighteen inches deep. The runoff from the main spring forms a small hot water fall (below) where you could sit and enjoy a shower.

902 PALOMAR CANYON HOT SPRINGS

● **Southwest of Mexicali**

Small wilderness hot springs in a remote palm canyon on the east slope of the Sierra Juarez Mountains, 45 miles from the nearest paved road. Elevation 1,500 feet. Open all year, but summer temperatures often reach 110°.

Natural mineral water bubbles out of three small source pools at 98° and then sinks into the sand as it flows down the canyon. A small cement pool at 96° is good for bathing but is only eighteen inches deep. A large rock and cement pool at 85° degrees has just been built. At this remote location, the apparent local clothing custom is the mutual consent of those present.

There are no facilities or services, but there is an all-year cold water stream in the canyon and excellent camping locations for backpackers. Four-wheel drive is required on the last few miles of the access road, and the springs are a two-hour hike up the canyon beyond the end of the road.

Directions to such a remote location are beyond the scope of this book. The use of a guide service is recommended.

903   VALLE CHICO HOT SPRINGS

●   **Southwest of San Felipe**

A remote, primitive hot spring in a barren canyon in the eastern escarpment of the Sierra San Pedro Martir. Elevation 1,500 feet. Open all year, but summer temperatures often exceed 110°.

Natural mineral water bubbles out of a large source pool at 144° and flows across the canyon into a year-round cold water stream. Volunteers could build a soaking pool at that confluence but have not yet done so. At this remote location, the apparent clothing custom is the mutual consent of those present.

There are no services at this location.

Directions to such a remote location are beyond the scope of this book. The use of a guide service is recommended.

In such remote areas it is not unusual to find the hot water simply flowing across the ground. This area could use volunteers to build more permanent pools.

A series of three soaking pools is revealed for a few hours each day at low tide. Located between the volcanic rocks, the pools need the cool ocean water to make the water temperatures comfortable.

The tiny pueblo of Puertecitos does provide such necessary services as gas, vehicle repair, a small store, campsites, a restaurant, fishing, and boat ramps.

904 PUERTECITOS HOT SPRINGS
On the Gulf of California

● **South of San Felipe**

Geothermal water bubbles up from under volcanic rock along the edge of the Sea of Cortez and collects in waist-deep soaking pools that are under water during high tide and useable only several hours each day during low tide. Elevation sea level. Open all year, although summer air temperature can soar above 110°.

Natural mineral water flows up through the gravel bottom of the soaking pools that have been blasted out of the volcanic rock. Two rectangular pools are large enough for a dozen people each; while a third round pool can accommodate six people. Pool temperatures vary widely, depending on the mix of geothermal water and sea water. There is only a brief time each low tide when the mixture makes it possible to soak. Bathing suits are recommended.

There are no services at this location. It is .25 miles to all services in the tiny pueblo of Puertecitos. Services include gas (honk your horn 8 AM to 8 PM for service), vehicle repair, a four-room hotel, small store for provisions, and campgrounds all along the Sea of Cortez south from San Felipe.

Directions: From the roundabout at the Pemex Station just past the arches in San Felipe, follow Hwy 5, which is the road toward the airport. At 6.4 miles take the turnoff toward Laguna Chapal, Percebu, and El Faro. Pay careful attention to signs along this road warning of "vados" (dips), which are deep, steep, and imperceptible until you are upon them. It is 53 miles from the roundabout in San Felipe to the town of Puertecitos, where the paved road ends.

In Puertecitos, just before the Pemex station, turn left toward the pink entranceway marked "Private Property: Puertecitos Hot Springs, boat ramp..." The owners collect a fee of $1.00 per person to go to the springs. At .2 miles past the gate, on the left is "Taller Panama," a large tin building where the dirt road veers to the right up a hill past the boat ramp. Follow this road for .6 miles to a cul-de-sac and turn around. The hot springs are in the tide pools on the right below a green building. There are parking turnouts on both sides of the road. There is a cement walkway through the volcanic rock down to the pools.

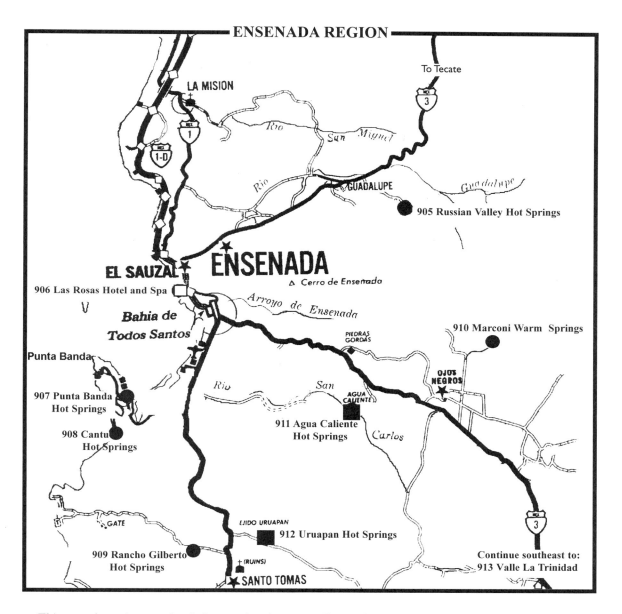

La Mision

To Tecate

Rio San Miguel

Guadalupe

GUADALUPE

905 Russian Valley Hot Springs

ENSENADA

△ Cerro de Ensenada

EL SAUZAL

906 Las Rosas Hotel and Spa

Bahia de Todos Santos

Arroyo de Ensenada

910 Marconi Warm Springs

PIEDRAS GORDAS

Punta Banda

Rio San

AGUA CALIENTE

OJOS NEGROS

907 Punta Banda Hot Springs

911 Agua Caliente Hot Springs

Carlos

908 Cantu Hot Springs

GATE

EJIDO URUAPAN

912 Uruapan Hot Springs

3

909 Rancho Gilberto Hot Springs

(RUINS)

SANTO TOMAS

Continue southeast to: 913 Valle La Trinidad

This map shows in more detail those springs in or near Ensenada. Use this map with a detailed road map.

As arid as this land appears, less than a quarter of a mile away is a lovely cold stream and waterfall.

905   RUSSIAN VALLEY HOT SPRINGS

(see map on page 195)

● **South of Tecate**

Several undeveloped wilderness hot springs near a beautiful waterfall in a remote valley that was named for an historic Russian settlement. Elevation 1,500 feet. Open all year.

Natural mineral water flows from two main source springs at 125°. In one sandy-bottom pool, the geothermal water bubbles up from below and is cooled by evaporation to maintain the pool temperature at approximately 110°. The other source spring flows out of a sandy bank into a rock-lined pool where it is mixed with creek water and the temperature is controlled by moving rocks to admit cold water. In this remote location, the apparent local clothing custom is the mutual consent of those present.

There are no services on the premises, but there is a delightful cold pool and waterfall beside the access trail a quarter mile from the springs. All services are twenty five miles away in Ensenada.

The hot springs area is located fifty miles south of Tecate and ten miles east of Hwy 3. See map at right for detailed directions.

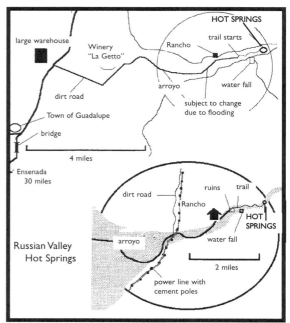

906   LAS ROSAS HOTEL & SPA

(see map on page 195)

Post Office Box 316   011-52-61-74-43-10

❏   Ensenada, Baja California, Mexico

A charming, upscale, small hotel/resort on the magnificent shoreline north of Ensenada. Elevation sea level. Open all year.

Tap water, heated with propane, is used in a seaside pool maintained at 80° and in a hydrojet spa maintained at 104°. Bathing suits are required. Pools are available for day use except during the busiest summer months. Inquire by telephone to determine current status.

Rooms, restaurant, fitness center, and racquetball court are available on the premises. It is two miles to all other services in Ensenada. Visa and MasterCard are accepted.

Directions: From Tijuana, take the Hwy 1 toll road south for 60 miles to Las Rosas, which is 2 miles north of Ensenada.

907   PUNTA BANDA HOT SPRINGS

Estero Beach   **(see map on page 195)**

●   **On the Punta Banda Peninsula**

A unique opportunity to literally dig your own hot spring pool at low tide on an easily accessible beach south of Ensenada. Elevation sea level. Open all year.

Natural mineral water (up to 170°) bubbles up through many yards of beach sand. During high tide swimmers can feel the extra warmth in the surf. During low tide it is possible to dig pools in the beach sand. These fill with a soakable combination of hot mineral water and cold sea water. Bathing suits are required.

Parking is available in the adjoining trailer camp, which offers its tenants hot mineral water piped from geothermal wells on the premises. It is eight miles to all other services in Ensenada.

Directions: From Ensenada, drive south on Hwy 1 to Hwy 23 Maneadero. Turn right on the paved road for approximately 8 miles to the Agua Caliente Trailer Camp. This beach is also known as La Jolla and is near the Baja Beach and Tennis Club.

Soakers travel thirteen miles of very scenic, improved, dirt road, climbing to 2,000 feet before crossing the Punta Banda ridge and dropping to a remote beach on the Pacific Coast.

908   CANTU HOT SPRINGS
(see map on page 195)
● South of the Punta Banda Peninsula

A small pool at the edge of the ocean on a remote rocky beach just past Rancho Cantu. Elevation 20 feet. Open all year.

Natural mineral water flows from a small, 90° stream down an arroyo to a shallow, hand-made pool about 100 yards from the beach. You may need to do some further digging to enlarge the pool to your specifications. Due to the remote location, clothing is optional.

There is free camping on the windswept bluffs, fifty feet above the beach. There are no services on the premises, and it is thirty miles (one hour driving time) back to Ensenada. This is a good area for fishing, diving, and surfing.

Directions: Take Hwy 23 .5 miles past La Jolla Beach and turn left onto graded dirt road. There is a sign for Ej. Cantu. The dirt road winds up the mountain and crosses over the top, then drops down to the Pacific Coast. Note the kilometer markers (small cement posts on the side of road).

909   RANCHO GILBERTO/ ST. TOMAS HOT SPRINGS
(see map on page 195)
● South of Ensenada

Hot water comes up in several locations in a small stream which flows down into a valley near Santo Tomas and is surrounded by farming areas and tree-covered hillsides. Elevation 500 feet. Open all year.

Natural mineral water flows up from the streambed at 100° in several places. You will need to dig your own pool and place rocks and sand around the edge to hold the water. Temperatures are regulated by mixing hot water with cold stream water. Bathing suits are required.

There are no services on the premises, but overnight parking is available at the farmhouse 100 yards away. It is fifteen miles to a campground at La Bocana Beach and four miles to a store and restaurant.

Directions: From Ensenada, travel 20 miles south on Highway 1. Turn right on the dirt road with a sign for La Bocana. Drive 4.1 miles on graded dirt road toward the ocean. Rancho is on the left side, no sign.

The only way to find out where the hot water comes up in this stream is to feel for it. Then, build yourself a pool to soak in.

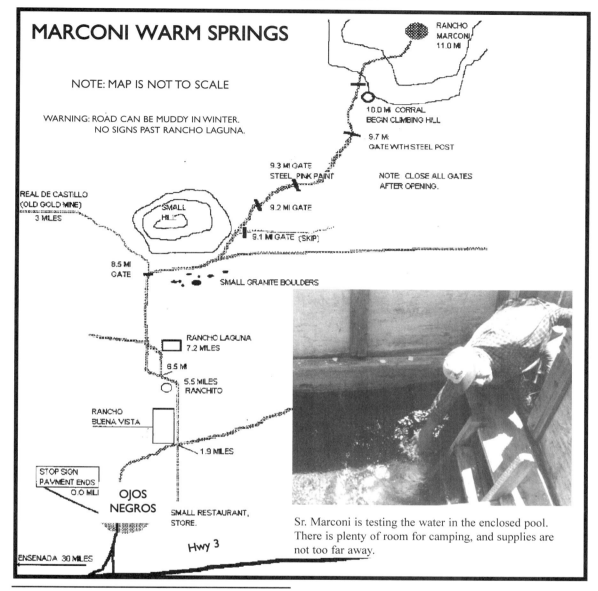

MARCONI WARM SPRINGS

NOTE: MAP IS NOT TO SCALE

WARNING: ROAD CAN BE MUDDY IN WINTER.
NO SIGNS PAST RANCHO LAGUNA.

RANCHO MARCONI 11.0 MI

10.0 MI CORRAL
BEGIN CLIMBING HILL

9.7 MI
GATE WITH STEEL POST

9.3 MI GATE
STEEL, PINK PAINT

NOTE: CLOSE ALL GATES
AFTER OPENING.

9.2 MI GATE

REAL DE CASTILLO
(OLD GOLD MINE)
3 MILES

SMALL HILL

9.1 MI GATE (SKIP)

8.5 MI
GATE

SMALL GRANITE BOULDERS

RANCHO LAGUNA
7.2 MILES

6.5 MI

5.5 MILES
RANCHITO

RANCHO
BUENA VISTA

1.9 MILES

STOP SIGN
PAVMENT ENDS
0.0 MLI

OJOS
NEGROS

SMALL RESTAURANT,
STORE.

Hwy 3

ENSENADA 30 MILES

Sr. Marconi is testing the water in the enclosed pool. There is plenty of room for camping, and supplies are not too far away.

910   MARCONI WARM SPRINGS

(see map on page 195)

● **East of Ensenada**

Located in the foothills of the Sierra Juarez Mountains at the norther end of the Ojos Negros Valley. Elevation 1,500 feet. Open all year.

Natural mineral water at 80° fills one enclosed six-foot by four-foot by three-foot deep pool. Considering the hot summers in the area, this water temperature should feel quite good. Clothing may be required outside the enclosed area even though there are very few tourists. However, this is a farming community.

There is one shelter for camping plus many open areas where camping is permitted. There is a $10 charge per night per car. The nearest food and gas are in in Ojos Negros, and all other services are found in Ensenada.

Directions: take Hwy 3 east of Ensenada for 30 miles and turn left at the sign to Ojos Negros. Pavement ends 1 mile later in the center of town. It is 11 miles to the springs (see detailed map above).

Relaxing, waiting for the pool to refill with fresh water.

911   AGUA CALIENTE HOT SPRINGS
(see map on page 195)
■   East of Ensenada

An older commercial hot springs "resort" located in an arid valley five miles south of Hwy 3. Elevation 1,500 feet. Open all year, but the bar and restaurant are open only during April through August.

Natural mineral water flows out of several springs at temperatures ranging from 80 to 108°. The warmest source spring supplies 108° water to the bathhouse tubs, which are drained and filled after each use. It also flows directly into a large concrete outdoor soaking pool which maintains a temperature of 97°. Water from the coolest spring is piped to a large swimming pool at a temperature of 75° which is drained and filled every week. No chemical treatment is added. Water from a third spring at 97° is piped to the motel rooms, bar, and restaurant as tap water. Bathing suits are required except in individual tubs.

Motel rooms with bar and restaurant service operating during spring and summer months only. It is sixteen miles to all other services in Ensenada.

Directions: (Do not attempt in wet weather.) From Ensenada, drive east on Hwy 3 to marker KM 26. Watch for "AGUA CALIENTE" sign and turn right on a 5-mile dirt road that ends at the resort. Not recommended for trailers or low clearance vehicles.

As there is no telephone or mailing address, it is not possible to secure reservations. It is very crowded during Easter vacation.

912   URUAPAN HOT SPRINGS
(see map on page 195)
■   South of Ensenada

A well-worn combination bathhouse and laundry in a green fertile valley at the base of coastal scrub foothills two miles from Hwy 1. Elevation 500 feet. Open all year.

Natural mineral water flows out of many pastureland springs at temperatures ranging from 118 to 138° and is piped to a cistern that supplies a fifty-year-old building with five individual bathtub rooms and five outdoor washing machines. Clearly, the tubs are for cleanliness bathing, not recreational soaking, and clothing is optional only in private spaces.

913 VALLE DE TRINIDAD/RANCHO LOS POZITOS

(see map on page 195)

● **Southeast of Ensenada**

Sandy bottomed, semi-developed pools, at the headwaters of a stream in an open valley. Surrounded by small hills, low mountains, and agricultural lands in the midst of old ranchos. Elevation 2,800 feet. Open all year.

Natural mineral water flows up from the bottom of the first pool at 105°. This eight-foot square pool has a sandy bottom, brick walls, and tin roof. The second pool is lined with rocks and located in the middle of the stream. In the third, water flows into a six-foot square brick pool. Bathing suits are required.

Overnight parking is permitted at the farm hous about 100 yards away. It is five miles to a store, restaurant and other services.

Directions: Go east from Ensenada on Highway 3 about 60 miles. Turn right toward Valle De Trinidad on paved road. After 1 mile turn right onto dirt road at church. Continue 2 miles toward west end of valley and follow dirt road about 5 miles with some signs for San Isidoro. Look for Rancho Los Pozitos, Family Arballo.

While it is always fun to soak in the middle of nature, having a pool with a bit of covering to offer protection from the sun is welcome in this hot, arid valley.

914   MISSION SAN BORJA HOT SPRINGS

● **East of the town of Rosarito**

A small, historic source pool on the grounds of a well-preserved mission in a remote and enchanting part of the Sierra La Libertad. Elevation 2,200 feet. Open all year.

Natural mineral water at 96° flows out of a rock-lined source pool built by the missionaries in the early 1800s. It is located at the edge of the mission cornfields, a five-minute walk southeast from the main building. The runoff from the spring was commingled with a nearby cold stream to water the mission's fields. Bathing suits are required.

There are no facilities or services, but camping is permitted anywhere among the ruins of the old mission buildings.

Directions: At Rosarito, from Hwy 1, turn east on a dirt road for 21 miles. There will be no sign for the mission, but there are two ranchos on the way, and the road ends in a remote valley where the mission is located.

The hot spring water was mixed with water from several cold streams to water the fields when the mission was in use in the 1800s.

BAJA SUR

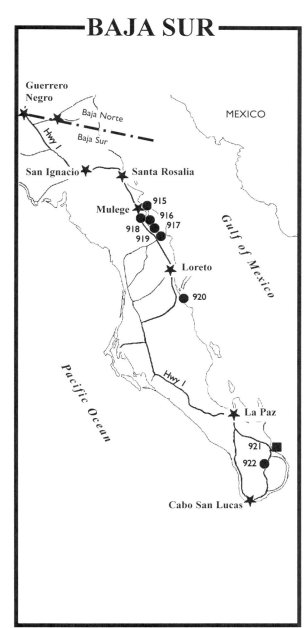

---

915   MULEGE MISSION WARM SPRINGS

● **Near the town of Mulege**

Warm water springs found in the middle of a stream creating a jungle-like oasis complete with fan palms and ponds surrounded by desert and a view of the mountains. Elevation 50 feet. Open all year.

Natural mineral water bubbles up through the sand into the cool streambed at 90°, creating an interesting effect as you sit in the stream. Bathing suits are required.

There are no services on the premises. It is two miles to a campground and one mile to all other services in Mulege.

Directions: Park at the mission and walk downhill. Cross stream in front of the dam. Continue 100 yards downstream; gas bubbles can be seen rising in the stream. Suggestion: On Hwy 1 at Mulege, ask for Arcadio Valle Somora at the ABC Bus Station and hire him to guide you.

This squishy-bottom pool at Santispac Beach is located above the tide line, so it is available for soaking all day.

916   SANTISPAC BEACH

● **South of Mulege, on Concepcion Bay**

Two squishy-bottom soaking pools built by volunteers near a mangrove swamp on the edge of the bay. Elevation sea level. Open all year.

Natural mineral water oozes up through the rock-encircled mud bottom of one source spring, maintaining a temperature of 106° except when flooded by high tide. A second source spring, on slightly higher ground, has been excavated by volunteers to create a squishy-bottom pool that maintains a temperature of 102°. Bathing suits are required.

Santispac Beach is a popular RV and camping destination on the Sea of Cortez. Camping is $5 per car per night, and there is a small restaurant on the beach. All other services are ten miles north in Mulege.

Directions: From Mulege, drive 10 miles south on Hwy 1 and turn left into the commercial parking and camping ground. Drive to the far right side of the cove, to a small area for parking, and walk approximately 100 yards on a dirt trail around the mangrove swamp to the two pools.

917   CONCEPCION BEACH

● **South of Mulege, on Concepcion Bay**

On the edge of a beautiful bay, very hot water flows from rock fissures into rock and sand pools which are usable only when the high tide brings cold water for mixing. Elevation sea level. Open all year.

Natural mineral water flows out of cracks above the high tide line at more than 135° into volunteer-built soaking pools on the beach below. Twice a day the high tide supplies enough cold water to bring the pool temperatures down to tolerable soaking levels. Bathing suits are required.

Directions: There are no direct routes down the steep cliffs that border this beach. Therefore, it is necessary to hike south along the tide pools from Santispac Beach (see 916) or north from Los Cocos Beach.

Since these pools require cold ocean water to cool them down to a soakable temperature, it would be a good idea to bring along a tide table to figure out when to expect a high tide.

● **South of Mulege, on Concepcion Bay**

A small permanent soaking pool in a fantastic setting on the edge of Concepcion Bay. Elevation sea level. Open all year.

Natural mineral water seeps into a tide pool at the base of a cliff. Volunteers have built a rock-and concrete wall around the tide pool, which maintains a temperature of 86° at low tide. Small shrimp have been observed in the warm, partly salty water. Bathing suits are required.

The camping fee at El Coyote Beach is $10 per night, but there is no additional fee for using the hot spring. There are no other facilities at the beach, but there is a restaurant at Rancho El Coyote across the highway. All other services are seventeen miles away in Mulege.

Directions: From Mulege, drive 17 miles south on Hwy 1 to the El Coyote Beach commercial campground. Park and follow a rocky trail 100 yards to the pool.

Waiting for the tide to go out so that you can build a pool where the hot water seeps up through the sand.

---

919 **BUENA VENTURA HOT SPRINGS**

● **South of Mulege, on Concepcion Bay**

Build your own pool in Concepcion Bay as hot water flows up through the sand at low tide on this beach twenty-five miles south of Mulege. Elevation sea level. Open year round.

Natural mineral water at 100° pushes up through various spots in the sand at low tide, just waiting for someone to build a small soaking pool with the available rocks. The apparent local custom is clothing optional.

The Playa Buenaventura Hotel and Restaurant is nearby. It is twenty-five miles to all other services in Mulege.

Suggestion: See Mike at the Playa Buenaventura Hotel and Restaurant for boat rentals and for progress on future plans to build a hot pool.

920   AGUA VERDE HOT SPRINGS

● **Near Agua Verde, south of Loreto**

Two pools in the Sea of Cortez, surrounded by a rocky, rocky coastline and panoramic ocean views. Elevation sea level. Open all year.

Natural mineral water percolates up through the sand into two large eight-foot and ten-foot rock pools. The temperature at low tide in the upper pool is 110° and 105° in the lower pool. High tide covers the pools. The apparent local custom is clothing optional.

There are no services available on the premises, but overnight parking is permitted (watch the tides). It is 200 yards to the nearest campground and thirty miles to all other services. This is a very good area for snorkeling.

Directions: Go 29 miles south of Loreto and turn at sign for Agua Verde. Go another 12 miles and take the first turn onto the beach. Go north on beach 1 mile. You must wait for low tide to drive to the site.

Along with some of the best diving, spectacular views, and an oceanside campground, there are two large soaking pools available at low tide.

921 HOTEL BUENA VISTA RESORT
PO Box 574   800 731-4914
La Paz, Baja California Sur, Mexico

This full destination resort is located on the coast between the Baja desert and the Sea of Cortez, southeast of La Paz. Elevation sea level. Open all year.

Natural mineral water flows up from several wells at 180° into pools that are drained and refilled once a week. The large swimming pool, with a swim-up bar, is maintained at 80°, and a smaller swimming pool is 80-100°. There is also a hydropool. All three use an ion filtration system. Hot water also seeps up on the beach next to the hotel at low tide. The pools are open to the public for day use for a charge. Bathing suits are required.

Luxurious rooms, tennis courts, gift shop, a restaurant, and entertainment on Saturday nights are available on the premises. The hotel also has its own fishing fleet. Deep sea fishing is legendary in this area. Major credit cards are accepted. Phone for rates, reservations, and directions.

922 AGUA CALIENTE (SANTIAGO) HOT SPRINGS

● **Near the town of Santiago**

Mountains and trees surround two small hot pools located in a canyon with fresh water streams and cold pools. Elevation 900 feet. Open all year.

Natural mineral water at 115° flows into a two-foot by three-foot source pool and then through a ditch to a three-foot by four-foot pool big enough for one or two people, where the water has cooled to 108°. The only way to further cool this tub is to block up or divert the water flow. The apparent local custom is clothing optional.

There are no services on the premises, but there is room for three or four cars to park overnight. It is seven miles to all other services.

Directions: From the town of Santiago, go east 5 miles to the town of Agua Caliente. Continue east 1.5 miles to Rancho El Chorro. Pass the nature preserve (El Santuario) .5 miles, then go .3 miles further to the end of the road and the springs.

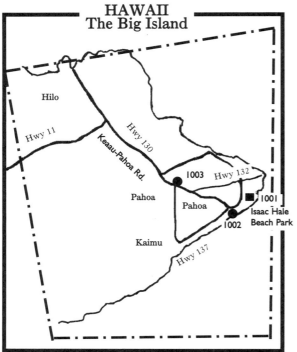

HAWAII
The Big Island

This map was designed to be used with a standard highway map.

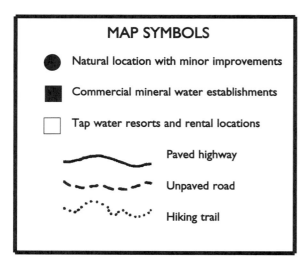

MAP SYMBOLS

● Natural location with minor improvements

■ Commercial mineral water establishments

□ Tap water resorts and rental locations

⎯⎯⎯ Paved highway

– – – Unpaved road

· · · · Hiking trail

You would think that with all the volcanic activity that created the chain of islands known as Hawaii hot springs would be prevalent over all the islands. Actually the only island that has any soakable pools is the Big Island which supports numerous springs—most of them warm, hardly qualifying as hot. (At this point, steam vents and caves, which are very hot, are being counted as hot springs.) Many of the springs are on private land or inaccessible; many appear and disappear with the tides, and even the steam vents are not always able to be accessed due to excessive heat and location. This section is based on the reports of Skip Hill, publisher of the *Hot Springs Gazette*; Oscar Voss, a hot springs soaker who wrote that Hawaii ought to be in the book; Philip Maise, who owns the guesthouse near the steam vent; and the super friendly owners of the Hale Kia O Kiana guest-house. Thanks to all of you.

The "Red Road" referred to in the directions is the meandering coastal road from Kaimu to Kapoho that winds along one of the most beautiful coast lines in the world. Pack a lunch, take a good book, your fishing rod, and enjoy the day.

While you may come across some warm shallow ponds off the beaten path, you should use a great deal of discretion when taking off your clothes. The native Hawaiians are very offended by nudity. It is illegal in most areas and you can be heavily fined. I understand that there is an explicit anti-nudity regulation covering the entire state park system, but no similar regulation for Hawaii county parks, which might lower the legal hazards. The steam vents are customarily clothing optional. Kehena is a clothing optional beach, pictured below.

Courtesy of Hale Kipa O Kiana

Just another beautiful beach with blue skies and white surf. Only at Kehena is clothing optional okay.

1001   AHALANUI WARM SPRING AND PARK

■   **East of the town of Pahoa**
808-961-8311 (Hawaii County Parks and
Recreation in Hilo, no phone on site)

Large pool next to the ocean, in Ahalanui County
Park, about a mile northeast of Pohoiki Hot Spring on the
Puna Coast of Hawaii's Big Island southeast of Hilo. (This
is part of the Isaac Hale Beach Park and managed by the
Department of Parks and Recreation for the County of
Hawaii.) Elevation sea level. Open all year.

Ground water, heated by the Kilauea volcano, flows
toward the sea where it comes in through cracks in the
lava bed up through the sandy bottom of the large rock
and concrete pool that covers about one-half acre. The
pool has an outlet to the ocean which allows sea water to
mix with the spring water. Pool depths vary from two to
eight feet, depending on tide levels and whether you are
in the shallow or deep end. The water temperature is
around 95-97°. Bathing suits required.

The pool is open 7 AM to 7 PM and has a lifeguard on
duty every day, but only during specific hours. Alcoholic
beverages, dogs, and unattended children are not allowed.
There are benches, tables, and portable toilets on site.
Other services are available in Pahoa, about eight miles
inland.

Directions: From Hilo, take route 11 south 7 miles toward
Keaau. Just north of Keaau turn left (east) onto route 130
(known as the Keaau-Pahoa Rd.) toward Pahoa. Travel
about 10 miles to the junction with route 132 (the Pahoa-
Kapoho Rd.) on the east side of Pahoa. Turn left (east)
onto route 132. After 2.5 miles, there is a sign for the
turnoff to Pohoiki. Go straight ahead onto the turnoff
(instead of left to stay on route 132). The road is paved
but narrow, sometimes one lane. Continue straight ahead
for 4.7 miles from the junction with route 130, passing an
unmarked turnoff for route 137 at mile 4.5, to the
entrance to Isaac Hale Beach Park. Turn left (northeast),
away from Isaac Hale. Continue about .8 miles. The park
entrance will be on the right (toward the ocean).

From points along the coast, take route 137 (the "Red
Road") to the park entrance at mile 10.6. To the east of
the pool are several warm springs that vary in temperature. They are more private and secluded but most are
very shallow.

Note: Be careful where you park, as route 137 in front
of the park entrance is very narrow. As with any tourist
destination in Hawaii, to reduce the risk of vehicle break-
in, do not leave valuables in your car.

1002 POHOIKI HOT SPRING (POHOIKI WARM POND)

● **East of the town of Pahoa**
   808-961-8311 (Hawaii County Parks and Recreation in Hilo, no phone on site)

Soaking pool about twenty yards from the ocean and an easy walk from the highway, in Isaac Hale Beach Park (county), off Pohoiki Bay on the Puna coast of Hawaii's Big Island southeast of Hilo. Elevation sea level. Open all year.

Ground water heated by the Kilauea volcano flows toward the sea, where it mixes with ocean water seeping inshore, and rises to fill a natural pool. The source comes in and around the lava boulders on the uphill end of the pool. The pool is approximately twenty-feet long by ten-feet wide by four-feet deep (depth fluctuates by a foot or so with the tides), with a temperature of about 98°. The pool is next to a rocky beach popular with surfers, and is near houses, so bathing suits are advisable.

The spring is within 400 feet of the boat ramp in Isaac Hale Beach Park, where there are portable toilets and an emergency phone. Other services are available in Pahoa, about eight miles inland.

Directions: From Hilo, take route 11 south about 7 miles toward Keaau. Just north of Keaau, turn left (east) onto route 130 toward Pahoa. Travel about 10 miles, to the junction with route 132 on the east side of Pahoa, Turn left (east) onto route 132. After 2.5 miles, there is a sign for the turnoff to Pohoiki. Go straight ahead onto the turnoff (instead of left to stay on route 132). The road is paved but narrow, sometimes one lane. Continue straight ahead for 4.7 miles from the junction with route 130), passing an unmarked turnoff for route 137 at mile 4.5, to a "T" intersection at the entrance to Isaac Hale Beach Park. Turn right into one of the parking areas on either side of the boat ramp. From the boat ramp, follow the path to the right, heading southwest along the shore. The spring will be about 400 feet from the boat ramp, on the right.

From points along the coast, take route 137 (the "Red Road") to the Isaac Hale boat ramp at mile 11.4, then follow the directions above from the boat ramp.

As with any tourist destination in Hawaii, to reduce the risk of vehicle break-in, do not leave valuables in your car.

GPS: N 19° 27.492', W 154° 50.602'

Skip Hill, above in the white cap, made three new friends from Sweden at *Pohoiki* and deemed it "a paradise." Thanks to Oscar Voss, pictured below, for all of his photos and information.

Top photo by Skip Hill
Bottom photo by Oscar Voss

1003　PAHOA STEAM CAVES
(PAHOA STEAM VENTS)

● **Southeast of the town of Pahoa**

Natural steam caves and open-air steam vents, within an easy hike from the road, in the Keauohana Forest Reserve (state) on Hawaii's Big Island southeast of Hilo. Elevation about 800 feet. Open all year.

Several open-air steam vents, and two steam caves, are scattered in the forest within 500 feet of a parking area on a state highway. They reportedly were created less than fifty years ago, by volcanic activity along the east rift zone of the Kilauea volcano, and emit steam from super-heated groundwater. The most popular steam cave is the most distant (about 500 feet) from the highway, in the bottom of a volcanic "splatter cone," with a volunteer-provided ladder down into the cave and also a changing bench at the top. It is the hottest and most humid cave, with temperatures fluctuating from day-to-day but feeling like it's above the 150° range. It is about five-feet square inside by four-feet tall, with a small bench inside that holds three to four people. A second cave is cooler and less humid, and somewhat roomier, but with a smaller entrance. It has wood planks inside for people to sit on. The open-air vents also usually have wooden benches, with room for one person each. The apparent local custom is clothing optional.

The trails up into the basalt cones where the caves and vents are located can be steep and/or slippery, over volcanic rock that can cause nasty cuts if you fall. Also, stay close to the cave entrances so you can get out if the heat becomes unbearable. The area is open twenty-four hours a day, but there is no artificial lighting, so bring a flashlight and use caution if visiting at night. There reportedly is a significant risk of vehicle break-ins at night (even in the day, do not leave valuables in your car). There are no services on site. The nearest services are in Pahoa, about five miles away.

Photos by Oscar Voss

Directions: From Hilo, take route 11 south about 7 miles toward Keaau. Just north of Keaau, turn left (east) onto route 130 toward Pahoa. Travel past Pahoa, about 10 miles, and start looking for the mile markers along the right side of the road. Across the road from mile marker 15, there is a posted "scenic overlook," with room for several cars to park along the westbound side of the road. Park there, and look for steam from mounds of small basalt cones rising out of the foliage. A web of trails from the parking area connects the vents and caves. The most distant cave from the road is in the last and largest of the splatter cones (once there, you'll see a guesthouse on adjacent property, and a steamy black field marked "no trespassing"). The other vents and caves are between the last splatter cone and the road.

GPS: N 19°26.431', W 154°56.527' (hot and humid steam cave, the one most distant from the road); GPS: N19°26.418', W154°56.555' (the cooler and less humid cave, closer to the road).

The steam caves are open to the public and anybody can just park their car along Hwy 130 at mile marker 15 at the turnout and go to them.

Entrances to the caves include one where you climb down a ladder. One of the caves has benches to sit on.

CLOTHING OPTIONAL ACCOMMODATIONS

Photos courtesy of Hale Kipa O Kiana

HALE KIPA O KIANA
RR 2, Box 4874   808 965-8661
Kalapana Shores, HI 96778
www.halekipaokiana.com
email: haleokiana@aol.com

Unique guesthouse hideaway with one large guest room with a double and single bed, sink in room, phone, small desk, private entrance, and private bath. There is a covered lanai with table, chairs, BBQ, and exercise machine. The house is in a private cul-de-sac facing the 1990 lava flow with the ocean beyond.

Located southeast of Hilo in Kaimu. Nearby surroundings include Kehana clothing optional beach and a natural outdoor sauna where clothing optional seems to be the custom. The owners are naturists and offer a topless friendly environment on the grounds.

Visit the web for a pictorial. For more information or to make a reservation, phone or email.

The owners describe themselves as "naturist friendly" and have provided a lovely setting in which to go topless. They will also be happy to give you directions to the Kehena clothing optional beach.

KALANI HONUA RETREAT AND CONFERENCE CENTER
PO Box 4500   808 965-7828
Kalapana, HI 96778
800 800-6886

Large swimming pool, soaking tub with jets, and watsu pond are filled with mineral water from their own well. Clothing optional in the pools after dark.

Can accommodate individuals or groups either camping, in lodge rooms, or in tree houses (bungalows in the trees) with great views of the ocean. Community kitchen, bath in each lodge, sauna, conference facilities.

Conveniently located to nearby Kehena Beach natural steam baths which are clothing optional, as well as Kehena Beach and Pahoa Steam Vents.

STEAMVENT GUESTHOUSE
        808 965-8800

Pahoa, Big Island of Hawaii
www.steamventguesthouse.com

Modern spacious guesthouse positioned next to a recent lava flow on the slopes of Kilauea. (Clothing optional facility, gay-owned and operated.) Elevation 1000 feet. Open all year.

Steam billows from the ground in many locations providing a unique opportunity to take a natural steam bath. Steamvent's guests can adjust the steam temperature within a custom-built steam bathhouse. The steam also heats pool water and rainwater for guest showers and baths. Clothing is optional.

Visitors that are not staying at the guesthouse can use the property next door. This property contains several steam caves. (See write-up on steam caves.) The deeper you go into the cave the hotter it gets.

Rooms with an ocean view, garden view and private or shared bath are available. The nearest restaurant is three and one-half miles away, and the nearest beach is six miles away.

Directions to the steam caves: From either Kona or Hilo take Hwy 11 South to Hwy 130. Park at "Scenic Turnout" located at mile marker 15. Walk over highway embankment where a bit of climbing will get you to the caves. Look for steam rising from large mounds.

Guesthouse is .1 mile west of mile marker 15 and guests can park at the house.

Note: Please keep Hawaii clean and leave the wild orchids for the enjoyment of future visitors.

GOING NATURAL IN PALM SPRINGS

❑ The following listings cover a growing industry in Palm Springs—going uncovered in lush, upscale surroundings. These clothing optional resorts have varying amenities, but all of them will arrange for airport pickup, are open all year, and accept credit cards. The pools use tap water and are gas heated and chlorine treated. Phone for rates, reservations, and directions.

John Samora

Moonlight and roses becomes sunshine and bougain-ville in Palm Springs as this romantic couple enjoys the day at the *Terra Cotta Inn*. It seems that all of the clothing optional resorts had romance in mind when they built their inns and hotels.

MORNINGSIDE INN
888 N. Indian Canyon   760 325-2668
                          800 916-2668

Palm Springs, CA 92262

www.morningsideinn.com

Exclusive, secluded, clothing optional bed and break-fast for couples in the heart of Palm Springs.

Suites and cabana rooms are available. Suites contain fully equipped kitchens, and some have patios. The pool and spa, a covered workout area, and a massage table are available for your use along with a barbeque area. A misting system operates to keep customers comfortable all year around.

Snacks, afternoon sweet tray and beverages, and lunch on the weekends are available for your enjoyment.

Courtesy of Morningside inn

VILLA ESCONDIDA

280 Mel Ave. 760 323-2676
Palm Springs, CA 92262 877-RELAX-US
www.villaescondida.com

Distinctive romantic hideaway rests on lush private grounds where the mission is to provide guests with a natural environment that enhances relaxation. Majestic mountain views and clear starry skies add to the ambiance.

A beautiful, large swimming pool and a spa, along with a misting system for those hot summer days encourage guests to relax and enjoy the gardens.

Eleven cabanas have been completely refurbished to meet the standards of a quality hotel. Nine rooms have well-stocked kitchenettes. All visitors are invited to use the communal barbecue and cooking area. Continental breakfast served daily. One room is fully handicap accessible. Massage available. Adult only policy.

Call for reservations.

Courtesy of Terra Cotta

"Palm Springs' Best Hideaway," according to *The Arizona Republic. Los Angeles Magazine* names it, "one of our four favorite resorts for couples in Palm Springs."

Courtesy of Villa Escondida

THE TERRA COTTA INN

2388 E. Racquet Club Rd. 760 322-6059
Palm Springs, CA 92262
www.sunnyfun.com

A premier clothing optional resort for couples surrounding a secluded, romantic garden. Situated on a private, colorful acre with magnificent mountain vistas.

A large, pristine pool is heated year-round, and the fifteen-person hydropool spa has fantastic mountain views. Both pool and spa are open twenty-four hours a day and are situated in a very spacious, private garden. The pool patio is micro-mist cooled for relaxing sunbathing in all temperatures.

The seventeen luxurious rooms are lavishly appointed. The charming grounds feature a private shade fountain retreat and several sun patios. A special suite is available with a private patio, sunken tub, and terrarium bathroom garden. Amenities include a sumptuous poolside breakfast, hot hors d'oeuvres in the afternoon, and pampering services such as massage and spa treatments.

Call or email (info@sunnyfun.com) for a free brochure, or check out the website for more information.

DESERT SHADOWS INN RESORT AND VILLAS

1533 Chaparral   760 325-6410
Palm Springs, CA 92262

A secluded retreat for the discerning naturist with a magnificent view of the San Jacinto Mountains. Only minutes away from downtown Palm Springs.

Three grand pools are heated to 86°. The main pool has a waterfall created by jets of water flowing from three stone lions. The "quiet" pool has classical music playing softly in the background from behind flowering bougainvillea and citrus trees. The "villa" pool has three distinct entrances and steps for sitting comfortably in the crystal clear water. Two magnificent outdoor spas are heated to 102°. The original spa rests under a canopy complete with skylights for stargazing and is surrounded by our unique misting system. The second spa is 250 square feet in a free-form clover pattern making pockets for relaxing or socializing au naturel.

Choose from the private courtyard rooms, the main chaparral rooms or the two-story deluxe villas complete with private whirlpool baths. A full service restaurant on the property means you never have to leave the acres of lushly landscaped grounds. Steam room, massage, facials, hair salon, manicures and pedicures, and herbal body wraps are offered at the spa at Desert Shadows. A handicap accessible room is available.

Gracious hospitality and luxurious ambiance make this the premiere resort location in Palm Springs.

GOING NATURAL—PLACES TO STAY

To help those of you who like to stay in places that cater to the naturist lifestyle, included is a list of clubs offering varying types of accommodations. Always call first to check on available amenities.

ARIZONA

Arizona Oasis of the Sun   520 568-4027
55551 W. La Barranca, Maricopa, AZ 85239

El Dorado Hot Spring   602 393-0750
PO Box 10, Tonopah, AZ 85354
(See listing in Arizona for full description)

Jardin del Sol   520 682-2537
PO Box 39, Marana, AZ 85653-0039

Shangri La II   623 465-5959
46834 N. Shangri La Rd., New River, AZ 85027

CALIFORNIA

De Anza Springs Resort   619 766-4301
1951 Carrizo Gorge Rd. Jacumba, CA 91934

Deer Park Nudist Resort   909 880-0803
1924 Glen Helen, San Bernardino, CA 92407

Glen Eden Sun Club   800 843-6833
25999 Glen Eden Rd., Corona, CA 92883-5223

Laguna Del Sol   916 687-6550
8683 Rawhide Lane, Wilton, CA 95693

Lupin Naturist Club   408 353-2230
PO Box 1274., Los Gatos, CA 95030

Mystic Oaks   909 678-2333
40051 Long Canyon Rd., Lake Elsinore, CA 92530

Olive Dell Ranch   909 825-6619
26520 Keissel Rd., Colton, CA 92324-9526

Chris Andrews

Lupin Naturist Club in California represents all that is fun and natural at this great resort.

Sequoians Family Nudist Park   510 582-0194
10200 Cull Canyon Rd., Castro Valley, CA 94546

Silver Valley Sun Club   760 257-4239
48382 Silver Valley Rd., Newberry Springs, CA 92365

Swallows   619 445-3754
1631 Harbison Canyon Rd., El Cajon, CA 92019

COLORADO

Mountain Air Ranch   303 697-4083
PO Box 855, Indian Hills, CO 80455

Wild Wood's Resort   719 NUDE-500
East of Colorado Springs

HAWAII

No landed clubs (see Hawaii section for places to stay).

NEVADA

Nevada Sun Rancho   702 723-5463, 888 786-LVSC
HCR 31, Box 351, Sandy Valley, NV 89019

NEW MEXICO
No landed clubs

TEXAS

Bluebonnet   940 627-2313
CR 1180, Box 146
Alvord, TX 76225

Live Oak Nudist Resort   409 878-2216
R#1 Box 916,
Washington, TX 77880

Acorn Acres Resort   409 657-3061
10220 F.M. 442, Boling, TX 77420

Riverside Ranch   830 393-2387
PO Box 14413
San Antonio, TX 78214

Sahnoans   512 273-2257
PO Box 142233
Austin, TX 78714

Sandpipers Holiday Park   210 383-7589
Rt 7, Box 309, Edinburg, TX 78539

Sunny Pines   903 873-3311
PO Box 133, Wills Point, TX 75169

Vista Grande Ranch   817 598-1312
1149 FM 1885 Road, Weatherford, TX 76088

UTAH

No landed clubs

BAJA (Mexico)

Eden Ranch (near Loreto, Baja Sur)
01152 (113) 30700

INDEX

This index is designed to help you locate a listing when you start with the location name. The description of the location will be found on the page number given for that name.

Within the index the abbreviations listed below are used to identify the specific state or geographical area of the location. The number shown after each state listed below is the page number where the KEY MAP of that state will be found.

AZ = Arizona / 92
BJ = Baja (Mexico) / 190
CCA = Central California / 124
CO = Colorado / 44
HI = Hawaii / 208
NV = Nevada / 14
NM = New Mexico / 72
NCA = Northern California / 106
SCA = Southern California / 164
TX = Texas / 68
UT = Utah / 34

NUBP = Not Usable By the Public
Some springs that have recently become NUBP are still included in the directory for your information.

If you discover that the description of a location needs to be revised, or you find a location not in the book, jot down the pertinent information below and send to:

ATA Directory Editor
55 Azalea Lane
Santa Cruz, CA 95060
831-426-2956

VISA & MASTERCARD orders only:
1-800-637-2256 (US & Canada) 24 hours

ALASKA   CANADA
IDAHO   WYOMING
OREGON   WASHINGTON
        MONTANA
            and
STATES EAST OF THE ROCKIES

$18.95 ISBN 1-890880-00-0

CALIFORNIA   UTAH
ARIZONA   COLORADO
NEW MEXICO   NEVADA
TEXAS   BAJA (MEXICO)
        HAWAII

$19.95 ISBN 1-890880-03-5

Order form can be found on our web page
www.hotpools.com

Name			
Street			
City		State	Zip
		Order Quan.	Amount
Hot Springs and Hot Pools of the Northwest $18.95			
Hot Springs and Hot Pools of the Southwest $19.95			
Postage: $3 first book, $2 each additional book			
Canadians: Please send in US dollars			
BOOK Make check to: AQUA THERMAL ACCESS (831) 426-2956			
MAIL ORDER Mail to: 55 Azalea Lane, Santa Cruz, CA 95060		TOTAL	

Unusual Recipes for Creative Cooks

A GOURMET'S GUIDE TO
MUSHROOM COOKERY
WITH SELECTED RECIPES
FROM MASTER CHEFS

EDITED BY MARJORIE YOUNG AND VINCE VIVERITO

"These recipes are a cut above the usual basic recipes...gustatory jewels. I felt as though the chefs were in my kitchen providing me with a private gourment cooking class."
Arleen Bessette, author *Taming the Wild Mushroom*

"This will sell well as the recipes are well chosen, easy to follow. The comments in the side bars are informative and add an interesting touch.
Arnika Gumbiner, owner World Coffees, Teas and Kitchen Things.

$12.95 120 pages trade paper ISBN 1-890880-02-7

SEASONAL FEASTS
55 Azalea Lane, Santa Cruz, CA 95060
Phone and fax: 831 426-2956